HUMANIZING AMERICA'S ICONIC BOOK

SOCIETY OF BIBLICAL LITERATURE
BIBLICAL SCHOLARSHIP IN NORTH AMERICA

Kent Harold Richards, Editor

Number 6
Humanizing America's Iconic Book
Society of Biblical Literature
Centennial Addresses 1980
Edited by Gene M. Tucker and Douglas A. Knight

Gene M. Tucker and Douglas A. Knight, Editors

HUMANIZING AMERICA'S ICONIC BOOK
Society of Biblical Literature
Centennial Addresses 1980

SCHOLARS PRESS
CHICO, CALIFORNIA

The Society of Biblical Literature gratefully acknowledges a grant
from the National Endowment for the Humanities to underwrite
certain editorial and research expenses of the Centennial Publications Series. Published results and interpretations do not necessarily
represent the view of the Endowment.

Library of Congress Cataloging in Publication Data
Main entry under title:

Humanizing America's iconic book.

(Biblical scholarship in North America ; no. 6)
(Centennial publications / Society of Biblical Literature)
(ISSN 0277-0474)
    Contents: America's iconic book / Martin Marty—
Scripture, history, and the quest for meaning / Langdon
Gilkey—To what we can still cling / Hans Küng—[etc.]
    1. Bible—Criticism, interpretation, etc.— Addresses,
essays, lectures. I. Tucker, Gene M. II. Knight, Douglas A.
III. Series. IV. Series: Centennial publications (Society of
Biblical Literature)
BS511.2.H78   220.06   82-836
ISBN 0-89130-570-X   AACR2

Printed in the United States of America

CONTENTS

Abbreviations vii

Foreword xi

I   America's Iconic Book
    Martin Marty 1

II Scripture, History, and the Quest for Meaning
    Langdon Gilkey 25

III To What We Can Still Cling: A Christian
    Orientation at a Time Lacking in Orientation
    Hans Küng 39

IV Parable and Performative in the Gospels
    and in Modern Literature
    J. Hillis Miller 57

V   Anthropological Approaches to the Study
    of the Bible during the Twentieth Century
    Edmund Leach 73

VI Is Historical Anthropology Possible? The Case
    of the Runaway Slave
    Gillian Feeley-Harnik 95

VII Treaty and Oath in the Ancient Near East:
    A Historian's Approach
    Hayim Tadmor 127

VIII Is the Temple Scroll a Sectarian Document?
    Yigael Yadin 153

Contributors 171

ABBREVIATIONS

Pseudepigraphical and Early Patristic Books

Jub.	Jubilees
Barn.	Barnabas
Did.	Didache

Rabbinic Literature

b.	Babylonian Talmud
Hor.	*Horayot*
Mek.	*Mekilta*
Qidd.	*Qiddušin*
Sanh.	*Sanhedrin*
Šebu.	*Šebu'ot*
t.	Tosepta

Periodicals, Reference Works, and Serials

AfO	*Archiv für Orientforschung*
AHW	W. von Soden, *Akkadisches Handwörterbuch*
AnBib	Analecta biblica
AnBoll	Analecta Bollandiana
ANET	J. B. Pritchard (ed.), *Ancient Near Eastern Texts*
AnOr	Analecta orientalia
AOAT	Alter Orient und Altes Testament
ARM	Archives royales de Mari
AT	D. J. Wiseman, *Alalakh Tablets*
ATR	*Anglican Theological Review*
BA	*Biblical Archeologist*
BAR	*Biblical Archaeologist Reader*
BASOR	*Bulletin of the American Schools of Oriental Research*
BCSR	*Bulletin of the Council on the Study of Religion*
Bib	*Biblica*
BibOr	Biblica et orientalia
BJRL	*Bulletin of the John Rylands University Library of Manchester*
BO	*Bibliotheca orientalis*

CAD	*The Assyrian Dictionary of the Oriental Institute of the University of Chicago*
CBQ	*Catholic Biblical Quarterly*
ConBOT	Coniectanea biblica, Old Testament
EAT	J. A. Knudtzon (ed.), *Die El-Amarna-Tafeln*
EncJud	*Encyclopaedia Judaica*
ExpTim	*Expository Times*
HR	*History of Religions*
HTR	*Harvard Theological Review*
IDB	G. A. Buttrick (ed.), *Interpreter's Dictionary of the Bible*
Int	*Interpretation*
JANESCU	*Journal of the Ancient Near Eastern Society of Columbia University*
JAOS	*Journal of the American Oriental Society*
JBL	*Journal of Biblical Literature*
JCS	*Journal of Cuneiform Studies*
JEA	*Journal of Egyptian Archaeology*
JJS	*Journal of Jewish Studies*
JNES	*Journal of Near Eastern Studies*
JPSV	*Jewish Publication Society Version*
JQR	*Jewish Quarterly Review*
JRH	*Journal of Religious History*
JSS	*Journal of Semitic Studies*
KAI	H. Donner and W. Röllig, *Kanaanäische und aramäische Inschriften*
KAJ	*Keilschrifttexte aus Assur juristischen Inhalts*, ed. E. Ebeling
MGWJ	*Monatsschrift für Geschichte und Wissenschaft des Judentums*
MIO	Mitteilungen des Instituts für Orientforschung
MLN	*Modern Language Notes*
OIP	Oriental Institute Publications
Or	*Orientalia* (Rome)
OTS	*Oudtestamentische Studiën*
PRU	*Le Palais royal d'Ugarit*
RA	*Revue d'assyriologie et d'archéologie orientale*
RelSRev	*Religious Studies Review*
RLA	*Reallexikon der Assyriologie*
SBLDS	Society of Biblical Literature Dissertation Series
SBLMasS	Society of Biblical Literature Masoretic Studies
SBT	Studies in Biblical Theology
TCS	Texts from Cuneiform Sources
UF	*Ugarit-Forschungen*
VT	*Vetus Testamentum*

VTSup	Vetus Testamentum, Supplements
WMANT	Wissenschaftliche Monographien zum Alten und Neuen Testament
WO	*Die Welt des Orients*
WZKM	*Wiener Zeitschrift für die Kunde des Morgenlandes*
ZA	*Zeitschrift für Assyriologie*
ZAW	*Zeitschrift für die alttestamentliche Wissenschaft*
ZDPV	*Zeitschrift des deutschen Palästina-Vereins*

FOREWORD

From 5 to 9 November 1980, the Society of Biblical Literature met to celebrate the hundredth anniversary of its founding. The Centennial Meeting was held in Dallas, Texas, at the Loews Anatole Hotel in conjunction with the regular meetings of the American Academy of Religion, the American Schools of Oriental Research, and the Scholars Press Associates. Total registration for the congress was 3,134, of which 1,059 were members of the Society of Biblical Literature. The Executive Secretary was able to report at the meeting that the Society of Biblical Literature included 4,936 members, making it the largest professional society in religion in North America, if not in the world. Those figures stand in dramatic contrast to the original eight who met in New York in 1880 to form the society, and to the first membership list of thirty-five.

In 1972 the Council of the society appointed a committee to plan appropriate ways of celebrating its centennial. From the outset it was assumed that the one hundredth year would provide the occasion for taking stock of biblical scholarship in North America and that the activities related to the centennial—including research and publications—would by no means be limited to the 1980 meeting itself. Consequently, in addition to developing plans for the centennial meeting, the committee initiated in 1973 a program unit in the annual meetings on "American Biblical Scholarship" and began to plan and develop—through the Centennial Publications Committee—an extensive publications program. Two major themes have guided the committee's work: the history of biblical scholarship, especially in North America, and the Bible in American history and culture. Centennial publications have begun to appear and will continue to do so over the next several years, appearing in four distinct series: The Bible in American Culture; Biblical Scholarship in North America; The Bible and its Modern Interpreters; and Biblical Scholarship in Confessional Perspective.

The Centennial Committee determined that the 1980 meeting, while including occasions for celebration, congratulation, and even nostalgia, should focus primarily on the history and future of American biblical scholarship and on the role of the Bible in American history and culture. The conference should have as its overall aim the assessment of biblical and related studies in retrospect and prospect but with emphasis on the latter; to state it differently, the aim was to assess the discipline's past as a means of enlightening its future. Consequently, a program was designed that facilitated this aim by a critical examination of various past and current approaches to biblical and related literatures and cultures and by a critical examination of biblical scholarship in itself and in its various contexts.

The entire program was organized under five headings, each with a range of subtopics and with a coordinating committee to determine the detailed format and contents of its program segments. In each case thought was given not so much to the history of the discipline but to those sources, methods, and movements that are likely to set the tone and determine the direction of future research and scholarship. Four of the program areas were perceived by the Centennial Committee to be particularly lively research fields in contemporary biblical studies. They were approaches to the Bible (1) through language analysis, (2) through social analysis, (3) through the question of meaning, and (4) through history and archaeology. The fifth area considered the history and sociology of biblical scholarship itself.

The program identified as "Approaches to the Bible through Language Analysis," organized by Robert C. Culley of McGill University and Dan O. Via of the University of Virginia, attempted to take account of the increasing activity in various disciplines that focus upon the Bible in terms of literature and language. Such activity is perceived, for example, in the reassessment of and changes in form-critical work in various programs and projects of the society—such as the New Testament Forms and Genre project—and in biblical scholars' appropriation of theories and methods from modern linguistic theory and practice. Programs under this heading acknowledged and evaluated the proposal by some scholars that a linguistic paradigm may be replacing a historical one in biblical studies as in other disciplines. The category included new approaches—or modifications of older ones—such as literary criticism, structuralism, discourse analysis, motif analysis, and linguistics. It included also programs on more familiar methods such as form criticism, tradition criticism, redaction criticism, and rhetorical criticism.

During the last decade scholars have become increasingly interested in using various forms of anthropological and sociological methods and data to explore biblical religion, literature, and history. The program sessions under the heading "Approaches to the Bible through Social Analysis," chaired by Wayne A. Meeks and Robert R. Wilson, both of Yale University, were intended to give a representative sample of the recent use of such approaches. However, rather than analyzing the current state of the discipline by reviewing recent publications or by making a comprehensive survey of the diverse and sometimes still experimental methods that are now being used, the sessions focused on issues that have grown out of recent research but have not yet been treated in detail.

The programs included in "Approaches to the Bible through the Question of Meaning" took into account matters conventionally identified as biblical theology and hermeneutic but were not limited to those categories. Topics for discussion included the influence of American culture on biblical interpretation, current issues and emerging possibilities in hermeneutic, and the purposes of biblical commentaries. Scholars who have advanced new proposals, e.g., concerning canon, authority, and inspiration, were asked to enter into conversation with one another and with the members of the society. This program area was planned by Robert Jewett of Garrett-Evangelical Theological Seminary and Kent H. Richards of The Iliff School of Theology.

"Approaches to the Bible through History and Archaeology" have been the dominant ones over the last century of biblical research, especially in North America. Such scholarly activity has yielded new insights and generated new methods; on occasion it has also been one-sided, obscuring other approaches to biblical texts. The programs under this topic, organized by Richard J. Clifford of Weston School of Theology and Helmut Koester of Harvard University, continued some of the fruitful avenues of the past while at the same time evaluating for future research the methods and perspectives currently operative. Topics included the history of Israel, early Judaism and the early church, the study of the cultural backgrounds of the Bible, and field archaeological data. Special attention was given to the assessment of the most recent data, e.g., from Qumran and Nag Hammadi.

Programs under the heading "The History and Sociology of Biblical Scholarship" were unlike the other four. While the others dealt with the substantive and methodological directions of research, these investigated the historical and social framework of the discipline itself. One program evaluated the Society of Biblical Literature, seeking to identify its successes and failures in influencing the course of scholarship and to propose directions for its future. Other programs examined the institutional contexts of biblical scholarship, including the church, the synagogue, and educational institutions; others addressed the role of women in biblical scholarship and the role of the Bible in politics and social reform in America. Edwin S. Gaustad of the University of California, Riverside, and Gene M. Tucker of Emory University were responsible for these sessions.

All five program categories involved the participation of numerous members of the society who were asked to address specific issues concerning the present status of the discipline. In addition, eight distinguished scholars were invited to present plenary addresses on the several themes, for the most part from the perspective of disciplines outside biblical studies. The papers themselves were representative of the diversity that prevails within biblical scholarship. Some reflected on the nature of the Bible and its status as an object for study; others addressed broad theological or methodological issues important for the discipline generally; still others focused on selected problems that are of special current interest. In common they share a humanistic approach to the Bible—this religious document that has enjoyed widespread attention and often reverence in the history of North America and beyond. In an effort to continue the discussion initiated at the centennial meeting, these eight plenary addresses are published here. While some of them have been revised slightly and expanded with footnotes, they all retain the substance and usually even the colloquial style of the original lectures.

As part of the section on "The History and Sociology of Biblical Scholarship," Martin Marty, a historian of American religion, evaluates directly the impact of the Bible and biblical scholarship on American culture. Two theologians, Langdon Gilkey and Hans Küng, consider aspects of "Approaches to the Bible through the Question of Meaning." J. Hillis Miller, a literary critic who in the past has brought his discipline to bear on biblical texts, contributes to the theme "Approaches to the Bible through Language Analysis." Two social scientists, Edmund Leach and Gillian Feeley-Harnik, engage problems of historical anthropology within the theme of "Approaches to the Bible through Social Analysis." Hayim Tadmor, an Assyriologist and biblical scholar, and Yigael Yadin, an archaeologist and biblical scholar, contribute to "Approaches to the Bible through History and Archaeology."

One of the papers published here, that of Yigael Yadin, could not be presented at the centennial meeting. Because of urgent responsibilities in his capacity as Deputy Prime Minister of the State of Israel, Professor Yadin was forced to cancel his participation. We are grateful that he has graciously agreed to have his paper published together with the other plenary addresses. We also join the members of the society in expressing our appreciation to Professor Frank Moore Cross, Jr., of Harvard University, who agreed at the last minute to replace Professor Yadin. Unfortunately, Professor Cross's paper had already been committed for publication elsewhere.

The full program for the centennial meeting, published in *Scholia XII* (Chico: Scholars Press, 1980), attests eloquently to the collaborative work and the extensive preparations of many members of the society. In addition to the above-mentioned persons who chaired the five program areas, the membership of the Centennial Committee deserves special note:

Paul J. Achtemeier, Union Theological Seminary, Richmond
Bernhard W. Anderson, Princeton Theological Seminary
Richard J. Clifford, Weston School of Theology
Robert C. Culley, McGill University
Eldon Jay Epp, Case Western Reserve University
Joseph A. Fitzmyer, The Catholic University of America
Stanley Gevirtz, Hebrew Union College, Los Angeles
Douglas A. Knight, Co-Chair, Vanderbilt University
Bruce M. Metzger, Princeton Theological Seminary
Elaine H. Pagels, Barnard College
Kent H. Richards, The Iliff School of Theology
James M. Robinson, Claremont Graduate School
Gene M. Tucker, Co-Chair, Emory University

A sincere word of appreciation is expressed to the National Endowment for the Humanities. It awarded the society a Conference Grant in the amount of $8,200.00 to underwrite expenses incurred in bringing the eight plenary speakers to the meeting. Moreover, a second NEH grant, which supports the wide-ranging research projects within the society's Centennial Publications Series, has met the editorial costs of preparing the present manuscript for publication.

Finally, we acknowledge gratefully the careful assistance rendered by three persons in editing and proofreading these manuscripts: Lamontte Luker of Vanderbilt University and Maurya Horgan and Paul Kobelski, both of The Iliff School of Theology. They and the other individuals who contributed directly to this volume and to the centennial meeting itself join the ranks of the many members who during these hundred years of the society's existence have sought through scholarship to humanize America's iconic book.

GENE M. TUCKER
Emory University

DOUGLAS A. KNIGHT
Vanderbilt University

I

AMERICA'S ICONIC BOOK*

Martin Marty

"We are all critics, I trust, and higher critics too." Thus Professor Angus Crawford, without spelling out the details of who "we" were, rushed to judgment from the Theological Seminary of Virginia during a debate at the Episcopal Church Congress in 1896.[1]

The public, be it churchgoing or in the general culture, did not share those conclusions. Four years before Crawford spoke, during critic Charles A. Briggs's heresy trial in New York, newspapers nationally covered the subject. Most of them pointed to the growing gap between the scholars and the public. One could choose from scores of sources, but this comment from the Savannah, Georgia, *News* is typical:

> The great majority of Christians regard the Bible as the inspired work of God, and therefore, cannot contain errors. An admission that it does contain errors opens the door to doubts, and when doubts are once entertained, it is a difficult matter to place a limit upon them. Professor Briggs's doctrines may be entirely satisfactory to those who clearly understood them, but it is about impossible to make them understood by the masses. To the average mind the whole Bible is true, or it is not the inspired work of God.[2]

Events during the first two decades of American biblical criticism before the turn of the century set the mold for controversy that has not ended at the end of a century of such scholarship. Crawford's word, "we are all critics, I trust, and higher critics too," is true of scholars at Jewish, Roman Catholic, nondenominational, mainline Protestant, secular graduate, and—their enemies would have it—some of the flagship evangelical schools. Wherever people in the humanities teach others how to analyze the historical, formal, and structural elements of texts and wherever there are no vested interests in fending off ecclesiastical resistance to the critical, the

---

* This is an expansion of a paper read at the centennial meeting of the Society of Biblical Literature in Dallas, November 1980. I wish to acknowledge the research assistance of Mr. R. Scott Appleby.
[1] *Papers and Speeches of the Church Congress* (New York, 1897) 104.
[2] Quoted in *Public Opinion* 14 (7 January 1893) 333.

critical methods and outlooks prevail. Yet the Savannah *News* report could be written even today about much of the churchgoing outlook and, if polls are a measure, also about much of unchurched America. The public still connects criticism with the spotting of errors and the planting of doubts. A century of biblical criticism, however presented to the public it may be, has produced little difference.

Recent Gallup Polls—shall we call them centennial presents to the Society of Biblical Literature—find that 42 percent of the general public finds the whole Bible to be inerrant. We must presume that at least that many are therefore resistant to critical scholarship. Gallup found 48 percent of the self-named Protestants in his sample and 41 percent of the Roman Catholics to be on the anticritical side.[3] This side is powerful beyond its numbers because its leadership has effectively mobilized sentiment. Anticritical forces have been outspoken in intradenominational warfare and in the 1980s are being heard in public school board rooms, where battles in defense of biblical creationism are being waged as intensely as they were in 1925 at the time of the Scopes trial in Tennessee.

In this division between camps and the opposition to critical study something is going on that reaches beyond the merely cognitive, beyond the critical-analytic method. The resistance to critical understanding, I propose, has its root in what Suzanne Langer would say lies "much deeper than any conscious purpose, . . . in that substratum of the mind, the realm of fundamental ideas."[4] Fundamental ideas which José Ortega y Gasset calls *creencias*, are ideas so deep that we do not even know we hold them. They are not the ideas that we "have" but the ideas that we "are." And these *creencias* hook up with certain *vigencias*, binding customs of a culture, customs that have a hold much stronger than that which law itself can impose.[5] Anthropologist George Boas showed his at-homeness with such notions when he urged students to pursue the locations of profound ideas: "When an idea is adopted by a group and put into practice, as in a church or a state, its rate of change will be slow."[6] An idea that the American churches and in some ways the society have adopted and put into practice is the uncritical acceptance of the Bible's worth. Thus Perry Miller observed of the role of the Old Testament in historic American society: it was "so truly omnipresent in the American culture of 1800 or 1820 that historians have as much difficulty

[3] Walter A. Elwell ("Belief and the Bible: A Crisis of Authority," *Christianity Today* [21 March 1980] 19–23) reports on the poll by Gallup.

[4] Suzanne K. Langer, *Philosophy in a New Key* (New York: New American Library, 1952) 41, 39.

[5] On Ortega's ideas, see Karl J. Weintraub (*Visions of Culture* [Chicago: University of Chicago, 1966] 261, 263) and Harold C. Raley (*José Ortega y Gasset: Philosopher of European Unity* [University, AL: University of Alabama, 1967] 81).

[6] George Boas, *The History of Ideas* (New York: Scribner's, 1969) 88.

taking cognizance of it as of the air people breathed."[7] It was Jacob Burck-hardt, I believe, who said that the most important things in life do not get written about by historians simply because they are *too* close to people, too taken for granted. This may account for the absence of good histories deal-ing with American attitudes toward the Bible.

An example of the way anticritical attitudes were locked in to the main-line culture appears in an often quoted trio of sentences by a great Ameri-can average mind and exemplar of its day-to-day and less than Lincolnesque civil religion, President Grover Cleveland: "The Bible is good enough for me, just the old book under which I was brought up. I do not want notes or criticisms or explanations about authorship or origin or even cross-references. I do not need them or understand them, and they confuse me."[8] What is going on here is a reference to an aspect of the American *consensus juris*, the minimal basis of consensus on which civil life is ordered. Such a consensus may be truly minimal, as cynical observers sometimes suggest. British student of politics Bernard Crick thought that he had the American version filtered down to something as terse as the *cri de coeur* of Groucho Marx, "Take care of me. I am the only one I've got."[9] But one does not need to spend much time regarding America from afar or near to see that this "nation with a soul of a church," to use G. K. Chesterton's phrase,[10] has more than the Declaration of Independence and the United States Constitution enshrined in a vault in its archival heart. The Bible also is there.

Nothing is supposed to be, say very sober historians. They find America seeing itself as an aniconic nation, one that lacks images or icons. In a brilliant epigraphic choice to illustrate the main theme of his book *The Genius of American Politics*, Daniel Boorstin, now the Librarian of Congress and thus keeper of the archive, compared the American aniconic intention to a scene in Heinrich Graetz's *History of the Jews*: "Pompey then penetrated into the Sanctuary, in order to satisfy his curiosity as to the nature of the Judaean worship, about which the most contradictory reports prevailed. The Roman general was not a little astonished at finding within the sacred recesses of the Holy of Holies, neither an ass's head nor, indeed, images of any sort."[11] A refusal to fill our sanctuary with ideological images characterizes American life, say historians like Boorstin. Yet if they stayed around and took a little longer look in that shrine they would not find it empty. In the corner, under a layer of dust, there is a leather-bound, gilt-edged, India-papered object, a

[7] Perry Miller, "The Garden of Eden and the Deacon's Meadow," *American Heritage* 7 (1955) 55.

[8] George F. Parker, *Recollections of Grover Cleveland* (New York, 1911) 382.

[9] Bernard Crick, *In Defense of Politics* (Baltimore, Penguin, 1964) 176.

[10] Raymond T. Bond (ed.), *The Man Who Was Chesterton* (Garden City, NY: Doubleday Image, 1960) 131.

[11] Daniel J. Boorstin, *The Genius of American Politics* (Chicago: University of Chicago, 1953) title page.

Bible, revered *as* object, *as* icon, not only in Protestant churches but in much of the public congregation as well.

Such an observation can be fighting words in a self-described aniconic culture or set of churches. Yet if we use our terms with conceptual propriety and great care and are willing to take some risks, this insight—if it holds up—can illumine the history of response to biblical criticism in America. It can help explain why so many found it possible to ignore or to resist the main line of biblical scholarship for a century.

Five risks come to mind at once. First, to use such a vivid image as "image" is to risk confusing instead of clarifying. A notable and notably difficult Catholic philosopher once made a distinction between types of abstractions that could apply here to types of images, metaphors, or similes. At a Catholic philosophers' convention he was comparing notes with his peer. They were discussing how many of their reviewers commented on the level of abstraction with which they both operated. "Yes," said the friend, "but there is a difference. I use enriching abstractions and you use impover-ishing ones." Some might say that they use clarifying images and I may be using a confusing one.

Second, the image employed may be inappropriate because it is too arcane. The icon, for example, is at home in an Eastern Orthodox Christian culture, where it congenially reposes among its connotations, but one may do violence by snatching it away from those connotations and resituating it on the more bare spiritual landscape of America.

At midpoint during our risk assessment we should mention that to some the image of the icon is so obvious, so lacking in subtlety, that to use it adds nothing but banality. "My love is like a rose." Of course, everyone knows my love is like a rose—to me. Americans use the Bible, even as a physical object, as an icon. Of course . . .

A fourth risk has to do with emotional connotations. The image can be so vivid that it diverts from inquiry. In the 1950s an opponent of the World Council of Churches who made his living staging protests against it, found that he scored the strongest points when he pointed to one of its constit-uencies: "the bearded Orthodox icon-kissers." Being bearded and kissing icons called to mind something so overpowering that it swept away all the more ordinary functions and images. Thus to say that America treats the Bible iconically will, in the minds of pure prophets, connote paganism and thus something bad. (Were this address an essay directed to the American Academy of Religion and not the Society of Biblical Literature, I would not have to apologize for mentioning paganism and would not dare mention it pejoratively. The historians of religion there would immediately score my implicit value judgment with a question, "What's the matter with pagan-ism?") In the context of this risk I can only urge that we must also keep in mind ordinary functions of the Bible. Sometimes an image *does* carry peo-ple away. One thinks of a moment when the late philosopher Herbert

Marcuse said something humorous; that was a noteworthy event, because he usually, figuratively, lumbered steatopygically across the stage in efforts at being humorous. But, once: "Yes, yes, I know that the jet airplane is a phallic symbol. But it can also get you from London to Brussels." Yes, yes, I know that the Bible is an icon, but its contents can also be read, marked, learned, and inwardly digested, and lived by.

A final risk is the notion of *pars pro toto*. One can concentrate on a subculture, Protestant conservatism, which guards the shrine and fights for the iconic object, without noticing that by 1980 the shrine itself is often neglected. Or if not neglected it is surrounded by other objects and symbols until it recedes from center stage, no longer informs, or is lost in a diffusion and confusion of symbols.

These risks notwithstanding, I believe there are values in using the image of the icon as an effort to lead beyond merely rational analysis to the root emotions of people in a culture. Only then can we assess the power situation, which has little to do with the *content* of ancient scriptures but much to do with the *form* of modern American life.

First we must establish the place of the Bible among the other fonts and sources of culture. The Bible is a book. The molecules that make it up constitute paper and ink. The ink is shaped in the form of letters whose agglomerations in the form of words, sentences, chapters sign something; they signify, they impart ideas, they at least potentially disclose meanings. Thus people gain access to other minds or learn something about their own. Since the meanings come from the past, they may study their history or analyze them structurally, with special interest in the cast of contemporary mind. So one would expect that the same Gallup Poll that showed Americans believing the Bible to be beyond criticism, without error, would also find it being used and find it informing life.

Strangely, significantly fewer people who consider the Bible to be the errorless book of God consult it first when in trouble. Forty percent turn to it, 27 percent to the Holy Spirit, 11 percent to the church, and 22 percent to "Other." So far, so good; the Bible outranks the other sources of wisdom or consolation. But, writes Walter A. Elwell in his comment on the disuse of the book, "It is apparently one thing to *believe* that the Bible is God's word [as 72 percent of the polled public simply does] and quite another to read it." The general public average daily readership is 12 percent, with the Protestant average being 18 percent and the Roman Catholic 4 percent. Who reads the Bible less than once a month? Fifty-two percent of the general public, 41 percent of Protestants, and 67 percent of Roman Catholics. As for knowledge of the content as opposed to claimed reading of the book, the figures are even lower. Asked to name the Ten Commandments, perhaps the most familiar part of both "testaments," 45 percent of the public could come up with four or fewer; this public found 49 percent of the Protestants and 44 percent of the Catholics able to do so. Elwell adds: "Belief in God is not

much affected by how often people read the Bible."[12] The public resists
critical analysis of its revered object, calls this object the Word of God. A
minority claims to consult it first in trouble; yet few read it regularly and
not many know its basic contents. This anomaly occasions an examination of
the iconic hold this book exercises.

Let me draw on a frequent experience of Marxian scholars when they
visit Marxist societies. They lecture on articulated and filiated aspects of *Das
Kapital*. They assume that assenting communists, be they university students
or peasants, would be conversant with many dimensions of the writings of
Marx. They report on responses that range from incomprehension through
bemusement to disdain. As one told a friend of mine, "You are not commu-
nicating well. You know too much Marx. You know where his ideas came
from and how he put them together and how they relate and what they
mean. We don't need all that Hegelian metaphysical stuff. We only need
the basic Marxian notion as a trigger to get our revolution going." A pro-
letarian or a peasant might not articulate it so well. What the people need is
the awareness that somewhere there *is* an authority and perhaps an elite
that regards it as, shall we say, inerrant? The society draws security from the
knowledge that an enclosure or a support exists, one that transcends mun-
dane and practical living.

So it is with the use of the Bible as an image in a society like that of
pluralist America. In a brilliant passage on icon and image, Rosemary
Gordon has written that "every man walks around in the world enveloped in
a carapace of his own images. Their presence enables him to structure and
to organize the multiplicity of the objects and the stimuli which throng
him. . . ."[13] A zoological carapace is "a hard bony or chitinous outer covering, such as the fused dorsal plates of a turtle, or the portion of the exo-
skeleton covering the head and thorax of a crustacean." But the dictionary
goes on to refer to it as "any similar protective covering." Here we are
speaking of the protective covering, the sort of cocoon that individuals,
subcultures, and in their own way societies need for the structuring of experience.

Far from using the iconic image disdainfully, then, I am trying to suggest
that it has a value of great anthropological and psychic significance; without
such carapaces people would likely go mad. Relate this to the observation of
Talcott Parsons that "good fortune and suffering must always, to cultural man,
be endowed with meaning. They cannot, except in limiting cases, be accepted
as something that 'just happens.'"[14] The Bible, in American history and in

---

[12] Elwell, "Belief and the Bible," 19–23.

[13] Rosemary Gordon, "A Very Private World," in *The Function and Nature of Imagery*, ed.
P. W. Sheehan (New York: Academy, 1972) 63.

[14] Quoted by Andrew Greeley, *The Denominational Society* (Glenview, IL: Scott, Foresman
& Co., 1972) 51.

much of present-day culture, provided and provides as an object a basic element in the carapace of images, and its presumed contents, that for which one would consult it if one did consult it, remove the "just happening" dimension from human existence.

A reach beyond churchly into public culture demonstrates this kind of location for the Bible as icon. Benjamin Franklin, who in 1749 chartered and called for "the Necessity of a *Publick Religion*," took pains to speak well of the Bible, whose contents he did not regard as supernatural at all but whose form he regularly printed and published. When asked to join John Adams and Thomas Jefferson on 4 July 1776 to prepare a great seal of the United States, this Franklin reached for biblical imagery (of Moses and the Red Sea), though the design was later compromised.[15]

Under the carapace of organizing images for the republic, the "founding father" of his country has a central place. So it is that George Washington is associated with the Bible, even though the most notable scholar of Washington's religion says he made "astonishingly few references" to it in his many volumes of literary remains. While he accepted a gift of Bibles as "an important present to the brave fellows" in the military during the Revolution, only one letter in his corpus has a reference to his own reading of the book. There are few biblical allusions in his writings, and they are in settings as near to the jocular as Washington ever came. Yet Washington was a Freemason, and the Masons regarded the Bible as their key icon, even though they did not regard it as supernatural. Observers took pains to notice the precedent at the Washington inaugural, when the first president brought along his Masonic Bible; "the president kissed the Bible after taking the oath of office." In 1789 he was thus an unbearded icon-kisser. Later presidents would upset the images under the carapace were they to neglect or despise the role of the Bible in their oath—even though the Constitution is silent on the subject.[16]

Thomas Jefferson did upset the images by taking the content of the Bible seriously. He appeared to be the great iconoclast among the fathers. Yet he read the book. We know of 271 religious titles in the Jeffersonian library. He collected editions of the Bible: two Greek Septuagints, ten Vulgates, ten Greek New Testaments, one French and six English versions, with four Apocrypha. "For a man with a reputation for being irreligious he had an amazing number," writes an analyst of that library. And Jefferson was not a collector but a student. From 1804 to 1819 he pieced together his "wee-little book," "The Jefferson Bible," which began as a moonlighting project in the White House. There he pasted together the nonsupernatural

[15] See Anson Phelps Stokes, *Church and State in the United States*, vol. 1 (New York: Harper Brothers, 1950) 293–99.

[16] Paul F. Boller, Jr., *George Washington and Religion* (Dallas: Southern Methodist University, 1963) 40–41; Stokes, *Church and State*, 1. 486, 244.

elements of the Gospels, clipped from English, French, Latin, and Greek versions, into *The Life and Morals of Jesus of Nazareth*. For this he came to be thought of as an infidel, and his place in the American evangelical pantheon was less secure than was that of owners-but-not-readers like Washington, who probably had the same hermeneutical principles as Jefferson but did not put them to use.[17]

Abraham Lincoln, the center of American public faith and its greatest theologian, illustrates the positive role of the iconic use of the Bible. In the library at Fisk University there reposes a Bible given Lincoln on 4 July 1864 by the "Loyal Colored People" of Baltimore. Lincoln responded: "In regard to this Great book, I have but to say, it is the best gift God has given to man. . . . All the good Savior gave to the world was communicated through this book. . . . To you I return my most sincere thanks for *the elegant copy of the great Book of God* which you present" [emphasis mine]. It was noted that Lincoln regularly read the Bible in the White House and that it was the old Lincoln family Bible, a version from the Society for Promotion of Christian Knowledge (S.P.C.K.) dated 1799—such details always mattered. While Jefferson was a church member but an infidel for his iconoclasm, Lincoln was well received by the churches, though he is the only president ever who was not a church member. He had the right attitudes toward the Bible, whose cadences entered his very speech.[18]

One could further survey the central figures who have sacerdotal roles in the public religion and hence in guarding the sanctuary. We have already heard Grover Cleveland, the first president to be vocal after critical views of the Bible reached America. Years later another priestly president, the well-informed historian Woodrow Wilson, made iconic use of the Bible. John Mulder says of him that "Wilson showed no awareness of problems in the Bible or controversies surrounding interpretation of its passages." The Bible was the standard for the culture, and it spoke to Wilson and the nation more in terms of law than of grace.[19] Wilson effectively mounted military crusades using biblical imagery.

One candidate for the presidency did more than any American scholar or cleric to harden public sentiment against biblical criticism. William Jennings Bryan was always a populist about religious knowledge. He spoke critically against the scholarly elite who wanted to make a different use of the arcanum. "A religion that didn't appeal to any but college graduates would be over the head or under the feet of 99 per cent of our people."

---

[17] Charles B. Sanford, *Thomas Jefferson and His Library* (Hamden, CT: Archon, 1977) 271. For Jefferson's interests in the Bible and religion, see Robert M. Healey, *Jefferson on Religion in Public Education* (New Haven: Yale University, 1962).

[18] On the Fisk Bible, see Elton Trueblood, *Abraham Lincoln: Theologian of Anguish* (New York: Harper and Row, 1973) 48–49, 55.

[19] John Mulder, *Woodrow Wilson: The Years of Preparation* (Princeton: Princeton University, 1978) 49; Stokes, *Church and State*, 2. 549.

Bryan, of course was not everyone's chosen keeper of the sanctuary, and many in his time and ever since repudiated him or even saw his latter-day opposition to criticism to be a mark of senility. Yet Bryan gained a broad following, and showed both an iconic and an unreflective use of the Bible in many exchanges during the Scopes trial, which had to do with biblical literalism. Asked by his antagonist Clarence Darrow about certain calculations of historical biblical accounts of the The Deluge, Bryan replied:

> I never made a calculation.
> Darrow: What do you think?
> Bryan: I do not think about things I don't think about.
> Darrow: Do you think about things you do think about?
> Bryan: Well, sometimes.

Liberal America scorned Bryan for his literalism and was sure that his fundamentalist outlook, soon a mark of disgrace, would disappear from the scene. It happened, however, that many to Bryan's right felt that he let them down because there were moments in the trial when he allowed cracks in their carapace. He was not perfectly literal about the biblical accounts at all times. Bryan never deserted or changed his boyhood biblical faith, which gave him security for political contingencies and defeats. "Give the modernist three words, 'allegorical,' 'poetical,' and 'symbolically,'" said Bryan in 1923, "and he can suck the meaning out of every vital doctrine of the Christian Church and every passage in the Bible to which he objects."[20] Darrow slew his thousands, but in pious America, Bryan slew his ten thousands.

This attitude in moderate form continues in the 1980s. President Jimmy Carter did what he could to evade questions that might draw him away from defense of biblical literalism. Whatever Americans thought of him politically, the polls found them admiring his moral construct based on reverence for the Bible. And his successor, Ronald Reagan, was not out of character or tradition when during the presidential campaign he pointed to the icon and said with an emphasis few evangelical clerics would be bold enough to use: "It is an incontrovertible fact that *all* the complex and horrendous questions confronting us at home and worldwide have their answer in that single book"[21] [emphasis mine].

Perhaps I have dwelt too long on presidential candidates, but vote-getters in their public expressions are custodians of the national carapace and the images under it. One could as well point to the role of the Bible as an object in legislative halls or, more vividly, to the part the Bible plays in

[20] Bryan is quoted in the *Truth-seeker* 26 (29 June 1929) 402. The exchange with Darrow is quoted in George Marsden, *Fundamentalism in American Culture: The Shaping of American Evangelicalism 1870–1925* (New York: Oxford University, 1980) 187. On the other attitudes of Bryan, see Lawrence W. Levine, *Defender of the Faith: William Jennings Bryan: The Last Decade, 1915–1925* (New York: Oxford University, 1965) 247, 281, 292.

[21] *New York Times* (25 September 1980) A27.

judicial history in the context of "the nine high priests in their black robes" in the Supreme Court. It is in the courts that all but a few dissenting individuals take their oath on the Bible so consistently that in colloquial America one swears on "a stack of Bibles," to prove one's seriousness. The Supreme Court has been seen as the great iconoclastic desecrator because it "took the Bible out of the schools," when it limited not the pedagogical but the devotional use of the book in public institutions.

The Court did no such thing. The public had "taken the Bible out of the schools," but, significantly for my thesis, it did not know or does not even now know that it did this. What mattered under the carapace of images in the national mind was that the Bible belonged in classroom devotion. Yet a year or two before the Supreme Court decisions of 1962 and 1963—according to social scientist Richard Dierenfeld, who took pains to take a survey—not many were reading the Bible in schools. Even "without comment," as one should read it if it is an icon beyond interpretation, few read it. About 42 percent of the respondents were still reading it, thanks to the heritage of the older parts of the country. The putatively profane East found almost 68 percent of its classrooms in public schools still using the Bible, and over 75 percent of the Southern districts reported such use. But in the other half of the Bible Belt, the Midwest, only about 18 percent did. And in the West, including California, whence came so many protests to the Court against "taking the Bible out of the schools," only 11 percent kept the practice. (By the way, where the Bible was used, 70 percent chose the King James Version, which until the 1950s was almost universally the iconic version.) But if the Bible survived *devotionally*, which usage underscores our point, its contents were not subjects of analysis. Are there Bible *classes* of any sort in your schools? Now *one-tenth* as many polled districts, 4.51 percent nationally, replied in the affirmative. In the South 9 percent, in the East barely 1 percent, in the Midwest 4 percent, and in the West fewer than 9 percent of the districts looked at the contents.[22]

The Bible worked its way into the schools as icon because in sectarian America it was seen as "nonsectarian," and the "not commented upon" aspect was to assure objectivity in its use. Horace Mann, a Unitarian cleric, as much as anyone else, helped establish this use of the Bible in schools. His form of comment or interpretation would have been abhorrent in most of the Protestant then-dominant culture of his own day. After World War II a follower of John Dewey and an advocate of a postbiblical nonsectarian religion of democracy, Chaplain J. Paul Williams, commented critically on this iconic use: "This belief in the efficacy of spending a few minutes daily in reading the Bible grew up in a time when it was almost universally believed by Protestants that there was some kind of magic in the Bible to which one

[22] Richard B. Dierenfeld, *Religion in American Public Schools* (Washington: Public Affairs Press, 1962) Chap. 4.

needed but to be exposed in order for it to have a very great influence on life."[23]

In the unofficial but privileged mainstream American literary culture there was an almost immediate acceptance of biblical critical outlooks, a fact that gave this culture a marginal status in what today we would call "Middle America." Already in his sermon of 1841 on "The Transient and Permanent in Christianity," Theodore Parker showed his awareness: "Modern criticism is fast breaking to pieces this idol which men have made out of the scriptures." Parker helped import radical German criticism, such as De Wette's *Einleitung*.[24] Others were iconoclastic enough to point to iconodulism among Bible-believers who were, they thought, not Bible-readers or Bible-followers. Thus Henry David Thoreau: "It is remarkable that, notwithstanding the universal favor with which the New Testament is outwardly received, and even the bigotry with which it is defended, there is no hospitality shown to, there is no appreciation of, the order of truth with which it deals. I know of no book that has so few readers."[25] This was still in the period before critical study was widespread.

A towering mainstream literary figure of the generation in which knowledge of biblical criticism reached the public was Oliver Wendell Holmes. In 1869 he wrote Frederic H. Hedge:

> The truth is staring the Christian world in the face, that the stories of the old Hebrew books cannot be taken as literal statements of fact. But the property of the church is so large and so mixed up with its vested beliefs, that it is hopeless to expect anything like honest avowal of the convictions which there can be little doubt intelligent church men of many denominations, if at all, entertain. It is best, I suppose, it should be so, for take idolatry and bibliolatry out of the world all at once as the magnetic mountain drew the nails and bolts of Sindbad's ship, and the vessel that floats much of the best of our humanity would resolve itself in a floating ruin of planks and timbers. . . .[26]

We do not need to accept Holmes's conspiracy theory about ecclesiasticism to agree with his understanding, one that under different images matches our own, that a carapace of images is necessary in order for individuals and society to function cognitively or morally.

As in public religion or literary culture, so in popular social behavior there are evidences on all hands of the iconic use of the Bible in America. These may be losing out in many elements of "postbiblical" pluralist America, and the recent distancing from the Bible may be part of the presumed

[23] J. Paul Williams, *What Americans Believe and How They Worship* (New York: Harper and Row, 1962) 46.

[24] Jerry Wayne Brown, *The Rise of Biblical Criticism in America, 1800–1870* (Middletown, CT: Wesleyan, 1969) 158, 66, 164.

[25] Henry David Thoreau, *A Week on the Concord and Merrimack* (Boston: Houghton Mifflin, 1906, 1961) 73–74.

[26] John T. Morse, Jr., *Life and Letters of Oliver Wendell Holmes*, vol. 2 (Boston: Houghton Mifflin, 1896) 296–97.

chaos, malaise, or anomie of such a culture. People suffer from what Robert Jay Lifton calls *"historical*, or *psychohistorical* dislocation,"* which he saw to be the "break in the sense of connection men have long felt with vital and nourishing symbols of their cultural traditions—symbols revolving around . . . religion." This breach in tradition is accompanied by a *"flooding of imagery* because of mass communications networks."[27] Some of the contemporary political polemics from the American right results from reaction against this breach, this flooding.

Only some of the rejection was thoughtless, thanks to the passing of time. At least in the years of the rejective counterculture or wherever "now" people advocated historical amnesia as liberating, it is the biblical culture that serves as a foil. But the rejection has not been successful or complete, so locked into the corners of the carapace of images have been awarenesses of the Bible. Culture critic Eugene Goodheart rose up at the height of such rejection to speak with historical sense and sanity about the moment. He referred more to the content of the traditions than I am in the present instance, but the point is still in place:

> The *tabula rasa* is a presumption of innocence. It is not the result of genuine discovery, for instance, that the Christian and classical traditions are no longer part of us. The enactments of our personality and character are involuntary, often compulsive. We are not free to choose what we are or even what we will do. We cannot simply wish away traditions that we have grown to dislike. The very dislike may be conditioned by the fact that they still possess us, if we do not possess them. If Judeo-Christian and classical traditions are still alive in all of us (and I suspect they are), despite attempts to deny them, then an education that fails to address itself to these traditions (I do not speak of arguing for or against them) would fail according to the ideal of relevance. The mere repudiation of these traditions does not have the effect of exorcism.[28]

No doubt I was invited to a centennial observance of biblical scholarship as a historian of American social and religious behavior. Here it would be easy to display expertise in that field and prolong the essay by showing all the ways in which the Bible as the object that embodies the center of Goodheart's "Judeo-Christian" religion endures iconically. Instead of documenting I shall only point, to stimulate the vision and imagination of professional biblical scholars concerning their context and environment. Some pointings:

Americans have an adjectival use of the noun "Bible" as one indicator: Bible belt, Bible camp, Bible believer, Bible Sunday, Bible week, Bible school, Bible institute, Bible college, Bible battle, Bible bookstore, Bible puzzles and crosswords and quizzes, Gideon Bible in airplane and hospital and hotel room (enhanced in the Mormon Marriott by a Book of Mormon).

---

[27] Robert Jay Lifton, *Boundaries: Psychological Man in Revolution* (New York: Vintage, 1970) 43.

[28] Eugene Goodheart, *Culture and the Radical Conscience* (Cambridge: Harvard University, 1973) 9–10.

There are tours to Bible lands, and Bibles brought back with covers made of wood from the Mount of Olives. The Bible is a gift at rites of passage, to new mothers, in Sunday school, at confirmation, in white covers for marriages, at graduations, for *bon voyage*. Protestants who always found the Catholic practice of burying grandmothers with an object like a rosary repulsive characteristically buried grandmother with a black Bible. The family Bible is also the place between whose testaments one is always going to fill out the family tree, as ancestors once did.

Bibles are as ubiquitous in hotel rooms as wire coat hangers. Have any of us ever seen an old one, a used one, a spinecracked version? What happens to them? A Second City comic would have it that one does not know either where wire coat hangers come from. They are absent when one checks in but still mysteriously proliferating by the time one checks out. Could the Gideon Bible be a wire coat hanger in its larval or pupal stages? No one has seen an old Bible in the garbage. Nor are Bibles burned, except when defenders of the iconic King James attacked the National Council of Churches' desecrating Revised Standard Version as "Stalin's Bible." When that RSV was issued, an iconodule figured out that the first edition consumed twenty million square inches of twenty-three carat gold leaf, enough to make a twenty-four foot wide sheet one mile long, and that the Bibles of that first year's edition, all of which soon were sold, could be stacked high enough to equal one hundred Empire State Buildings. In 1954 *Catholic Digest* estimated that two hundred million Bibles were in circulation, far more than one per citizen of all ages—and probably a low figure, were one to add all the atticked and betrunked versions in semicirculation.[29]

The Bible legitimates other expressions. Cecil B. De Mille learned that he could serve up magic and miracle and sex as long as the main images were sanctified by reference to the Bible. A few biblical lines about Bathsheba or Delilah were enough to keep Susan Hayward or Gina Lolabrigida in motion on screen for an hour and a half, before a public that was not then yet free to watch in clear conscience similar unclad secular imagery.

Even in those parts of Protestant culture that do not favor magic, superstition, or relics, the Bible is allowed a special role. The stories of soldiers whose lives were spared because they had a bullet-proof covered New Testament in their breast pocket are so frequent that one almost pictures an army with people tilting by the weight of the book to their left sides. In frontier folklore there were stories of infidels and deists who on death beds faced the horror of hell because they had "burned all the Bibles they could get." A Methodist itinerant, it was said, faced off a robber in Chillicothe, Ohio, who let him go when he saw the Bible. The victim was "more than thankful for my Bible, which had served me better than a revolver. This was a new kind of weapon, the merits of which he appeared

[29] Claire Cox, *The New-Time Religion* (Englewood Cliffs, NJ: Prentice-Hall, 1961) Chap. 15.

to have no desire to contest." The wife of a circuit rider needed money for provisions while her husband was on the road and she was ill. She asked for a Bible, "intending to seek comfort from its holy counsels, opened it, found a five dollar bill."[30] These stories have not disappeared from the culture of television evangelism, where miracles associated with the physical object of the Bible continue.

So much for the Protestant/Enlightenment-formed general culture. The case is little different in Judaism, which in America has been forced to be "more biblical than it is." Jewish scholars constantly point to the transformations of Judaism and its texts during the past twenty-seven centuries, showing that the Bible is only a part of their tradition. But just as rabbis, who are lay people in Europe, have to be clerics in American culture to round out the priest-minister-rabbi trifaith triad, so Jews have had to be "people of *the* book" in America in a special normative sense. Literalist understandings of the Bible among premillennial fundamentalists in America have blunted anti-Semitism and led to surprising coalescences between Jews and evangelicals who must keep respect for Jews because of Jewish reverence for the Hebrew Scriptures.

Solomon Schechter, dedicating the Jewish Theological Seminary in New York in 1903, summarized the case for America and Judaism:

> If there is a feature in American religious life more prominent than any other it is in its conservative tendency. . . . This country is, as everybody knows, a creation of the Bible, particularly the Old Testament, and the Bible is still holding its own, exercising enormous influence as a real spiritual power in spite of all the destructive tendencies, mostly of foreign make. . . . The bulk of the real American people have, in matters of religion, retained their sobriety and loyal adherence to the Scripture, as their Puritan forefathers did. America thus stands for wideness of scope and for conservatism.[31]

The iconic case is weakest in the instance of Roman Catholicism, as Gallup polls and cultural evidences show. In the liturgy the priest kisses the Gospel. Catholic conservatives point to *Providentissimus Deus* of 1893 to certify their at-homeness with Protestant doctrines of inerrancy. But Catholicism was not under the carapace in the nineteenth century. It was the fact that Catholics had other icons, talismans, relics, amulets, and sacramentals that kept them in part from being seen as "true Americans" by the others. The Nativist battles of the 1840s make this clear. In October of 1842 an overfervent priest in Carbeau, New York, angry because the King James Version was being distributed in his parish, burned some Bibles. Bishop John Hughes, "Dagger John," spoke up: "To burn or otherwise destroy a spurious or corrupt copy of the Bible, whose circulation would tend to disseminate erroneous principles of faith or morals, we hold to be an act not only justifiable

---

[30] Folkloric treatment is in Donald E. Byrne, Jr., *No Foot of Land: Folklore of American Methodist Itinerants* (Metuchen, NJ: Scarecrow, 1975) 85, 134.

[31] Solomon Schechter, *Seminary Addresses and Other Papers* (Cincinnati: Ark, 1915) 48–49.

but praiseworthy." A wave of Bible burnings was said to ensue, and this was followed by larger waves of Nativist anti-Catholic sentiment.[32]

Yet even if the Catholic case for faith did not depend only on the Bible but also on "the tradition," Catholics were also wary of anything that touched this icon. Cardinal William O'Connell, later Archbishop of Boston, remembered how in the 1880s at the American College in Rome students had discussed higher criticism, which had its source "mostly in Germany, from a group of clever agnostics whose plain purpose was to destroy completely the fundamentals of the Christian faith by a well-planned attack upon the whole system of divine revelation. . . ."[33] To Catholics as to others, higher criticism was un-American, foreign, alien. The Americanist and Modernist controversies found the few early Catholic critics undercut and displaced. And today, as Catholics link up with conservatives in many causes, the polemical columnists—one thinks of the weekly efforts in the *National Catholic Register*—consistently attack biblical criticism as a desecration of the book that—according to Gallup—few Catholics read.

The case for seeing the Bible as America's iconic book is both most important and most startling in the instance of Protestantism—most important in that today it is hard to picture how dominant was Protestantism for three centuries, while the *creencias* and *vigencias*, the root ideas and the binding customs, of the culture were being programed and set. Yet in the British colonies that made up the original United States, non-Protestant religious expression was almost nonexistent outside Maryland, southern Pennsylvania, and on occasion Rhode Island and New York City. Not until the great continental Catholic migrations to America in the 1840s and the Jewish influx after the 1880s did other religious voices begin to gain power and privilege.

If important, it was also startling that the Bible became an icon, for Protestantism for the most part—except in its liturgically high wings—has seen itself as aniconic and even iconoclastic. C. J. Jung wrote from a psychological point of view about a stereotype cherished in many disciplines:

> The history of the development of Protestantism is one of chronic iconoclasm. One wall after another fell. And the work of destruction was not too difficult, either, when once the authority of the church had been shattered. We all know how, in large things as in small, in general as well as in particular, piece after piece collapsed, and how the alarming impoverishment of symbolism that is now the condition of life came about. The power of the church has gone with that loss of symbolism, too.[34]

Protestants were nervous because, while images also represent other things, they *could* displace unseen realities and thus lead to the worship of

---

[32] Ray Allen Billington, *The Protestant Crusade 1800–1860: A Study of the Origins of American Nativism* (Chicago: Quadrangle, 1964) 157–58.

[33] William H. O'Connell, *Recollections of Seventy Years* (Boston: Houghton Mifflin, 1934) 120–22.

[34] C. J. Jung, *The Integration of the Personality* (New York: Farrar and Rinehart, 1939).

created objects or, in short, to idolatry. Protestants failed to discriminate between reverence for icons and worship of images. Albert C. Moore draws the distinction finely, and I quote him because this is crucial for my theme, which is *not* a charge that America worships the Bible as an idol. "When the icon is treated with reverence in the context of worship, this attitude can be described as 'iconolatry', veneration of the icon. This term should be used in preference to the term 'idolatry' which has so many censorious and pejorative associations in Western usage. . . ."

Are the objections raised against idolatry applicable to the use of images? At the very least one must ask what is the source of the information concerning alleged idolators; was it, asks Moore, from biased observers?

> For instance, at the Reformation both Catholics and Protestants agreed that idolatry was forbidden to Christians by the Bible; but they disagreed over the question as to when an image became idolatrous: 'At no time was it possible to prove that idolatry was taking place, since the worship of a created thing in place of God occurs in the mind of the worshipper rather than in the image addressed.'[35]

In other words, were some Protestants and other Americans "Bibliolators," as beleaguered biblical critics sometimes cried out in counterattack? They may have *acted* like idolators. But, following Moore, how do we know if they were? It is far fairer to say that they were iconodules or iconolatrous people, so long as this observation does not include an implied theological denunciation. It means taking believers at their word and watching them at their work.

If I may condense more of Moore's argument to explain why Americans of Protestant stripe could reverence the Bible as an icon, there are five points to stress. First, an image evokes the experience of the numinous. Second, it captures a religious experience that is valued as a continuing reality, so that each confrontation of the image allows for repetition of the experience even if in 'frozen' form. Third, the image embodies a manifestation of sacred power and presence that is then celebrated in myth and ritual, in sacred space and time. Thus the Bible is the book of worship as well. Fourth, the image offers the worshiper an ideal archetype or sacred model for the sake of regular transformation. One "grows into" the plot of the Bible, and in the child's imagination its landscape and characters are as familiar as is the view out the window. Finally, the image enables one to be related to the cosmos, for it is a microcosm with which one can identify. One almost needs a physical object for gathering images under the individual and collective psychic carapace.[36]

Ordinarily the books on religious iconography include images taken from the Bible, but they rarely if ever notice the Bible itself as icon. Yet on

---

[35] Albert C. Moore, *Iconography of Religions: An Introducton* (Philadelphia: Fortress, 1977) 28; Moore quotes from John Philips, *The Reformation of Images* (Berkeley: University of California, 1973) 201.

[36] Moore, *Iconography of Religions*, 34–35.

soil where other icons were prohibited, the same five needs or roles that Moore cited remained operative, and Protestant-minded America took to the use of the Bible to fill them.

On American Protestant soil, the Quakers come nearest to being aniconic people, at least in relation to the Bible, though not a few prophets in their midst accused their fellow believers of "lapsing" in this respect. And latter-day (but by no means early) Unitarian-Universalism may have moved far enough from biblical norms to have put the book aside. Beyond that, it survives. In colonial Puritanism where there was to be no adornment or distraction in the beautifully simple meeting house, the Bible was allowed to be oversize far beyond the function. Certainly not all the buildings were so dark or the preachers' eyes so weak that such enormous print in such huge volumes was necessary. The leather binding, the high placement on reading desk or pulpit, the focus of eyes on the Book—all these enhanced the iconic aspect of worship and the Bible. In paintings of pilgrims heading for worship in colonial New England, the gun and the Bible are the standard images.

On the frontier, the circuit rider had to be a light traveler. A bit of rum under the saddlebags (until temperance made its way), a few personal necessities, perhaps a Book of Discipline—these were all that went along with the evangelist on the trail. Except for the Bible. Even Quakers used the Bible as a "civilizing" instrument in their work among the Indians.

As for blacks, what Hylan Lewis said about "Kent" applies widely: "References to the Bible—which are frequent—are verbal props used to prove, document, underscore, or just to display a kind of erudition. 'The Bible says . . .' is an expression used by even the most profane and secular when occasion demands."[37] The slaves were not permitted the Bible, but every chronicler reports their love for it and on the way the book itself became a symbol of liberation. Carter G. Woodson says that "Negroes . . . almost worshiped the Bible, and their anxiety to read it was their greatest incentive to learn." Reports of fugitive slaves liked to stress that they carried "a big Bible," hardly a useful object in the precarious passage on the underground railway. Of course, the content of the Bible, its message of hope and liberation, meant much to people denied the book as object or literacy as access, but they regarded the book numinously as did their white brothers and sisters.[38]

As for recent times, Protestant America by mid-century was taking on the attitudes the Gallup survey found to be extant in 1980. In a *Catholic Digest* survey, 83 percent of the Protestants regarded the Bible as the

---

[37] Hylan Lewis, "Blackways of Kent: Religion and Salvation," in *Hart M. Nelsen, Raytha L. Yokley and Anne K. Nelsen* (New York: Basic, 1971) 103.

[38] See the section on "Bible Christians," in *Slave Religion: The "Invisible Institution" in the Antebellum South*, by Albert J. Raboteau (New York: Oxford University, 1978) 239–43.

revealed word of God, but 40 percent of the Protestants read it "never or
hardly ever."[39] In a survey of a very Protestant county in Bible-believing
mid-America, Victor Obenhaus found that 63 percent of churchgoing
Protestants could not designate any differences between the Old and New
Testaments, few knew a single thing about the prophets, few could apply
the story of the Good Samaritan to life, and biblical materials as such were
"only slightly comprehended,"[40] despite weekly access to these themes in
church. I have often suggested that this same population cohort could spend
one evening of three hours in a community college on the Bhagavad-Gita
and know more of it than they gain by way of knowledge of the Bible
through a lifetime. Yet all reverence the book; they might join in denominational warfare against critics who might challenge its literal truth or in political conflict against courts that would "take it out of the schools." The
knowledge that the Bible is cherished, is a supreme authority, and is available to experts like preachers who can consult it is more important than
exploration of the contents. Bible classes seem most popular where the contents of the Bible are least critically examined, whereas when the Bible is an
object of scrutiny and study the iconic sense disappears and the crowds
dwindle.

In the political realm, iconoclasts have learned to keep their distance
from the Protestants on the subject of the Bible if they wish to win any
causes. In the 1890s radical feminists began to prepare a *Women's Bible* in
order to counteract what they felt were anti-women passages and emphases
in the use of the Bible. But in 1895 Susan B. Anthony showed political savvy
when she wrote Elizabeth Cady Stanton: "*No*—I don't want my name on
that Bible Committee—*You* fight that battle—and leave me to fight the
secular—the political fellows. . . . I simply don't want the enemy to be
diverted from my practical ballot fight—to that of scoring me for belief one
way or the other about the Bible." Stanton went ahead, and lost power. She
had no idea about the level of denunciation she would receive, including
from Protestant male clerics who supported both the Bible and the rights of
women. She made the mistake of saying, "We have made a fetich [*sic*] of the
Bible long enough. The time has come to read it as we do all other
books. . . ." Even nonreaders who were supporters of the Bible were not
ready to hear that.[41]

In a centennial observance of biblical scholarship in America it is natural for us to test the iconic thesis on the founders of the discipline. The last
thing any of them wanted to be was a destroyer of the Bible. They were

---

[39] Quoted by Will Herberg, *Protestant, Catholic, Jew* (New York: Doubleday, 1955) 236.

[40] Victor Obenhaus, *Church and Faith in Mid-America* (Philadelphia: Westminster, 1963)
72–82.

[41] Quoted in *The Ideas of the Woman Suffrage Movement, 1890–1920*, by Aileen Kraditor
(New York: Columbia University, 1965) 78, 80.

virtually unanimous in their theme that biblical criticism, historical and structural and analytic in character alike, would enhance faith in an age of science. To this day biblical scholars in the ecclesiastical community are frustrated when given no chance to show their fellow believers among the laity how much more exciting is one's pursuit of the "acts of God" through the environmental and contextual studies they cherish or the formal inquiries that lay bare so many dimensions of a text. They have fused critical scholarship and faith, and wonder why others are not allowed to share their enthusiasm. Yet in most denominations they know that partisans of anticritical outlooks can always exploit the iconic sense of people and go on to suggest that there will be less, not more, Bible as well as less, not more, faith, once one enters the mental furnished apartment in which the critic has no choice but to live.

In the beginning, when critical scholarship had its first pre-Civil War hearings, Edward Robinson was the patriarch, the only American to gain an international hearing. Robinson set the theme: "It has ever been the glory of the Protestant Faith, that it has placed the Scriptures where they ought to be, above every human name, above every human authority. THE BIBLE IS THE ONLY AND SUFFICIENT RULE OF FAITH AND PRACTICE."[42]

In the first critical generation, the celebrity preachers, the ones Winthrop Hudson called "Princes of the Pulpit"[43] almost to a person—T. DeWitt Talmadge was the exception—accepted biblical criticism as an advancement of the Protestant principle and an enhancement of faith in a scientific age. Only a few critics who were spoiling for a fight made their case less plausible by doing violence to the iconic sense of the Bible or the iconolatry of their attackers. Thus Charles Briggs was sarcastic about the "Bibliolatry" that treated the Bible magically instead of as "paper, print, and binding." Yet even such iconoclasts felt that they were helping the Bible in the public arena: "We have forced our way through the obstructions; let us remove them from the face of the earth, that no man hereafter may be kept from the Bible."[44] Briggs and other early critics regularly defended themselves by saying that no scholars would give a lifetime to the study of a book in which they did not believe. That, however, was not a telling point among conservatives who were fed a diet of stories that told how infidels from the Enlightenment to Robert Ingersoll studied the Bible in order to destroy it.

William Rainey Harper is an ideal type of the reverent biblical critic who did expend his energies sharing the critical outlook for the purpose of

[42] Edward Robinson, *The Bible and Its Literature* (New York: Office of the American Biblical Repository, 1841) 17.

[43] Winthrop S. Hudson, *The Great Tradition of the American Churches* (New York: Harper and Brothers, 1953) Chap. 8.

[44] Quoted by William R. Hutchison, *The Modernist Impulse in American Protestantism* (Cambridge: Harvard University, 1976) 94.

extending and deepening faith also among the laity, and for half a generation it worked. In 1892 he gave a speech on "The Rational and the Rationalistic Higher Criticism" at Chautauqua. First, the iconic regard:

> Can we, in the multiformity of the work which lies before us during the few weeks of
> our sojourn together, find anything in which we possess a common interest? At first
> thought it would seem impossible to name a subject related directly or indirectly to the
> work of all of us; but if we think again, if we recall the place occupied among us by
> the Bible, a place fundamental in all thought and life; if we recall the conflict of opin-
> ion which to-day rages on every side about the Bible, a conflict in which most vital
> interests are concerned; if we remember that in this conflict the principles at stake are
> principles of universal character and application—if we think of all this, I fancy we
> shall agree that the question of the higher criticism of the Bible is one in which we
> have a common interest, and one, the consideration of which at this time and place
> will not be inappropriate.

In other words: only the Bible would bring them together, and only
biblical criticism would quicken their inquiries. Harper recognized that
"criticism" conveys "to some minds an unpleasant idea, but the right usage
of the word carries with it nothing of this kind. . . . Do you ask what criticism is in its technical sense? I answer in a single word, 'inquiry.' The whole
business of a critic is to make inquiry." Then Harper went on to criticize the
rationalism of both the conservative scholastic defenders of the Bible and the
rationalists themselves. He wanted a scientific not a "scientistic" view of the
Bible.

Then came the pastoral and faith-building sense of the critic:

> Great care, therefore, must be exercised, lest the learner, whether a professional stu-
> dent or a casual listener, be led to give up old positions before new positions have been
> formulated. The proper spirit is the building spirit, but the more natural spirit and the
> more easily developed is the destructive spirit.

Harper was confident, as were most of the other pioneers, that if the rever-
ently critical approach were to be adopted, "the man who has believed without knowing why will have an intelligent basis for his faith," but Harper did
not recognize that "believing without knowing why" better satisfied the
wishes and wants of people whose view of the Bible as icon did not need
another base. The critical approach would further remove grounds of hostility and skepticism. And the large class of people who had been coolly indif-
ferent would learn "that this Book is what it purports to be, the word of
God. . . . It will become to them a thing of life, not because it has
changed—it has always been alive—but because they have changed toward
it." To a "destructive" or "objective" critic, of course, Harper would have
been dismissed as an iconolatrous believer programed by his Sunday school
faith in childhood with presuppositions that would not let him read the
Bible as he would "any other book."

As Harper heard it, "the cry of our times is for the application of scientific methods to the study of the Bible," but he heard the cries of University

of Chicago students and the lay elite, while Grover Cleveland probably spoke for louder cries when he wanted an uncommented-upon Book. "If," Harper continued, "the methods of the last century continue to hold exclusive sway, the time will come when intelligent men of all classes will say, 'If this is your Bible we will have none of it.'" And Harper wrote an epitaph for himself that he could have applied to most of his contemporaries in the critical circle: "He has done what he could to build up not only an interest in the study of the Scriptures, but a faith in their divine origin."[45]

For half a generation, Harper and the Chautauquans, the university extension propagators, and some of the lay elite or princes of the pulpit made some progress, but in the end it was not the scientific outlook that drew the masses but the pre- or anticritical views of the Dwight L. Moodys and Billy Sundays that prevailed. There is some pathos in the attempt of Harper and the "scientists," one that I am reminded of in the similar courting principles of a modern young subject of a limerick:

A free-living damsel named Hall
Once went to a birth control ball.
   She took an appliance
   To make love with science;
But nobody asked her at all.

Harry Emerson Fosdick from the twenties through the forties of this century was the last "prince of the pulpit," the last celebrity cleric, who effectively propagated the biblical critical view as an enhancement of faith to huge audiences and readerships. Since then we have seen a "collapse of the middle" between the world of the scholars on one hand and the lay and sometimes the preaching public on the other.

Believing critics have seldom gotten much help in the larger culture. The press, beginning early in this century, knew it could always create sensation by dwelling on the iconic regard for the Bible and then "exposing" the iconoclasm of critical elitists. The *Cosmopolitan* magazine turned loose a writer named Harold Boice, who month after month toured the major campuses and spread shocking news of how the scholars treated the Bible as a great spiritual book but not as the unique book of God.[46]

Through the twenties of this century humanists like H. L. Mencken, Ben Hecht, Clarence Darrow, Joseph Wood Krutch, Walter Lippmann, and others found it convenient, however historically inaccurate it was, to treat fundamentalist biblicism as normative Christianity from which modern biblical

---

[45] Reported on in *Chautauqua Assembly Herald* 17, no. 14 (4 August 1892) 2, 3, 6, 7. For more on Harper's view, consult Robert W. Funk, "The Watershed of the American Biblical Tradition: The Chicago School, First Phase, 1892-1920," *JBL* 95 (1976) 4–22.

[46] Sample titles of Boice articles in *Cosmopolitan* 47 (June–November 1909) were "Polyglots in Temples of Babel," "Avatars of the Almighty," "Christianity in the Crucible," and "Rallying Round the Cross."

critics were falling. In fact, this spirit lived on into the 1970s in the hands of Princeton philosopher Walter Kaufmann, who accused anyone of a developmental view of "gerrymandering" theology. The biblical critic has therefore progressively withdrawn into the company of other professionals and has become inept when denominational politics or cultural assault see him or her as an iconoclast.

Where does this history leave us? I shall set forth a few summary remarks, each of which needs further development.

(1) The critical approach in the course of the century established itself in the academy. Opponents on their turf seem apologetic and defensive, knowing that their battle for scholarship that would repeal "the crisis of historical consciousness" or would move people out of the mental furnished apartments characterized by the critical outlook is an uphill task.

(2) Biblical scholars in the *academy* are expected to reflect only humanistic (humanities-based) concerns, employing critical methods on the Bible just as they find their colleagues using them on the *Iliad* or Shakespeare. They are not to claim special privileges for their work or their texts. And like all other humanists, they can expect the respect and curiosity of a small circle of colleagues.

(3) Biblical scholars in the context of *religious* communities, in church-related colleges, theological schools, church and synagogue, or the proreligious but nonpracticing public have no such luxury. They deal with texts that are engendered by a community and that engender community and, though some complain of this situation, it is from such communities that they gain a kind of power. But they have reason to complain when political forces in those communities keep them from gaining a fair hearing.

(4) About half the Protestant community, some of the Jewish community, and an indeterminate number in the Catholic community, have *ignored or resisted* the century of scholarship. The critic is in a position not unlike that of the poet in Dylan Thomas's vision, whose "craft and sullen art" concern the lovers who lie abed, unheeding. The believing public, for reasons of preoccupation, faith, or whatever, pays little notice.

(5) I have argued that the main reason for ignoring or resisting critical scholarship has been the iconic regard for the Bible as an object in the national shrine, whether read or not, whether observed or not: it is seen as being basic to national and religious communities' existence. They hold it in awe and give *latreia* to it.

(6) This iconic sense puts critical scholars at a disadvantage because they will also appear to be *iconoclastic* by the mere fact that they engage in inquiry. The media show that one can always be controversial if treating the Bible in any way other than iconically.

(7) Biblical *scholars* for the most part are aware of this situation because the vast majority of them—can we get surveys to confirm or refute the impression?—were nurtured in childhood in "Jerusalem," not "Athens." Few

come to critical study of the Bible through a random search for texts in the context of humanities. Most come through the passages of faith and life inspired by childhood experience of the Bible as icon in mind, home, church, and culture. Since the critical sense has enlivened their adult lives, they are often mystified about why everyone else does not make their passage. This seventh point has to be based more on personal observation than extensive defensible empirical inquiry, and I can only invite the community of scholars to begin to test it on each other.

(8) As for the future, it may be that our secular-pluralist culture is becoming so differentiated, its norms so diffuse, that each generation will see the Bible surrounded by an increasing number of icons, until it *loses centrality*. It is not likely that in foreseeable futures there will be no icons in the subcommunities of national life, for under the carapace of individual and social existence it remains necessary to have a framework for organizing effects and impressions. That the Bible has held such a position for such a significant number of Americans has been good for biblical scholars, who cannot help being curious about the future and who are not likely to be on the sidelines as that future unfolds. The second century of biblical scholarship in America therefore promises to be anything but settled and stale. That, I should surmise, is how biblical scholars would choose to have things.

II

SCRIPTURE, HISTORY, AND THE QUEST FOR MEANING

Langdon Gilkey

First of all, let me express my utter delight at being asked to present an address on the occasion of the one hundredth anniversary of the Society of Biblical Literature. This is for me a very signal honor—an honor both to me and to my craft, theology. And let me admit, perhaps in more muted voice, my surprise: not only that a theologian has been asked by the officers of this society to interpret the significance and meaning of what they have been about, but an *American* theologian. Continental theologians are born—so I have been assured—already speaking biblical sentences, replete with biblical categories innately structured into their most trivial nursery chatter; they may *seem* to have had to learn the biblical words and languages; but that is, as Valentinus said about Jesus' habit of eating regularly, "merely to avoid comment." It would, therefore, be highly natural, if risky, for these innately biblical thinkers to speak to biblical scholars. American theologians, on the contrary—at least according to the same oral tradition—are reported to inherit only cultural genes, to harken therefore only to cultural voices in their work, and to speak only cultural wisdom in their theologies. I trust my appearance here may mark a break in these oral traditions, in these rumors of legendary wars. There may be mutants even among theologians; or, put better, what others have by nature we may possibly inherit through grace. In any case I am very glad and proud to be here, and I hope my remarks may represent a genuine synthesis of our domestic theological style with the strange yet exciting and healing "world" of the Scriptures.

Our theme this evening is the relation of Scripture and its understanding to the understanding of history, to the discernment in the sequences of history of meaning or the promise of meaning. This relation may seem an obvious one to this society; and, to be sure, it has been taken for granted in the long tradition of Hebrew and of Christian thought about history and its meaning. For most of us, it is here—in *this* volume, in these two Testaments—that are contained the light that illumines the dark, terrifying mystery of historical existence and the grace that offers promise not only of understanding but also of creative courage and hope. And yet we must recognize that this correlation of scripture and history appears to most of the world around us—not to mention most of the American Academy of Religion—to be anachronistic, parochial, and bizarre, a kind of methodological version, so to say, of Lessing's "ugly ditch." If it seemed absurd to Lessing's age to derive a truth of universal scope from one historical event, surely it is equally backward in our own to interpret universal history on the basis of one text—and one text at that which represents a variety of epochs and cultural situations and is crammed with diverse materials and wildly divergent viewpoints.

Clearly, as Barth would say, this queer claim for one text to manifest the universal can become intelligible only through the category of revelation: only the divine Word can leap that "ugly ditch" from the particular to the universal; only through the Word can one text bear this transcendent role in truth and in grace. That point being granted to Barth, however—and speaking as a systematic theologian, I agree completely with him on it—it is, I think, nonetheless true that this correlation of one text, especially a religious text, with the interpretation and comprehension of history is not as bizarre and naive as modern culture tends to see it. To most of the modern consciousness—liberal or Marxist—history is not at all opaque, much less an impenetrable mystery. On the contrary, all one has to do is "to look at it" carefully and responsibly, "empirically and scientifically" as we would say, to see its structure and so to understand the principles of its sequences and changes. In such an endeavor, how can one text or one tradition be given a crucial role? And in such an obviously *secular* endeavor, comprised at best of economic, political, psychological, and especially sociological and historical learning, insight, and methodologies, how can a *religious* text be relevant or helpful, let alone decisive?

It is this viewpoint that I wish here to contest as a misunderstanding of the way, as humans, we are in history and the way consequently we understand history and find meaning in it. Texts, religious symbols, and participatory principles of interpretation, I shall argue, dominate and shape every approach to history and to life within it; this is a pattern pervasive in cultural and communal interpretations of history. And not only that, I shall seek to suggest that an understanding of history based on scripture, on the two Testaments, fits the contours of history as we experience it. This dual argument does not constitute a natural theology. Only in the brightest and happiest of epochs, and then only among the privileged classes, is a natural theology based on the character of *history* conceivable—and on this 5 November 1980 I can hardly say ours is the brightest of epochs! Thus our argument presupposes some transcendent principle of meaning, that is to say, it presupposes revelation which no natural theology can establish or encompass. Nevertheless, it is an argument in apologetics based on the compatibility or correlation of history as experienced and comprehended with history as interpreted in scripture, a correlation basic, I believe, to scripture's own understanding of itself and its historical world.

o   o   o   o   o

Let us begin this discussion with what will seem obvious about human being in time as we experience it. Humans, it has often been said, are both in and out of history, immersed in it and yet in part transcending it. Moreover, it is evident that human existence is in and out of history in two related but distinct ways. First of all, our being in history is characterized by the polarity of destiny and freedom; of a given (destiny) from our own past and that of our world, a given that constitutes us, forms and shapes us, pushes us inexorably in a definite, determined direction, and with which, whether we will or no, we must deal in all our actions. This unremovable destiny is, however, balanced by the unavoidable requirement to decide and to act now, to act in creative response to that given, within its limits but in the light of its possibilities (freedom). Thus is history characterized on the one hand by trends and continuities arising out of a given destiny and on the other by contingency and novelty arising out of the unpredictability of human response, decision, and actions in the face of that given. The given was once itself undetermined, itself mere possibility; now it is there, shaped, unavoidable; what we do with it is limited by these conditions but never determined by them. Conditions, said Gordon Leff, become *history* only when they elicit a human response. History is destiny in union with freedom, neither one alone. We are in history as dependent on the conditions given from beyond ourselves; we are "out" of it as capable of responding in novel ways to those conditions. In history, actuality is balanced by possibility and destiny by freedom; and union of the two makes historical events.

Second, while humans are *in* the stream of history, pushed by it in unwanted directions, threatened by its plethora of menacing forces and lured by its unexpected possibilities, humans are also "out of it" in memory and anticipation. Spirit transcends history by surveying its past and in that light envisioning its possible future, by uniting, in other words, its destiny and its freedom, its unavoidable actualities from the past and its range of possibilities for the future. In each act of freedom in relation to destiny—in each personal act by an individual *and* in each political act by a community—remembered past and anticipated future are brought together first in comprehension and then in decision. Again, embeddedness in time and transcendence over it unite to make event. Thus does eternity, transcendence over time but a transcendence united with time, invade personal and communal life in historical understanding and in political actions alike. In any case, it is for this ontological reason, because of the character or structure of human being in time, that there is the necessity of bringing what is remembered and interpreted and what is perhaps to come into a meaningful unity, a unity of understanding and of meaning—so that historical understanding be achieved, personal or political acts take place, in other words—so that ongoing life, creative action towards the future, be possible. The deep involvement of human being and meaning *in* historical passage, *in* history, and yet their ability to survey and partially to direct that passage, create together the necessity of giving to the sequences of time a *logos*, a structure of order and meaning in terms of which both understanding and purposive action become possible. Political consciousness is requisite for political action, and for both a *theory* about the sequence of events is necessary.

Political action is both unavoidable and central in historical existence. It represents the centered action of a unified community, through its "legitimate" leaders, in response to the given crises and opportunities of its common life. Since we all exist communally, political action is, therefore, the way human freedom expresses itself and is present communally—that is to say in historical life. For history is constituted by the life and action of groups. Moreover, for a political act expressive of freedom, as for historical reflection itself, a unified understanding of the past, of the present, and thus of the possibilities of our future, is necessary. Also involved or presupposed in creative political action is a firm grasp of the norms and of the potential meanings of life in time. In history and so in communal life the practical and the theoretical tend to fuse into one—as the continuous role of savants or sages in active political life illustrates. Both presuppose a vision of the structure and the meaning of the total sequence of events in which that community finds itself.

It is for these reasons, deeply embedded in our ontological structure as "finite freedom," as in yet out of history, that myths—symbolic visions of history as a whole—appear as basic to all important political speech and that a general vision of history is presupposed in all historical understanding, even that which claims to be "scientific." Ingredient in these myths or visions of history—at least as they function communally—is some understanding of, or theory about, the ultimate sovereignty that rules history, its magisterial or ruling forces, be they evolutionary, economic, psychological, or theological; some view of an ultimate order in these sequences; some vision of an ultimate norm for communal life in history; and some sense of its ultimate meaning and so for grounds of shared hope. Organized "religions" have traditionally provided that symbolic structure orienting communal life in time to some permanent order and meaning. In a secular world so-called ideologies, for example, liberal progressivism and Marxism, have done the same thing. Thus are politics and religion always interrelated in communal life. For it is the mythical vision (religious or secular) structuring this order and meaning of history that provides the basis for legitimate political rule, the guidelines for acceptable political action, the standards and goals for society's vocations, and the aims for its patterns of education. Every culture, as Tillich reminded us, has such a "religious substance," an apprehension of ultimate being that structures our ultimate concerns, and that, as we have indicated, symbolically structures the ultimate and sacred horizon within which each community and each facet of its culture live and become in time.

It is consequently no wonder that history, politics, and religion have always been so deeply intertwined. It is in the ongoing stream of historical process that communities face the crucial issues of their life and death, of security and insecurity, of freedom from fate or subservience to it, of the enhancement or the loss of meaningful existence—that is to say that they face "religious" issues. Moreover, it is here in the sequences of temporal change that their freedom is most sorely tempted to actions of vast sin or self-destruction or that they are called on for strength, courage, justice, and compassion. The issues of our being and of our non-being, our ultimate concerns, appear as much for communal life as for individual existence *within* historical sequence, in dealing with an unavoidable given and in facing an unknown and often uncontrollable future.

Despite all their knowledge and their technology, modern men and women have not transcended this ontological structure of temporality and finitude nor escaped the terrors and anxieties of history, the threats of fate and of non-being menacing their future, nor lost their need for confidence and hope in the open possibilities for that future. As much as older cultures, therefore, modern life has needed, and depends on, a "mythical" vision of history such as we have described. Thus is there a religious dimension in all cultural life and to all political speech and understanding, as much in contemporary as in ancient times. As a consequence, theological understanding—the understanding of the meaning of historical being in terms of some constellaton of religious-type symbols—is always relevant to the comprehension of history. Or, to put it another way, any global understanding of history—again one thinks of liberalism or of Marxism—foundational for political and theoretical life alike has a religious or a theological dimension or component. It includes a mythical structure providing for those who are committed to it an understanding of their own role in the global history of good and evil, an ultimate norm for cultural life, and a sense of meaning and of hope for the unknown future. To correlate *religious* documents structured by *religious* symbols with the interpretation of history is, therefore, by no means aberrant or merely traditional. Each modern secular ideology, however it may strain to be based on science or historical understanding alone, takes to itself religious elements whenever it functions as the common schema for the interpretation of a community's vital history.

Despite their necessity, such global visions of history are hard to come by and harder to verify. As every culture (except perhaps our own) has realized, the order and meaning of the structure of historical events is at best opaque, its key elusive; it represents a mystery with only dim and fragmentary facets of meaning. Furthermore, it is certainly true that history presents us with an exceedingly complex and rich scene. As the story of collective human action in relation to natural and social changes and to unexpected historical events, history includes all the multifaceted dimensions, factors, and "causes" characteristic of individual human existence. To seek to understand it as if it were merely an aspect of changing nature characterized by invariant and determined physical relations alone, by so-called "social laws," is thus a serious methodological error. Contingency and freedom are deeply ingredient in its structure, and so the possibility of real alternatives and the actuality of unexpected novelty continually upset any simple causal or rational order.

Three other factors add to the complexity and opaqueness of history.

(1) The curious observer of history, however objective he/she may seek to be, is herself involved in the history she observes, ultimately concerned with the direction of its current—for her life itself glides on them or sinks because of them. Thus is her vision shaped by her interests, and her interests by her location in the historical order. The fortunes or misfortunes of her class, sex, race, nation, epoch give form to her view and shape the optimistic or pessimistic mood that governs every such vision. For this reason myths about history, unless subjected radically to critique, are both partial and ideological; each is a limited perspective directed all too sharply by special interest as well as by particular insight.

(2) The sequences of history that are surveyed are always incomplete. The significance of each event, like election returns early on, is not yet "in," and so the meaning—even of a short span of events—is as yet neither settled nor evident. Consequently, visions of history are at best studied guesses, projected hypotheses, matters as much of communal commitment and hope as of any precise verification or clear conceptual understanding. They are in fact "religious myths," held communally for existential as well as theoretical reasons, massively influencing life but limited in their universality and verifiability.

Any tomorrow can effect radical changes in the meaning of every piece of the data on which a vision of history is built. In a brief span of time a novel sequence of important events can sink the most formidable and apparently permanent social or economic trend almost without a trace. Two examples come immediately to mind: predictions of a stable future for an agrarian society made in the Richmond or Montgomery of 1856 would have seemed bizarre indeed in 1875. And even Herman Kahn, who boasted that a "scientific futurology" could at last peer reliably into our probable future, had in his book on the year 2000 published in 1970 as yet no intimation at all of the ecology crisis, the crisis of world natural resources, that two short years later was to explode and qualify, if not falsify, every one of his scientific graphs and expectations about our common world future. The past is itself not yet finished, and the future is radically unknown and unknowable. These ontological facts both elicit our *need* for a meaningful vision for this opaque passage in which we are, and yet they also prevent us both from being too clear about what we dimly see or from being too certain about the validity of our reports and our vision of things to come.

(3) History is alienated or estranged from its own structure. It seems never to be what it could or should be, what its possibilities either promise or require. Since this alienation arises in large part from our freedom, it includes our common responsibility. History, said Tillich, is estranged, and its estrangement is sin; or, as Augustine and Niebuhr said, history is "fallen," and we are each alone and all together involved in that fall. As theory this sounds old-timey, moralistic, and even "small town" or naive. As historical experience, however, it is continually validated and revalidated. Glowing possibilities, both personal and social, do sour and become tasteless or demonic. Think of the waxing power of Europe in the seventeenth and eighteenth centuries, or that of America in the postwar world. And yet now the power of Europe is gone and that of America declining—and each is for the foreseeable future paying dearly for the exploitation, the oppression, and the conflicts that characterized the ways each actualized their own possibilities. The "given" that each older generation presents to its children—what they have done with their world so full of possibilities in their youth—festers as they hand it on with hidden or open sores that cause endless pain and can become lethal for the new generation that follows. My father's generation inherited from its parents the world of the First World War; mine, from that generation, Hitler's world and with it the Second World War; and *think* what a mass of tangled corruption—a world fraught with injustice, oppression, greed, and demonic possibilities—our children will inherit from us! This corruption of history's ideal possibilities is the experienced actuality of history. The estrangement of actuality, to be sure, is clearer in some ages and to some groups than it is to others, but it is characteristic of all times and places. Yet it is also true that in the midst of this deep alienation characteristic of actuality, still possibilities of the creative new do appear, hope and confidence are deeply felt, and unexpected healing is experienced.

Thus is there added to the complexity of history and the involvement of every observer in it a further dialectical complexity that requires a very subtle and rich—and also "religious"—set of categories. First, there is the ontological-anthropological structure of history of destiny and freedom whereby each finite actuality is or can be given new possibilities for the future. Second, there is the experienced alienation whereby destiny becomes fate and freedom seems stripped of genuine possibilities. Finally—a "fact" expressed in all religious visions—there appear redemptive forces of healing, of reconciliation, of reunion, and of new beginnings. Because of this dialectical complexity, secular theories of history become "ideologies" when they begin to function socially; that is, they all include finally a depiction of the career of good in the midst of evil, a story of redemption, however unintelligible or unempirical their version may be, from the evil that obscures our historical present. And for this same reason, explicit religious visions of history are often more subtle and therefore more empirical (that is, closer to the facts of history) than are most purely cognitive "scientific" or philosophical visions. For each religious view tends to include some version of this religious dialectic established by alienation and redemption as well as the ontological limits and possibilities inherent in finitude and in freedom. No general interpretation of history can ignore the pervasive patterns of evil that engulf historical life, any more than it can ignore the possibilities implicit in freedom. Without a religious dialectic of alienation and redemption, however, such views *mis*interpret those patterns evident in historical life; they either emphasize the positive structure and harmony of passage and so the possibilities of historical life (if the observer belongs to a fortunate group in a fortunate epoch) in an unwarranted and soon-to-be falsified optimism, or, concentrating so heavily on the actuality of evil, they speak only of fatedness, failing to discern the new possibilities and the forces for reconciliation latent in historical experience.

Biblical symbolism includes each of these levels of dialectical complexity, and that is perhaps the explanaton for whatever persuasive theoretical power it may possess. In its symbols of creation and providence, and its consequent understanding of human existence as dependent finitude, and yet a free finitude directed to the ultimate and the sacred, that is, as creaturely and yet made in the Image of God, it presents a structural or ontological understanding of existence that clarifies and affirms the finitude and yet the self-transcendence characteristic of human life in time. With its further "religious" categories of estrangement and sin on the one hand and of revelation, redemption, and reconciliation on the other, it encompasses the second dialectic pervasive in existence we have just outlined.

It should be noted, however, that this illuminating complexity has led to two divergent and often clashing interpretations of biblical symbolism, that of natural theology and Pelagianism, and that of sin and grace. Seen from the perspective of this dialectical complexity, each of these antithetical traditions takes its rightful place on the one hand as legitimate but on the other as partial. The first of them, conceived usually in an optimistic era, and from a privileged spot in which personal and historical possibilities seem plentiful, sees clearly history's fundamental ontological structure of creative destiny and of pervasive freedom for new possibilities. Thus, discerning an order and meaning to history's sequences, it concludes "rationally" that this evident goodness of life requires and so implies a divine power, a divine wisdom, and a divine bounty. When through the "good luck" of a fortunate epoch the ontological structure of history can be clearly seen, natural theologies, philosophical theisms, and an emphasis on human freedom abound and dominate theological reflection—but understandably such theologies, based on an apprehension of the obvious goodness and meaning of ordinary life, can only dimly discern the tragic elements of existence and so barely appreciate the full scope and meaning of the Gospel.

In contrast, for other biographies, other classes, and other epochs, the alienation, the fatedness, and the suffering of history are deeply experienced.

Destiny with its promise has seemed consistently to become a stifling fatedness to suffering and to meaninglessness, and the hope for new possibilities seems only an illusion. Freedom is aware only of its own bondage and its responsibility for that bondage. Sin, fate, and death appear to be factors that alone rule actuality. In *that* sort of situation, the ontological structure of history as characterized by freedom and by novel, creative possibility disappears as do landmarks in a heavy fog at sea. At that point, suave clerical assurances of the goodness, order, and possibilities of life and of a benevolent ruler of events seem to be a cruel jest if not an ideological sham, a turning away from obvious injustice in order to maintain and justify exploitative privilege. The longing for rescue from the anxiety, terror, and guilt of historical actuality replaces grateful celebration of its maker and serene confidence in divine justice. Understandably now the more "religious" and less philosophical categories of sin and grace come to the fore as characterizing experienced actuality. Creation and providence, although still providing the ontological grounds for God's judgment and God's grace alike, seem ideologically suspect, a self-interested justification and blessing of an evil world. Here, too, however, a theological error can appear if this emphasis is pushed too far. For the Gospel and the promises of grace make no sense unless the world is God's creation and under God's ultimate sovereignty. Both of these interpretations are, therefore, genuine intuitions of the character of historical existence, and both emphasize essential and so crucial biblical symbols—and both consistently detest the vision of history and of the Christian religion that the other proffers! Possibly an awareness of the complexity and the opaqueness, even the mystery and depth, of historical process will help us to appreciate the dialectical richness and even the apparent paradoxes of our common biblical symbolism.

In any case, the main thrust of our argument is that both the character of human participation in history and the consequent complexity of history call for mythical and theological understanding. We cannot just "look at" history to uncover either the structure or the meaning of its sequences. Some deep, assumed principle of interpretation is always at work whenever we think about temporal passage or seek to act within it. Such presupposed principles answer questions about the relation of determinism and freedom, about the meaning and scope of evil in time, about the possibilities available to life in time, about the redemptive forces available or not in history—in short, a global or mythical vision compounded of metaphysical, psychological, and religious elements. The history of religions provides us with explicitly religious variants of these global symbol systems; modern ideologies such as liberalism and Marxism provide us with secular versions of the same. Each shapes and gives substance to a community's life by uniting that community through its vision of history and the role it gives that community in history. The religious substance of each creative culture is largely constituted by such a vision of history and of its meaning. Each is in turn quite particular; each arises out of a religious or a cultural tradition; each has crucial texts to which to appeal. Thus not only religious symbols but also participation in a tradition, and attention if not adherence to the texts formative of that tradition, are constitutive elements of any communal interpretation of history. The logos of history is in each case borne by a given tradition and embodied in a given set of "scriptures," and both are crucial for communal and for political existence. History and interpretation, history and texts, are correlative. For historical beings, the universal is only available *through* the particularity of a given tradition and its texts, the meaning of history through a particular cultural or religious viewpoint. The role of scripture or its equivalent in human life in history, in shaping and unifying community, in guiding action and in comprehending the future with courage and hope, is no Christian or Jewish aberration destined to die out. It is essential to our human historicity.

o   o   o   o   o

Having discussed and defended the particular—in tradition, symbolic structure, and scriptural texts—as essential to the interpretation of past history and to action within present and future history, let us now turn directly to *our* particular case, to *our* scriptures, and see how they serve to discern the meaning of events as we experience the latter. Are they illuminative of the structure and meaning of historical passage, and does this illumination provide a creative framework, inspiration, and guide for praxis? I think they do—although any arguments at this level are so circular in character as hardly to count as demonstrations.

As I have argued in other contexts, in the Old Testament understanding of history there are three distinct moments or stages characterizing historical passage as Israel experienced that passage. First of all, there was the divine constitution or "creation" of the people as a people and of their cultural life in all its facets. There can be little question that for Israel cultural life had been constituted by Yahweh as probably the paradigmatic act *within* the history of creation: it was God, not they, who established the covenant, who gave the sacred law covering all aspects of cultural life, and even who established the political institutions (the judges and later the kings) who governed them. The main continuing role of Yahweh in relation to this people was the parental one of nurturing, fostering, and protecting, not so much of individual Hebrews but of the community as a community and the culture as a culture. Israel's culture was, if there ever was one, one explicitly with a "religious substance," one founded directly by God and one preserved and ruled by the divine actions in history. It is not inappropriate, therefore, to regard as "biblical" the viewpoint that each creative culture, insofar as it lives on a religious substance, is established in and through the presence of the divine, apprehended or received to be sure in ways different from this but nonetheless grounded there.

The second moment, as we have noted, is the appearance of estrangement or alienation, of the "fallen" character of the life of even a chosen people. Specifically this estrangement appears in scripture as the betrayal of their covenant, a corruption of the gracious gifts received in and through the creative divine constitution of their communal life. This betrayal and corruption characterized the entire extent of Israel's experienced and recorded life within the covenant, whatever minimal "doctrine" of the fall they might have explicitly expressed. As they knew well and repeatedly experienced, the sins of the fathers *are* visited on their children's children. Thus for them this alienation was one root, if not *the* root, of the tragic events and ultimately of the nemesis that increasingly threatened Israel's existence, as what we call the "prophetic interpretation" of their history makes clear. For she finally came to see this nemesis as God's judgment on her, a judgment so severe and total that it seemed (at least to Isaiah and Ezekiel) to betoken the *un*creation, the *un*ravelling, and the *dis*integration of the creative culture Yahweh and this people had together raised up. It is surely no exaggeration to claim that this experience of betrayal, a betrayal of *our* creative covenant, and this threat of tearing down and even of approaching nemesis, apply equally to our *own* experience, whether to the experience of Western culture generally or to that of our own American commonwealth.

The final moment is also prophetic, although it was so to speak "signalled" throughout the history by Yahweh's frequent and unexpected acts of repentant mercy. This is the promise of a new covenant beyond the destruction of the old—a new creative, redemptive act of Yahweh, the promise of new possibilities in historical life even though the old had become corrupted, judged, and dismantled. The promise of such a new covenant—of new religious and cultural possibilities—was what provided, in the midst of the experience of social disintegration, hope for the future—although, let us recall, it was rarely welcomed by those presently in power. This theme too finds its echo in our modern experience: confidence in its validity provides the hope so often proclaimed in liberationist movements, and fear of the appearance of the radically new characterizes every established or First World power, capitalist and socialist alike.

These three moments characteristic of ongoing history as a whole have been drawn from the Hebrew scriptures. They are—as a moment's thought will confirm—expanded, deepened, and refocused around one event or series of events in the New Testament, the life and destiny of Jesus who is the Christ. There divine constitution, divine judgment, and new creative act become incarnation, atonement, and resurrection/parousia—aspects of *history* to be sure but not of *ordinary* history. While this deepening and refocusing in the New Testament is central to any Christian interpretation of history, we have no time to develop its full implications here. Thus I would in closing like to return to the three moments that to me delineate a biblical interpretation of the general structure of ongoing history and ask how they illumine for us the contours of our own historical experience. Certainly they are not, as we have seen, totally strange either to ordinary experience of history or even to ordinary views of history. Of what, then, does their difference consist; and what does this difference or uniqueness add to our understanding of history and to our praxis within it? What we shall find, I think, is that on the one hand each of these three moments—divine constitution, divine judgment, and divine restitution or renewal— appears in its biblical form as apparently increasingly *incredible*; it is a truth about history and ourselves that is steadily harder to recognize and, to be honest, that we do not *want* to recognize. Still, on the other hand, we shall see that a closer and more careful look at the real situation shows each to be increasingly validated by that real situation.

Every creative movement or epoch in history believes in divine constitution. They may not put it *that* way, but intrinsic to any communal myth or vision of history is the deep belief that now at last the essential purpose and goal of history have manifested themselves embodied in historical community—and, needless to say, in *our* community. It is as if the ultimate grain of history has at last revealed itself in us; the center and goal toward which events had been moving and the patterns that will set the form of subsequent historical life are now plain and embodied in our communal life. So Christian nations and empires interpreted themselves in contrast to their pagan, infidel, or heretical contemporaries. So had China and Japan alike understood their role or destiny; and, ironically, despite their deliberate repudiation of the category of the sacred, so did the Enlightenment and its two children interpret themselves: liberal/democratic culture (this *was* the theory of progress) and now most recently Marxism. What distinguished the biblical (and possibly the Chinese) account from those others is that the divine is not regarded as indissolubly bound to the culture in question, as intrinsic to it, however creative it may have been. Rather, in the scriptural view the divine constitution eventuates in a *covenantal* relation in which betrayal and even abrogation are possible and can result in judgment and ultimate repudiation. In other words, the divine creative act has become characterized by a *moral* relation in which the issue of the *justice* of the community is crucial to the relation of the divine and its constituting power to that community. As a new and unexpected dimension of historical life, the norm of justice has become central to history, and with it the conceivability and so the possibility of communal self-criticism at the deepest level appear.

Likewise every culture has the experience of and belief in estrangement, alienation, and guilt. To all cultures evil is well nigh pervasive, human life by and large wrongly lived, immorality generally rife, and whatever good there may be vastly precarious and even endangered. To be sure, they manifest widely differing interpretations of these aspects of historical life and of what makes up good and evil, and each culture locates good and evil in vastly different places. To most cultures evil lies in those who are deviant from the community and its ethos, and especially it lies in whatever forces are opposed to the community, in other words, "our enemies." There among the "bad guys," deliberate wrongs are visible, malice and self-interest obviously rule, and thus the presence of real guilt is undeniable. Modern theory, social-scientific or Marxist, tends to deny guilt as a false category, itself expressive only of sociological or psychological alienation. Modern politics, on the other hand, domestic or international, is as replete with it and with the moral judgments that lie back of it as was that of any epoch.

Again, what is unique about the biblical interpretation of this aspect of history is that the pervasiveness of evil, of moral wrong and so of guilt, is made universal or all-inclusive. Thus, and here surely is the crucial point, it includes *us* as well as the enemy, the good guys as well as the bad. Clearly, the possibility of a new sort of communal self-understanding is appearing here and a new sort of transcendence: a self-understanding that can be self-critical and still affirm its own destiny and a transcendence that yet remains constitutive of the creative value and the potential moral health of the historical community. The biblical interpretation is becoming increasingly strange and incredible to ordinary wisdom and yet—as we promised—more and more in tune with the actual contours of concrete historical experience.

In a sense too hope is universal, at least wherever a culture or a community is on the rise, feels itself to be gaining strength, and thus finds itself facing a brightening future. However, despair and hopelessness are also in the same sense universal. For the historical forces that impel a movement forward can also, and frequently do, desert it or turn against it; or, as we have noted, a cultural community may well bring about its own nemesis. Confidence in liberalism and Marxism alike as opening up a new future has waned for our immediate generations. Each in its own way seems to many of its adherents spent as a historical force, its glowing possibilities corrupted into sordid actuality and its theories contradicted by too many historical facts. In such a situation promise and hope for the future, requisite for creative political action, seem impossible, and as a consequence, forces representing only the past or representing only sheer power move to the center of the stage. To believe in new possibilities in the midst of an apparently desperate situation, a situation with *no* possibilities, is therefore almost impossible; existentially the promise of a new covenant can be quite incredible. Such belief depends not only on a confidence in the sovereign forces of history; it also requires a mode of transcendence in the object of faith of which few visions of history are capable. Such a situation of despair about the future seemed itself incredible short decades ago, but such may well become our situation in the near future.

The uniqueness of biblical hope, however, is not only that it promises new possibilities in even the darkest hours. It is also that what we can genuinely and creatively hope for is not necessarily what we expect or even count on. It is a *genuinely* new possibility, upsetting and even contradicting what *we* are as well as what our opponents are, against *us* as good Democrats as well as against them as bad Republicans or Communists! Again transcendence has creatively entered the scene and made all the difference. But because the divine remains constant, it is a covenant new and yet in continuity with the old that we have experienced and loved and thus a valid object of our hope for the future. The cultural epoch that follows the demise of ours will not represent what either Washington or Moscow or Peking wants; of that we may be certain. But because it is the *same* Lord that rules the future and its possibilities, that promise of the unknown may be faced with confidence and with hope. And this, I suspect, is at this precise moment both the most incredible and the most important of all the biblical words about history to us.

III

TO WHAT WE CAN STILL CLING
A Christian Orientation
at a Time Lacking in Orientation*

Hans Küng

Crisis of Orientation and Basic Orientation

To what can we still cling today? To what can we hold fast? I am not a pessimist, but in view of the many complaints of so many people we scarcely need any demonstration, documentation, or illustration to prove that we are involved in a crisis of orientation as profound as it is far-reaching. Particularly after the youth revolts and student revolts of the late 1960s there are no agencies of orientation, no traditions of orientation, that have not been involved in this crisis or—as others would say—radically called into question. Where today is there any undisputed authority? Formerly we were simply told: the pope, the bishop, the church says; or the president says, the government or the party says; or the teacher, the professor, the parent says. Where today could we close a discussion with such an appeal to authority? No, both state and church, judiciary and army, school and family, seem to be insecure. They are no longer accepted without question—least of all by young people—as agencies of orientation. Neither Christianity nor non-Christian humanisms, neither nationalism nor Marxism, is any longer (if they ever were) a universally authoritative tradition of orientation.

With the critical questioning of hitherto accepted authorities, agencies, traditions, ways of life, and ideas of value, the norms linked to these also are brought into question. Liberalization was necessary but often went farther than had been foreseen or planned. Great processes to get rid of taboos frequently turned out to be processes of erosion, with the result that for many people today morality as a whole seems to be relativized. The effects of all this were anything but liberating. The ground was taken from under the feet of some people, especially the young, and they now find themselves

---

* Translated by Edward Quinn, Sheffield, England.

abandoned to meaninglessness, to practical nihilism or youthful criminality, or even—and not only in California and Guyana but also in Europe—to a religious youth sect or to sectarian quasi-religious political fanaticism, even terrorism.

This large-scale crisis of orientation threw modern society into conflicts that are not yet by any means settled nor presumably even seen in their full significance. For our grandparents, religion—Christianity—was still a matter of personal conviction. For our parents it remained at least a matter of tradition and good manners. For their emancipated sons and daughters, however, it is becoming increasingly a matter of the past that is no longer binding—*passé et depassé*, passed away and obsolete. Moreover, there are parents today who observe with perplexity that morality has vanished together with religion, as Nietzsche predicted. For, as is becoming increasingly clear, it is not so easy to justify ethics purely rationally, by reason alone, as Sigmund Freud and others wanted to do; we cannot explain why freedom under any circumstances is supposed to be better than oppression, justice better than avarice, nonviolence better than violence, love better than hate, peace better than war. Or more brutally: why, if it is to our advantage or contributes to our personal happiness, we may not lie, steal, commit adultery, or murder; or even why we should simply be "fair." Is not, perhaps, the good simply that which is to my advantage, to the advantage of my group, party, class, race, or even to the advantage of my business or trade union? Is it not a question of individual or collective selfishness? Individual biologists and ethnologists in fact try to persuade us that for human beings as for animals any sort of altruism, any sort of love, is merely the supreme form of biologically inherited self-interest. Furthermore—this question was raised at the world congress of philosophy in Düsseldorf in 1978—from where then are we to draw the criteria to judge the interests lying behind all knowledge: to distinguish between true and illusory, objective and subjective, acceptable and reprehensible interests? At the same time how are we to lay down, purely rationally, any priorities and preferences? Here even philosophical arguments for concrete ethical norms did not hitherto take us very far; they did not get beyond problematic generalizations and utilitarian pragmatic models. But these break down precisely in the exceptional case in which one is required to act in a way that is by no means to one's advantage or for one's personal happiness and may even in an extreme situation involve a sacrifice, perhaps the sacrifice of one's life.

Do we then know today to what we have to cling, in the last resort? Certainly we receive every day more and more rules of behavior, traffic regulations, maxims. It is obvious, however that regimentation is not the same thing as orientation. On the contrary, the more that regulations and regimentation, planning and organization, laws, prescriptions and clauses gain control in all spheres of life, the more people feel disoriented, lose insight and oversight, miss the great direction in their lives and the more—in the chaos of prescriptions and regulations, data and facts, operations and processes, structures and methods—they demand fixed signposts. At a time lacking in orientation they long for a firmly established orientation, for a basis or orientation—in short, for a *basic orientation*. And this is my theme: not any sort of orientation but this basic orientation.

I am not a pessimist. People today are not worse than they were in former times with more abundant orientation; young people of course, according to their elders, were always "bad." But this much must be said if we are to understand particularly the present younger generation, our students: social change, in which we all find ourselves involved, never came about formerly with such speed and complexity, making a basic orientation increasingly difficult. Consequently everyone helps oneself, often in a very simple fashion. One person orients one's life by the horoscope, and another—more scientifically minded—by biological rhythm; one person organizes everything according to a planned diet, and another according to yoga; one person swears by group-therapy, and another by meditation. But it is a question of orientation, not only in individual but also in social life. And from atomic power to gene manipulation and test-tube babies, from environmental protection to East–West and North–South conflicts, it is becoming increasingly clear how the ethical questions exceed the comprehension and overtax the powers of the individual human being. Today we can do more than is permissible, and we do not know what we ought to do.

It is obvious that I cannot answer all these extremely complicated questions in this one lecture. Yet I can perhaps say something of fundamental importance for the solution of all these individual and social questions— something that again provides some ground under our feet and makes possible a standpoint in the light of which all individual problems may be judged. That is, a *basic orientation* and, in fact, a *Christian* basic orientation. But it is at this very point that inhibitions set in. I hope I may be permitted, therefore, after this first part on the crisis of orientation and on basic orientation to make some observations in the second part leading to an answer and at the same time to introduce the distinction between what is nominally Christian and what is truly Christian.

The Nominally Christian and the Truly Christian

I should like to address not only Christians but also non-Christians, as well as all those who remain doubtful between the two groups. Perhaps it would be possible first of all to aim at agreement between Christians and non-Christians on three important points:

(1) In the present crisis of orientation most of our contemporaries remain convinced that human life together is impossible without a minimal *agreement* on existing *standards of orientation*. Without a minimal agreement about existing basic norms, basic attitudes, basic values—as these are

seriously discussed at the present time even in the different political parties—in the face of all the conflicting interests, even the functioning of democracy, of state, becomes questionable. In fact, we may take it as agreed that no civilized society and no state can exist without some kind of legal system. However, there can be no legal system without a sense of law; and no sense of law without a moral sense, without an ethos; and eventually no ethos without basic values, basic attitudes, basic norms (as in China, for instance).

(2) If (as indicated) it is extremely difficult or practically impossible to justify ethics purely rationally, by reason alone, then the meaning and function of that factor which has provided the justification for an ethos, for humanity's basic orientation, throughout the millennia from the time when the human being became human may not be carelessly ignored: *religion*, therefore, cannot be set aside with impunity. In fact, we may likewise assume here that there is no unconditional obligation to a particular form of action without the assumption of an absolute, without the assumption of an absolutely binding authority. That is to say, there is no unconditionally moral action, no unconditionally binding ethos without religion. Moreover, if true religion does not serve this purpose some kind of pseudo- or quasi-religion will be used. For true religion, however, the sole authority that can claim unconditional obedience is not anything that is human and relative but only the absolute itself, the Ultimate Reality.

(3) As Westerners, whether Christians or not, as members of one political party or the other, we must admit that the purely human basic values and basic norms have remained *in practice under Judeo-Christian influence*. This has been wholly for humanity's well-being and advantage. Inviolable human dignity, freedom, justice, solidarity, and peace still bear the mark of the Judeo-Christian spirit. Without that content they would be and are formal and ambiguous terms that—as is shown notably in Nazism and the peoples' democracies and George Orwell's *Nineteen Eighty-Four*—can be and are arbitrarily manipulated in East and West. On the other hand, whatever attitude we adopt, it cannot be disputed that the Judeo-Christian tradition gives not only a theoretical-abstract but also a completely practical-concrete answer to the question of basic values and basic norms.

Thus for the younger generation, to whom the future belongs, the question arises whether we should not perhaps again take more seriously that which guides us anyway. Not that we should return nostalgically to the past, still less to the Middle Ages. But certainly that we might, should, could go on our way into the future with the aid of what is indeed an old but perhaps not yet worn-out compass. A compass that, after so many other means of orientation have proved to be unreliable in the storms of modern times, perhaps could again point the way to a future more worthy of human beings: at a time lacking in orientation then once more—all over again and in a new way—a *Christian basic orientation*. But here a distinction must be made. I can already hear the protests of non-Christians. Christian basic orientation—what is "Christian" supposed to mean today? Christianity is finished. But I would like to explain myself to these also, to the non-Christians, to the unbelievers—not only to the unbelievers outside but also to the unbelievers within, in ourselves, who repeatedly raise doubts and objections, who say, "I believe," but—like the man in the Gospel—add: "Help my unbelief." We have to answer frankly and sincerely.

Frankly and sincerely: if you, whether you consider yourself a believer or an unbeliever, reject any Christian element for your orientation that has to do in any way with an authoritarian, unintelligible dogmatics or an unrealistic, narrow-minded, casuistic morality, then I cannot contradict you. If you are exasperated by the legalism and opportunism, arrogance and intolerance of so many ecclesiastical functionaries and theologians, if you want to attack the superficial piety of the pious, the boring mediocrity of the church papers, the absence of creative persons in the church, then I am on your side. Nor am I by any means ignorant of the failure of Christianity in history. I have no intention of whitewashing the history of Christianity, withdrawing it apologetically out of time, painting over its defects: the persecutions of Jews above all, but also the Crusades, trials of heretics, burnings of witches, and wars of religion; the Galileo trial and the countless false condemnations of solutions to problems, and condemnations of people—scientists, philosophers, theologians; the involvement also of the church in certain systems of society, of government, of thought, and all the many failures in the slavery question, the question of war, the question of women, the social question, the race question, the manifold complicity of the churches in various countries with the rulers; the neglect of the despised, downtrodden, oppressed, and exploited; religion as the opium of the people. . . . At all of these points criticism, severe criticism, is appropriate.

But one thing I can give you as food for thought. Is all this Christian? Neither believers nor unbelievers will deny that it is "Christian" only in a traditional, superficial, and untrue sense—at best as some faulty developments, wrong decisions, barbarities, and atrocities in recent German history are described as "German." Christendom certainly cannot shed its responsibility for what is called "Christian." However, none of this is Christian in the deep, true, original sense; none of it is truly Christian. As Christians often now quite clearly observe, it has nothing to do with Christ, whose name it invokes, but in many ways it is part of that which brought him to the cross. It is at bottom pseudo-Christian and even anti-Christian.

What is there indeed that is not *called* "Christian": groups, schools, associations, political parties, churches? But *is* it all Christian just because it is *called* "Christian"? I cannot and must not pass over critical questions to Christian churches and to Christian political parties such as those in European countries. For is it not true that even someone who declares membership in a Christian political party—and I am not saying anything against this here—will not want to claim that everything that party represents is wholly and entirely Christian or is even specifically Christian? Indeed it would be interesting to know what—over and above what are known as "Christian tradition" and "Christian virtues"—is specifically Christian here at all (and not merely "Western" or "European"). Some socialists—whether we share their opinions or not—are more interested in this question today than some Christian Democrats who continually avoid using the name of Christ, attach little importance to the Sermon on the Mount, but nevertheless think that what is Christian is in the secure possession of their party. I am not passing judgment here, only raising queries. I am not defending any politicizing theology of the right, left, or center. But, precisely because the German Bishops' Conference generally speaks only on one side, I must clearly state here that Christian parties also—not only the other parties—can produce disorientation instead of orientation.

Moreover, anyone who professes attachment to a Christian church—and I do so with conviction—will not want to claim that all that these institutional bearers of Christianity defend is Christian, still less specifically Christian. Indeed, here too it would be interesting to know what is specifically Christian and not merely "ecclesiastical," "Roman Catholic," "official teaching," or "Protestant." No, speaking about my own church, with the best will I cannot regard it as Christian or as having a genuine Christian orientation when only our own ecclesiastical authority and not Jesus Christ is invoked in questions that are important for millions of Catholics and non-Catholics alike. With the best will, I cannot think that he whom Christianity invokes, Jesus of Nazareth, if he came again today, would himself take up the same attitude now as the Roman authorities in controversial questions:

—that he, who warned the Pharisees against imposing intolerable burdens on others' shoulders would today declare all "artificial" contraception to be mortal sin;

—that he who particularly invited failures to his table would forbid all remarried divorced people ever to approach that table;

—that he who was constantly accompanied by women and whose apostles, with the exception of Paul, were and remained each and every one married would today have forbidden marriage to ordained men and ordination to all women and thus increasingly deprive parishes of their pastors;

—that he who took the adulteress and other sinners under his protection would have passed such harsh verdicts in delicate questions that require discriminating and critical judgment—issues like premarital sex and homosexuality.

Nor can I think that, if he came again today, he would agree in the present ecumenical climate that the difference of denomination should be maintained as an impediment to marriage; that the validity of the ordination and the eucharistic celebration of Protestant pastors should be disputed; that open communion and common celebration of the eucharist, shared church buildings and parish centers, and an ecumenical instruction should be prevented; that, instead of giving convincing reasons, the attempt should be made to tame our own theologians, student chaplains, teachers of religion, journalists, and functionaries of associations, responsible people in Catholic organizations, with decrees and "declarations" (and, whenever possible, with disciplinary or financial measures). No, if we want to be Christian, we cannot demand freedom and human rights for the church externally and not grant them internally. We cannot replace urgently needed reforms in the church with fine words at synods or congresses, or at papal demonstrations, about the Third World and the North–South conflict. Justice and freedom cannot be preached only where it costs the church and its leaders nothing. We cannot fight about matters of secondary importance and allow both the great Christian conception of the future and clear priorities to be missed. Yes— unfortunately, this too must be said—even Christian churches can produce disorientation instead of orientation.

I mention all these desiderata so clearly not because it gives me any pleasure to do so but simply because it is my duty and responsibility. But now, aware particularly of the sinister background of what is called Christian and aware also of the most important popular or scientific, historical, philosophical, psychological or sociological objections to Christianity, I should like to say in this time so lacking in orientation that I promise myself despite everything a basic orientation from Christianity—not indeed from what is simply called but from what is truly Christian: from the Christian message itself, from faith in Christ that is living and not merely believed, from *being* a Christian. However, here a question arises that must form the theme of our third section.

Why Precisely a Christian Basic Orientation?

Yes, why? Why be a Christian specifically? Permit me to reflect a little and not attempt to produce a quick answer to a question of principle. Recently in Israel the thought again occurred to me that as for a Jew or Muslim so also for a "born Christian" it cannot be entirely unimportant that we were born into a particular tradition of belief and community of belief and that we remain (whether we want it or not) positively or negatively influenced by it. The situation is like that of the family, where it cannot be entirely irrelevant whether we have maintained or—in anger or indifference—broken off contact.

In this light, could not even non-Christians or former Christians understand the many Christians who—and there are such—oppose completely and no less intelligently and critically the rigid Christian traditions and institutions that make it difficult to be a Christian and yet who do not want to give up living in the great and good Christian tradition of twenty centuries? Yes, why am I a Christian? First of all, simply because despite all criticism of often shatteringly wrong attitudes and wrong developments I can nevertheless approve a history that is significant for me, a history in which I live with so many others in the past and present, including many Jews for a large part of it; because, that is, I would not dream of confusing the great Christian cause with the often so pettifogging machinery and its administrators or leave to the latter the defense of the Christian cause; in brief, because despite my violent objections to what is often called Christian I find in Christianity a basic orientation for the questions of the great whence and whither, why and wherefore of humanity and the world: a basic orientation for my individual and social life. At the same time I find there a spiritual home on which I do not want to turn my back any more than I want in politics to turn my back on democracy, which in its own way has been and is no less misused and discredited than Christianity. But, admittedly, all this only hints at the decisive factor. I must make myself more clear.

There are in fact many non-Christians or former Christians who say that they would like to believe in such a great whence and whither, that they wish they could believe in an Absolute or a Supreme Being, a Deity or "God," that atheism leaves them intellectually and emotionally unsatisfied. But they have little idea of what to do about this "God," scarcely know what, how, or who God is. In this sense if they are not atheists, they are at least agnostics. This does not, of course, surprise me. I certainly do not want to belittle the *God of the philosophers*, of whom agnostics generally speak, nor declare this God, as a certain form of Protestant theology has done for a long time, to be an idol fabricated by humanity. How could I do so when I consider Aristotle, Plato and Plotinus, Descartes, Spinoza and Leibniz, Kant and Hegel? For it is still a great thing for a human being to know of this great whence and whither, why and wherefore of humanity and the world, of the great mystery of reality, and so to have a certain basic orientation. However, I readily admit that it is not very easy to live with this mystery which remains hidden, with this abstract God of the philosophers, to know what, how, or who God is. This God is a God without a countenance, is the "unknown God," the *theos agnostos* of the Acts of the Apostles, and thus easily remains a God of the agnostics. This, at any rate, is so unless, like the great philosophers of modern times (and also their atheistic opponents), we allow ourselves to be influenced by the Christian idea of God everywhere present even today.

Yet, looking more closely at that more philosophical or generally religious orientation, if we are to speak in this way of God as the great whence, the cause of causes, and the great whither, the goal of goals, how am I really to know what is concealed in the cause of causes and what awaits us in the goal of goals? Might not the primal ground perhaps be a dark abyss and not a bright ground of light? The primal support an enticing illusion and not a real support in life? The primal goal eventually a definitive breakdown and not ultimate fulfillment? How am I to know whether the primal meaning for myself and the world will not turn out ultimately to be nonsense, the primal value ultimately non-value? Such doubts are truly justified and make a basic orientation difficult.

Yes, *what, how, who is God* who is supposed to provide my basic orientation? In the light of the Old and New Testaments I know an answer to this question. The God of Jewish–Christian faith does not remain abstract and undetermined like the God of the philosophers; God is concrete and determined, not simply hidden but revealed in the history of the people of Israel and of Jesus Christ. And, unlike the God of the philosophers and scholars— to take up Pascal's contrast—this God of Abraham, Isaac, and Jacob, the God of Jesus Christ, is anyway not enigmatic like the Egyptian sphinx, the strangler of passers-by. Nor is God ambivalent, equivocal, two-faced, like the Roman God Janus; nor capricious, incalculable, like Tyche-Fortuna, as goddess of happiness and unhappiness, guiding the course of the world.

No, the God of the Jewish-Christian faith proves to be unambiguously— and this is by no means obvious—a God not against humanity but *for humanity.* "Emmanuel," God with us. A God who should mean for human beings not, as often in supposedly Christian education, fear but security, not unhappiness but happiness, not death but life; even in the Old Testament, despite some persistent pagan features, not a slave-owner but a God of the Exodus from Egypt, of liberaton, of mercy, of salvation, of grace; a God beside whom there are no other gods. This one and only God is that one very last, very first reality which Muslims also worship in Allah (a fact by no means unimportant for Camp David and the efforts for peace in the Near East), which Hindus also seek in Brahma and Buddhists in the Absolute, as do the Chinese in heaven or in the Tao. For Jews and Christians this one true God is not the unknown but the good, kind God in whom a person— even in doubt, suffering, and sin, in all private distress and all social affliction—can place an absolute and unreserved trust, in whom one can place one's faith.

God as the all-embracing and all-permeating is certainly not a person as a human being is a person. What determines every individual existence is not an individual person among other persons, is not a super-being or super-ego, is not "big brother." God then cannot be fitted into the notion of person; God is more than person. But, conversely, a God who establishes human personality cannot himself be non-personal. God is not sub-personal. God then cannot be fitted into the notion of the impersonal; God is also not less than a person. We might describe God as "trans-personal" or "super-personal." In any case God is a genuine partner who is kind and absolutely reliable, a partner to whom we can speak. Certainly we can speak about and to this God only in analogical terms, in metaphors and images, in ciphers and symbols. But we can speak to God appropriately with human words—how could we do otherwise? And, as you will understand, it is on this possibility that the possibility of prayer and worship depends, a possibility that—I think—is enormously important particularly for modern humanity and for one's basic orientation, which of course should not be purely intellectual. For in simple prayer and genuine worship even the modern man or woman can be oriented in a wholly different depth of his or her existence and can truly experience where we come from, where we are, and where we are going.

I need scarcely add to all that I have explained at length elsewhere. The assent to God does not involve a rational proof. Here a human being is faced with an alternative. One has to decide whether in one's life and in the history of humanity and the world one will accept an ultimate groundlessness, unsupportedness, and meaninglessness or on the other hand a primal ground, primal support, and primal meaning of everything: in personal terms, creator, ruler, and finisher. We can mistrust reality in its ground, support, and meaning and say "No," or we can trust it and say "Yes" to God. The "Yes" to God is thus a matter of trust—but in itself a completely reasonable trust. There is no rational proof for such an act of trust, but there are many reasonable grounds. For only a trusting assent to a primal ground, primal support, and primal meaning can answer the question of the origin, support, and goal of the world process and of my own life. Only a trusting "Yes" can provide a human being with an ultimate certainty, security, and in fact a genuine basic orientation. Seen in this way, only the "Yes"—not the "No" that ultimately leads to meaninglessness—is characterized by radical rationality.

Truly, we do not need, as many fear, to be irrational when we want to orient ourselves in faith to God, to the Judeo–Christian God. What happens is that understanding ripens under the influence of faith, and harmony is established between reason and faith. The God of the philosophers, who is closer to some, is not thereby by any means abolished but, in the best triple sense of the German word *aufgehoben*, is affirmed, negated, and transcended in one: affirmed, relativized, and elevated to the infinite. This God—I think—is what can be called the "more divine God": the God before whom the modern person, who has grown so critical, without having to give up reason can again, as Martin Heidegger once expressed his hope, "pray and offer sacrifice, again fall on his knees in awe and make music and dance." Thus my first fundamental answer to the quesion of the basic orientation is that I know to what I can hold fast, to what I may hold fast, because *I believe in this living God*.

It should be noted that each person has his or her own God: a supreme value by which one regulates everything, to which one orients oneself in practice, for which, if need be, one sacrifices everything. And if this is not the true God, then it is some kind of idol, an old or a new one: money, career, sex, pleasure. None of these is evil in itself, but they may not become God for a person unless he or she is to be enslaved. Orientation to the one true God, to the sole Absolute, relativizes all these things and permits a human being to use them to the extent that they make the person human.

Orientation to the one true God thus makes a human being truly free in this world. However, in all this we are speaking very generally. We must continue our reflections and speak more precisely.

What Is the Source of this Basic Orientation?

It is not a secret. I get it from him whose name is so readily passed over in silence in Christian political party programs and so readily venerated in Christian institutions merely as honorary president without any real influence. I get this basic orientation from *Jesus of Nazareth*, who is a historical figure and not a myth but is for that very reason the *Christ who is authoritative* in all things for Christians of all times. He proclaimed the one and only God who had spoken and been addressed in the history of the people of Israel, in the experiences of humanity; he proclaimed this God with a human face, as living and close. In his whole life and action he made this face of God shine out. When Jesus spoke of this God and acted in his name, he made clear what was vague in the Old Testament, made unambiguous what seemed ambiguous there. The one true God of Israel is now understood in a new way: in brief, he might be described as the Father of the "Prodigal Son" and indeed of the abandoned all together, not simply Father of the devout and of those who were righteous from the very outset.

This God, as Jesus proclaimed him, is not—as has often been instilled in children—an all-too-masculine, arbitrary, or legal-minded God without maternal features; God is not a God created in the image of kings, tyrants, and dictators. This God really is—and I beg you to take the word not in its sugary, superficial meaning but in its deepest sense—the loving God: that is, the God of love who in all justice is committed unreservedly to human beings, their needs and hopes (a consideration that is important also for questions of sexual morality); a God who does not always merely demand but gives, who does not oppress but raises up, who does not make people ill or poison them but heals them; a God who spares those who fall—and what person does not fall?—a God who forgives instead of condemning, liberates instead of punishing, makes grace rule instead of law; who rejoices over the repentance of one sinner more than over ninety-nine just persons; a God therefore who prefers the prodigal son to the one who stayed at home, the tax collector to the Pharisee, the Samaritan heretics to the orthodox, the prostitutes and adulterers to their self-righteous judges. As you see, this preaching of Jesus was offensive and scandalous not only for that time but also for today, particularly since it was accompanied by an equally offensive and scandalous practice—not excommunication but communication and even communion. He sat down at the table with the despised and the failures, "sinners" of every kind.

It is obvious that this God's name of Father is not merely an echo of the experience of parenthood in this world. It is not a projection that serves merely to transfigure the conditions of earthy parenthood and rulership. Not then a God as seen by the former theology student and later atheist, Feuerbach: not a God of the hereafter at the expense of the here and now, at the expense of human beings and their true greatness. Nor a God as criticized by Karl Marx: a God of the rulers, of unjust social conditions, of deformed consciousness, and of false consolation. Nor the God rejected by Friedrich Nietzsche: a God engendered by resentment, the leader of a pitiable loafers' morality of good and evil. Nor, finally, the God rejected by Freud and a number of psychoanalysts: a tyrannical super-ego, the false image of illusory infantile needs, a God of obsessive ritual arising from a guilt-complex, a father-complex, an Oedipus complex.

No, this God is a different God: a God who sets himself above the formalistic, casuistic, merciless righteousness of the law and has a "better" righteousness proclaimed; who even justifies the transgressor of the law. A God for whom the commandments exist for the sake of human beings and not human beings for the sake of commandments. A God then who does not have the existing legal order and consequently the social system, the temple and its worship, abolished, but for humanity's sake relativized. And who consequently wants to have the natural barriers removed between comrades and non-comrades, distant people and neighbors, friends and foes, good and bad. How? By straightforwardness, self-restraint, love in the sense of the Sermon on the Mount: a forgiveness without end, a service regardless of rank, a renunciation without compensation. In this way God places himself alongside the disadvantaged, the underprivileged, the oppressed, the weak, the poor, the sick, and—as opposed to the self-righteous—alongside the irreligious, immoral, godless. As you see, a God who is kind, amazingly kind, to human beings.

Jesus stood up for this God and his amazing kindliness. He spoke, fought, suffered, and was executed for him. At this point the question always arises: Did it not all end with Jesus' death? The answer, carefully phrased, is one that even the non-Christian could perhaps accept. For it is a historical fact that Jesus' death did not mean the end of everything but only the beginning: that his first community in a veritably foolhardy fashion proclaimed him—the heretical teacher, the false prophet, the seducer of the people, the blasphemer, allegedly condemned by God—to be Messiah of God, Christ, Lord, Son of Man, Son of God. Why? According to the New Testament sources, they were convinced—and only this faith explains the emergence of Christianity at all—that Jesus had not died into nothingness but into God. This means that Jesus is living: living through, with, in God, for our sake and for us as hope, as obligation, as orientation.

From that time onward both Christians and non-Christians have been faced with a clear alternative for the orientation of their lives. *The one possibility is*: we die into nothingness. I would not deny my respect for anyone who adopts this position. This is a view that sometimes demands heroism and anyway can scarcely be refuted. Not of course that anyone has proved it positively; never yet has there been anyone who could prove that we die into nothingness, that all our living, laboring, loving, and suffering are in vain and lead to nothing in the end. But to me this possibility does not seem reasonable, under no circumstances does it seem reasonable. *Or, the other possibility*: we die into an absolutely final reality that is also the absolutely first, incomprehensible-comprehensive reality, which for want of a better name we call God. This alternative likewise cannot be rationally proved, nor of course can it be refuted. Every human being is here faced with a decision that no one can take away from another.

As already stated, we can commit ourselves to this in a completely reasonable, enlightened trust—truly, not to console ourselves with the promise of a hereafter but to place ourselves so much the more decisively in the here and now, in this life, in this present-day society. And it seems to me the more reasonable, it seems reasonable under any circumstances that we die not into nothingness but into God. Think: if God really exists and really is God, he cannot be merely the God of the beginning but must also be the God of the end. Then God is both our Creator and also our Finisher. And it is this God, the Creator and Conserver of the cosmos and of humanity, who alone—also in dying and at death, beyond the frontiers of all that has hitherto been experienced—can be expected to have one more word to say: to have the first and the last word. If I seriously believe in an eternal, living God, I believe also in God's eternal life, in my eternal life. If then I begin my Credo with the belief in "God, the almighty Creator," I may—so I think—finish it reasonably with belief in "eternal life."

A firm faith of this kind changes completely even the present life. It enables us to live this life quite differently, more meaningfully, more responsibly, with greater involvement—in fact to live precisely in accordance with the standard of this Christ. With his proclamation, his way of action, his lot in life, he became the standard for those who believe in him, the standard for their relations with their fellow human beings, with society, and particularly with God. To put it briefly, the true human Jesus of Nazareth has thus been for believers up to the present time the real revelation of the one God—in biblical language, his Word, his image, his Son.

In this very way, however, he is truly a human being, *the* true human being. By his proclamation, his behavior, his whole destiny, he provided a *model of being human* that—if we commit ourselves trustingly to it—enables us again and again freshly to discover and to realize in existing and in involvment with our fellow human beings the meaning of our being human, of our freedom, of our life. As confirmed by God in the resurrection he thus represents for us the abiding, reliable, ultimate standard of being human. This also is something that has become clear in recent theological discussions. Christology and Christ-theory may be important, especially for theologians and bishops, but belief in Christ and the following of Christ are decisive. The important thing is being a Christian, and it is he, the historical Christ who is identical with Jesus of Nazareth, who makes this possible for me.

That means that I can now provide a more precise answer to the question of the basic orientation. I know to what I can hold fast, to what I may hold fast, because *I believe in this Jesus Christ*, who did not only preach the word of God but who *is* the Word God, the Son of God. But this also raises the question that cannot be passed over under any circumstances: What does all this mean in practice?

What Does This Basic Orientation Mean in Practice?

Here I can only suggest and outline the main direction to be followed. I said at the very beginning that it would be presumptuous to attempt in one lecture to offer an orientation for all possible urgent and immediate problems, particularly since different problems are urgent and immediate for different people. No, I must continue the general line of this lecture. I am concerned here and now with awareness of Christian fundamentals, the basic orientation that of course must have its effect on all the concrete questions of the individual and of society. This influence was described in *On Being a Christian* with reference to the problems of war and peace, violence and nonviolence, struggle for power and the pressures of the consumer society, education and service to others. Here I must restrict myself to some observations on the essential principles behind Christian practice. At the same time of course it is important to note that what I am suggesting and outlining here is not merely what is often criticized as "pure theory" but the theory behind a practice that is realized quite concretely in the daily lives of countless people in our churches—or, better, a theory that people one way or another attempt to live. In this sense—after so much criticism I can say this—our churches, despite all merely nominal Christianity, are also (and often more than people see) truly Christian.

Marx is master and teacher for Marxists, and Freud for Freudians. Jesus of Nazareth is certainly also master and teacher for the life of Christians. But he is also essentially more than this. As the one who was killed and raised to life, he is in person for believers the living authoritative embodiment of his cause. In all that he is, in all that he did and suffered, he personifies the cause of God and the cause of humanity. And so he calls us to follow him. "Following Christ": for some this is *too* lofty an ideal, its challenge almost alarming. But have we got it right? Certainly the living Christ does not call merely for worship without practical consequences, not merely for us to say: "Lord, Lord" or "Son of God, Son of God." However, neither does he call for literal imitation. It would be presumptuous to want to imitate him. No, he calls for personal discipleship—not for imitation but for correlation and adaptation, which means that I commit myself to him and pursue my own way in accordance with his orientation. Each has his or her own path to follow. It is not that we must. We are not compelled. To make his orientation our own was understood from the beginning as a very great opportunity, not a "must" but a "may," not a law to be slavishly observed but an unexpected chance and a true gift: that is—and the word has often been misunderstood—a genuine grace, to which we *may* cling; a grace that presupposes no more than this one thing, that I grasp it confidently and try to adapt my life to it.

Christian churches and political parties also ought to note that this Jesus Christ himself, who personifies his cause, is the specifically Christian factor, the distinguishing Christian feature, and not abstractly some kind of "Christian" or Western idea, some kind of principle, a mentality, a tenet, or a system. He, this concrete Jesus as the living Christ, is for believers in all situations the ultimate authority, to whom we may cling. He who is called in the light of the Old Testament the rising "sun of justice" is able to convey to us that fundamental "orientation"—a word that means, although this is often forgotten, a basic turning toward the East, the "Orient," the rising sun. He is—to adapt a Pauline saying—"our orientation."

This basic model for orientation in individual and social life is obviously aimed not merely at massage of souls but at conversion of hearts: a change of awareness. It makes possible quite concretely what so many are calling for today in view of the lack of orientation, lack of norms, lack of meaning, in view of drug addiction, criminality, and violence, and what is so important for religion *and* politics, for social and economic policy. This Jesus Christ, his Spirit, who is the strength and power of God, makes possible—if I may set it out systematically—quite concretely:

(a) *A new awareness, a new basic approach and basic attitude.* He makes possible a standpoint in the light of which a number of other things can ultimately be critically judged. He provokes a new, more human attitude to life and a new life style. As individuals and as a community, we may and can live differently, more authentically, more humanly, when we have before us this Jesus Christ as concrete guiding principle and living model for our basic relationship to human beings and society, the world and God. We thus gain identity and coherence in our individual lives, advantage and involvement in present-day society.

(b) *New motivations.* From his "theory" and "practice" we can deduce new motives of individual and social action. In his light it is possible to answer those questions from which we started and which are so difficult to answer purely rationally: why we should act just in this way and not in another, why we should be good and not bad, why love and not hate, why promote peace and not war. In his light it is possible to answer even that question which Sigmund Freud with all his brilliant insight could not answer: why we should be honest, considerate, kind whenever possible, even if this is to our disadvantage and we are made to suffer by the unreliability and brutality of others.

(c) *New dispositions.* In his Spirit we can develop and maintain new, consistent insights, intentions, tendencies. By him, not only for isolated passing moments but permanently, readiness to help is produced, attitudes created, qualifications conveyed that are capable of guiding individual and social behavior; dispositions of unpretentious commitment for our fellow human beings, of identification with the underprivileged, of struggle against unjust structures; and also dispositions of a new gratitude, freedom, magnanimity, unselfishness, peace, also of consideration, pardon, service; dispositions that are proved even in borderline situations in readiness for sacrifice out of the abundance of self-giving, in renunciation sometimes even if it is not necessary, in readiness for involvement for the sake of the great cause.

(d) *New enterprises.* By his Spirit we are enabled to undertake new actions on a great or small scale that begin—as they did with him—at the very point where no one is helping. By this are meant not only general programs for social change but also concrete signs, testimonies, witnesses of humanity, of the humanization of both the person and the society.

(e) *A new horizon of meaning and a new objective.* In his Spirit there dawns upon us that which so many people miss today: the meaning and ultimate purpose of our life and our history in that last and first reality that is the consummation of humanity by God's kingdom. It is precisely this meaning and this purpose that permit us to live our present, earthly life differently, life not only as a history of success but also the history of suffering, to which an ultimate meaning is promised from the same source.

This last point needs to be expressed more precisely. Non-Christians often describe themselves as humanists, but we too are no less humanists. And do you not think also that the crucial test of both Christian and non-Christian humanisms lies in their capacity to master the negative aspect of reality? It is easy to say that we approve everything that is human, everything that is truly human, whatever is true, good, and beautiful. However, what if we constantly in both individual life and society meet with the inhumane, the inhuman, the untrue, the bad, and the unsightly—the negative aspect which cannot by any means be simply talked out of existence? But how is this negative element to be mastered? It is only now and with the utmost carefulness that I introduce a word that has been misused by so many to enslave humanity and put people off with false consolation. The *cross* or—better—the Crucified enables us to cope meaningfully with the negative element. Who can deny that the life of a person—under whatever social and economic system and even after all reforms and revolutions—is and remains a life marked by pain, trouble, sin and suffering, sickness and death, and in this sense "criss-crossed," frustrated existence? This criss-crossed existence of ours acquires an indisputable meaning. For no cross in the world can refute the offer of meaning—it is no more than an offer—presented in the cross of the One who was raised to life: that, for the one who trusts in God, even the negative, even the greatest danger, the utmost loneliness, futility, nullity, sin and emptiness, are encompassed by a God who identifies himself with humanity, even if we do not perceive this at the time. We are not thereby under any illusion; there is no way of bypassing the negative element. What we are given is endurance without whining or tears, a way through the negative element, a future on our own way of life and suffering. This means certainly not seeking out what is negative but enduring it. And again, not merely enduring but fighting it.

In the Spirit of the Crucified, a struggle against the negative element and its causes is possible at a very much deeper level in the life of both the individual and society. That is, a struggle for respect of human dignity against all disregard of humanity, even going so far as love of enemies. A struggle for freedom against all oppression, even going so far as selfless service. A struggle for justice against all injustice, even going so far as the voluntary renunciation of rights. A struggle for solidarity against all selfishness, even going so far as involving all that we have. A struggle for peace against all discord, even going so far as reconciliation without limit.

Why then do I accept a Christian basic orientation? This is a third answer, which needs further clarification: I know to what I can hold fast, to what I may hold fast, because *I believe in the Spirit of Jesus Christ, who is the Spirit of God himself, the Holy Spirit.* This living Spirit enables me and countless others to be truly human: not only to act in a truly human way but also to suffer; not only to live but also to die—since in everything both positive and negative, in all happiness and unhappiness, we are sustained by God and can remain helpful to our fellow human beings. In this sense as Christians we stand not for just any kind of humanism but for a truly *radical* humanism: a humanism that goes to the roots since it is able to incorporate and—suffering and struggling—positively to cope not only with the true, good, and beautiful, the human-humane, but also with the untrue, the bad and unsightly, the all-too-human, and even the inhuman.

Conclusion

Whether believer or unbeliever, Christian or non-Christian, no one will deny that such a basic orientation provides an answer to the crisis of orientation with which we began. A basic orientation that can give to our individual and social life a new direction, a new meaning, a new support, a new meaningful shape. A way between revolution and servility, between hypercritical radicalism and uncritical conformity—a way precisely for the younger generation. What each individual initiates with this sort of answer depends of course on his or her own decision. There can be no pressure or compulsion here. But this much is certain:

—The more a *human being*—man or woman, worker or academic— makes this basic orientation his or her own, so much freer, so much more open, human, philanthropic does he or she become.

—The more an *older* person keeps to this orientation, so much more sympathetically will he or she also approach the younger generation but also more firmly and making no false concessions.

—The more a *younger* person commits himself or herself to this alternative, to a Christian way of life and a Christian life style, so much more will he or she overcome the unfruitful, sullen discontent and animosity so widespread today, in order to gain a new sense of reality and get oneself involved meaningfully for one's fellow human beings.

—The more a *church*—whether Catholic, Protestant, or Orthodox—is not only called Christian but also behaves in a Christian way, so much the more will it become freshly open, hospitable, truly credible, and so much more easily can it solve even what were regarded at the beginning as critical internal church problems and truly give hope to humanity.

—The more a *society*—whether formally Christian or pluralistic in the modern sense—is sustained by such human beings, authorities, and churches, for whom Christianity has come to mean something again, so much the more will it again be not only a happiness-oriented but also a truth-oriented society. And, as the physicist and philosopher Carl Friedrich von Weizsäcker said recently, "Only a truth-oriented, not a happiness-oriented society can exist." In fact, not a happiness-oriented but only a truth-oriented society can survive.

IV

PARABLE AND PERFORMATIVE
IN THE GOSPELS AND IN MODERN LITERATURE

J. Hillis Miller

A large contradictory modern secondary literature now exists on the parables of Jesus in the New Testament and on their relation to the tradition of secular parable in modern writers like Kleist and Kafka.[1] Since I am not a biblical scholar, I cannot hope to add much to this discussion except possibly from the point of view of secular literature; but I can begin here with several axioms or presuppositions to guide my investigation, if only as grounds to be ungrounded by what is discovered later on.

The first presupposition is the assumption that it ought to be possible to identify specific differences, in the language, between the parables of Jesus and any secular parables whatsoever. Much is at stake here. The distinction between sacred scripture and secular literature would seem to depend on being able to identify the difference. The authority not only of the Bible as in some sense or other the word of God but more specifically of the words of

---

[1] See, for example, William Beardslee, *Literary Criticism of the New Testament* (Philadelphia: Fortress, 1970); Charles Carlston, *The Parables of the Triple Tradition* (Philadelphia: Fortress, 1975); Dominic Crossan, *In Parables* (New York: Harper, 1973); idem, *Raid on the Articulate* (New York: Harper, 1976); C. H. Dodd, *The Parables of the Kingdom* (New York: Scribner, 1961); Robert W. Funk, *Language, Hermeneutic, and the Word of God* (New York: Harper, 1966); J. Jeremias, *The Parables of Jesus* (New York: Scribner, 1972); Norman Perrin, *Jesus and the Language of the Kingdom* (Philadelphia: Fortress, 1976); Norman Petersen, *Literary Criticism for New Testament Critics* (Philadelphia: Fortress, 1978); Jean Starobinski, "Le Combat avec Légion," *Trois fureurs* (Paris: Gallimard, 1974) 73–126; Mary Ann Tolbert, *Perspectives on the Parables: An Approach to Multiple Interpretations* (Philadelphia: Fortress, 1979); Dan O. Via, *The Parables* (Philadelphia: Fortress, 1967); Andrzej Warminski, "'Patmos': The Senses of Interpretation," *MLN* 91 (1976) 478–500; Amos Wilder, "The Parable," *Early Christian Rhetoric: The Language of the Gospel* (Cambridge: Harvard University, 1971) 71–88. A collection may also be mentioned, *Analyse structurale et exégèse biblique* (ed. François Bovon; Neuchâtel: Delachaux et Niestlé, 1971), which also contains the essay by Jean Starobinski listed above. In addition, two journals, *Semeia* and *Linguistica Biblica*, have contained many essays on the parables of Jesus. I owe most of this brief bibliography of recent work on the parables to Amos Wilder, who has kindly assisted in educating me in this area, as he has educated me in other ways over the years. I am glad to be able to thank him here for manifold kindnesses.

Jesus as speech of God would seem to hang in the balance here. If the Middle Ages needed a distinction between "allegory of the poets" and "allegory of the theologians," we moderns would seem to need a firm distinction between "parable of the poets" and "parable of the theologians."

The second presupposition is no more than a definition of parable. Etymologically the word means "thrown beside," as a parabolic curve is thrown beside the imaginary line going down from the apex of the imaginary cone on the other side of whose surface the parabola traces its graceful loop from infinity and out to infinity again. Comets on a parabolic trajectory come once, sweep round the sun, and disappear forever, unlike those on a large elliptical orbit which return periodically, Halley's Comet for instance. When this is taken as a parable of the working of parable in literature or in scripture, it suggests that parable is a mode of figurative language which is the indirect indication, at a distance, of something that cannot be described directly, in literal language, like that imaginary invisible cone or like the sun, single controlling focus of the comet's parabola, which cannot be looked in the eye, although it is the condition of all seeing, or like that inaccessible place from which the comet comes and to which it returns. A parabolic narrative is, my parable of the comet would suggest, in some way governed, at its origin and at its end, by the infinity distant and invisible, by something that transcends altogether direct presentation. The correspondence between what is given in parable—the "realistic" story represented in a literal language—and its meaning is more indirect than is the case, for example, in "symbolic" expression, in the usual meaning of the latter, where, as the name suggests, one expects more of interpenetration, of participation, and of similarity. One German name for parable is *Gleichnis*, "likeness." This is what Luther calls a parable of Jesus. The paradox of parable is that it is a likeness that rests on a manifest unlikeness between what is given and what cannot by any means be given directly. A parabolic "likeness" is so "unlike" that without interpretation or commentary the meaning may slip by the reader or listener altogether.

Hegel's discussion of what he called "conscious symbolism" provides a definition of parable that corresponds to the one I have been making. The sublime (*das Erhabene*) is, strangely enough, included by Hegel with fable, parable, apalogue, proverb, and metamorphosis as a mode of "conscious symbolism."

> What has emerged from sublimity as distinct from strictly unconscious symbolizing consists on the one hand in the *separation* [*in dem Trennen*] between the meaning, explicitly known in its inwardness, and the concrete appearance divided therefrom; on the other hand in the directly or indirectly emphasized non-correspondence of the two [*Sichnichtentsprechen beider*] wherein the meaning, as the universal, towers above individual reality and its particularity.[2]

---

[2] G. W. F. von Hegel, *Aesthetics: Lectures on Fine Art* (trans. T. M. Knox; 2 vols.; New

If "separation" and "non-correspondence" characterize all such forms of symbolism, including parable, then the meaning of the parable can hardly be expected to be perspicuous to eyes that cannot see the tenor of which such symbols are the vehicle. For example, says Hegel when he comes to discuss parable in particular:

> The parable of the sower [in all the Synoptics] is a story in itself trivial in content [*für sich von geringfügigem Gehalt*] and it is important only because of the comparison with the doctrine of the Kingdom of Heaven. In these parables the meaning throughout is a religious doctrine to which the human occurrences in which it is represented [*vorgestellt*] are related in much the same way as man and animal are related in Aesop's Fables, where the former constitutes the meaning of the latter.[3]

In parable, human is to religious doctrine as animal is to human. The latter constitutes the meaning of the former across the gap of their separation and non-correspondence.

On the basis of this definition, a distinction, in principle at least, between sacred parable and secular parable may be made. The parables of Jesus are spoken by the Word, the Logos, in person. Even if this terminology is fully present only in the Gospel of John, it is already implicit in the characterization in the first three Gospels of Jesus as the Messiah. The fact that the Messiah speaks the parables guarantees the correspondence between the homely stories he tells of farming, fishing, and domestic economy on the one hand, and the spiritual or transcendent meaning on the other, the meaning that tells of things beyond the threshold of the domestic and visible, the meaning that nevertheless can be spoken only in parable, that is, indirectly. Christ as the Logos is not only the basis of the analogies, echoes, and resemblances among things of the world created in his name and between things created in his name and things hidden since the creation of the world. Christ as Logos is also the basis of the correspondences within the realm of language, for example the correspondence between visible vehicle and invisible and unnamed tenor in a parable. When Jesus speaks the parables, Christ the Word stands visibly before his auditors, for those who have eyes to see and ears to hear, as support of the correspondence between his realistic narrative of sowing, fishing, or household care and those unseeable things of which the parable "really" speaks. This guarantee is, I take it, one of the fundamental meanings of the Incarnation. Believing in the validity of the parables of the New Testament and believing that Jesus is the Son of God are the same thing.

The speakers or writers of secular parables stand in a different place, even though their parables too may deal with religious or metaphysical matters. They are down here with us, and their words about things visible

---

York: Oxford University, 1975) 1. 378; *Vorlesungen über die Ästhetik, Werkausgabe* (Frankfurt am Main: Suhrkamp, 1970) 1. 486.

[3] Ibid., English, 391; German, 502-3.

can only be thrown out or thrown beside things invisible in the hope that their narratives of what can be spoken about, the fencing bear in Kleist's "Über das Marionettentheater," for example, will magically make appear the other invisible, perhaps imaginary, line to which their realistic stories, they hope, correspond. The editor of the Greek New Testament I have consulted, Henry Alford, a nineteenth-century Anglican biblical scholar, put this clearly in his preliminary note on Matthew 13. A parable, he says,

> is *a serious narration within the limits of probability, of a course of action pointing to some moral or spiritual Truth* ("Collatio per narratiunculam fictam, sed veri similem, serio illustrans rem sublimiorem." Unger, de Parabolis Jesu [Meyer]) ["some moral or spiritual truth," it might be noted, is a loose translation of "rem sublimiorem"]; and derives its force from real analogies impressed by the Creator of all things on His creatures. The great Teacher by parables therefore is He who needed not that any should testify of man; for He knew what was in man, John ii.25: moreover, He *made* man, and orders the course and character of human events. And this is the reason why no one can, or dare, teach by parables, except Christ. We do not, as He did, see the inner springs out of which flow those laws of spiritual truth and justice, which the Parable is framed to elucidate. *Our* parables would be in danger of perverting, instead of guiding aright.[4]

The fact that Alford a page later commits the crime he warns against is an amusing example of the *odium theologicum* but also an example of a problem with Christ's parables. Any interpretation of these parables is itself parabolic. In one way or another it must do what Henry Alford warns against, that is, claim to understand "the inner springs out of which flow those laws of spiritual truth and justice, which the Parable is framed to elucidate." Which of us, reading Matthew 13, would admit to being one of those who seeing see not, and hearing hear not, neither understand? So Alford, speaking of that terrifying law of parable Jesus enunciates whereby "For to him who has will more be given, and he will have abundance; but from him who has not, even what he has will be taken away" (Matt 13:12), applies it to the biblical commentators of his own day, doing in the process what he has said a page before no mere human being should dare do, namely, teach by parable: "No practical comment," says Alford, "on the latter part of this saying can be more striking, than that which is furnished to our day by the study of German rationalistic (and, I may add, some of our English harmonistic) Commentators; while at the same time we may rejoice to see the approximate fulfilment of the former in such commentaries as those of Olshausen, Neander, Stier, and Trench."[5] No doubt Olshausen, Neander, Stier, and Trench were worthy scholars, but there is also no doubt a grotesque incongruity or bathos in using the parable of the sower as a means of dividing the sheep from the goats in the parochial

---

[4] H. Alford, ed., *The Greek Testament* (4 vols.; Boston: Lee and Shepard; New York: Lee, Shepard, and Dillingham, 1874) 1. 136–37.

[5] Ibid., 138.

warfare of biblical scholarship. In any case, there is great temerity in doing so, just that merely human preaching by parables against which Alford has warned on the page before. Yet it is obvious that whoever speaks of the parables at all runs the risk, perhaps must endure the necessity, of doing this. The language of parable contaminates, or perhaps it might be better to say inseminates, impregnates, its commentators. Such language forces them to speak parabolically, since it is by definition impossible to speak of what the parables name except parabolically. Commentary on the parables is, or ought to be, an example of the dissemination of the Word, its multiplication thirty-, sixty-, or a hundredfold.

This need to distinguish secular from sacred parable and yet difficulty in doing so leads to my third presupposition. This is that the two kinds of parable may be distinguished by recognizing that both are performative rather than constative utterances but that two radically different kinds of performative would appear to be involved. A parable does not so much passively name something as make something happen. A parable is a way to do things with words. It is a speech act. In the case of the parables of Jesus, however, the performative word makes something happen in the minds and hearts of his hearers, but this happening is a knowledge of a state of affairs already existing, the kingdom of heaven and the way to get there. In that sense, a biblical parable is constative, not performative at all. A true performative brings something into existence that has no basis except in the words, as when I sign a check and turn an almost worthless piece of paper into whatever value I have inscribed on the check, assuming the various contexts for this act are in correct order—even though as the phenomenon of counterfeit money or the passing of bad checks indicates, the performative may make something happen even when some aspect of the contexts is amiss. Secular parable is a genuine performative. It creates something, a "meaning" that has no basis except in the words or something about which it is impossible to decide whether or not there is an extralinguistic basis. A secular parable is like a piece of money about which it is impossible in principle to know whether or not it is true or counterfeit. Secular parable is language thrown out that creates a meaning hovering there in thin air, a meaning based only on the language itself and on our confidence in it. The categories of truth and falsehood, knowledge and ignorance, do not properly apply to it.

My final presupposition is that both kinds of parable tend to be parables about parable. They are about their own efficacy. Jesus' parable of the sower in Matt 13:1–23, with its parallels in Mark and Luke, is a well-known example of this.[6] Its topic is the efficacy of the word. The distinction is between those who have eyes and ears for the Word and those who do not, or rather the parable distinguishes four possibilities, that the seed will fall by

---

[6] As Jean Starobinski observes, "Le Combat," 111ff.

the wayside, in stony places, among thorns, and in good ground, with an appropriate psychological interpretation for each of the different predispositions to receive the Word, as the thorns stand for "the care of this world, and the deceitfulness of riches," which "choke the word" (Matt 13:22). What in fact is the "word"? It is the good news, the gospel of salvation, the "secrets of the kingdom of heaven" (Matt 13:11), "what has been hidden since the foundation of the world" (Matt 13:35). A whole series of paradoxes operates at once in this parable about parable.

First paradox: The presupposition is that the mysteries of the kingdom of heaven cannot be spoken of directly. The things that have been kept secret from the foundation of the world can only be spoken of in parable. Christ as the Logos is in the awkward position of not being able to speak the Logos directly but of being forced to translate it into a form suitable for profane ears. The Word cannot speak the Word as such.

Second paradox: Unless you understand the Word already as such, unless you are already fertile ground for the Word, which means somehow already grounded in it, sown by it, you will not understand it when it is expressed in parable. When the disciples ask, "Why do you speak to them in parables?" Christ's answer is: "To you it has been given to know the secrets of the kingdom of heaven, but to them it has not been given. For to him who has will more be given, and he will have abundance; but from him who has not, even what he has will be taken away. This is why I speak to them in parables, because seeing they do not see, and hearing they do not hear, nor do they understand" (Matt 13:10–13). The parables are posited on their own inefficacy. If you have knowledge of the kingdom of heaven already, you do not need them. The parables are superfluous, a superabundance, a surplus, a gift beyond gift. If you do not have that knowledge, you will not understand the parables anyhow. They will be a way of covering your eyes and ears further, not a breaking of the seals or a form of unveiling, of revelation. The things that have been kept secret from the foundation of the world will remain secret for most people even after they are spoken in parable. Such things are perhaps made secret by that foundation, veiled by the creation itself rather than revealed by it, and so kept secret by parables that name those secret things with names drawn from familiar created things. The parables translate the Word, so to speak, into the language of familiar things, sowing, fishing, household work. Even so, those for whom the parables are intended are like those to whom one speaks in a foreign language or like someone who does not know Greek presented with the Gospel of Matthew in Greek. The parable, as they say, is all Greek to that person. Such persons lack the gift of tongues or the gift of translating the parable back into the original word. "Hearing they do not hear, nor do they understand." Such people are like Belshazzar confronted by the handwriting on the wall, or they are like those auditors who are not going to understand the prophecy of Isaiah, a failure in understanding that Jesus says the failure of his parables will fulfill. Here is the great text in Isaiah on which Jesus' parable of the sower is a commentary:

> Then flew one of the seraphims to me, having in his hand a burning coal which he had taken with tongs from the altar. And he touched my mouth, and said: "Behold, this has touched your lips; your guilt is taken away, and your sin forgiven." And I heard the voice of the Lord saying, "Whom shall I send, and who will go for us?" Then I said, "Here am I! Send me." And he said, "Go, and say to this people: 'Hear and hear, but do not understand; see and see, but do not perceive.' Make the heart of this people fat, and their ears heavy, and shut their eyes; lest they see with their eyes, and hear with their ears, and understand with their hearts, and turn and be healed." (Isa 6:6–10)

The parables, however, are intended for just such people, and so they are posited on their own inevitable misreading or nonreading. The problem, once more, is how to cross over from one kind of language to the other, from the word of God, "Whom shall I send?" to the word of the human: "Here am I! Send me." If you can understand the parables, you do not need them. If you need them, you cannot hope to understand them. The parables are not a way of giving the Word but a way of taking away, a way of adding further deprivation to a deprivation that is already total: "From him who has not, even what he has will be taken away."

Third paradox: The disciples are said by Jesus to be those to whom it is given to know the mysteries of the kingdom of heaven. It would seem that this means they already have the Word and therefore have open eyes and ears, are able to understand the parables spontaneously, translate their displaced language back to the original tongue, and at the same time do not need the parables. The parables give them more when they already have and so do not need. For them the parables are superfluous. "For to him who has will more be given, and he will have abundance." The paradox is that, having said that, Jesus proceeds to explain to the disciples the parable of the sower, spelling it out, translating it back into the language of the kingdom of heaven, as if they could not understand it without his interpretation. He has said they understand, but he goes on to speak as if they could not possibly understand: "Truly, I say to you, many prophets and righteous men have longed to see what you see, and did not see it, and to hear what you hear, and did not hear it. Hear then the parable of the sower. When any one hears the word of the kingdom and does not understand it, the evil one comes and snatches away what is sown in his heart; this is what was sown along the path . . ." and so on through the explicit application of each of the clauses of the parable to each of the four kinds of people in relation to the proffered insemination or dissemination of the Word, down to: "As for what was sown on good soil, this is he who hears the word and understands it; he indeed bears fruit, and yields, in one case a hundredfold, in another sixty, and in another thirty" (Matt 13:17–23).

Fourth paradox: The economy of equivalence, of giving and receiving, of equable translation and measure, of the circulation of signs governed by the Logos as source of proportion and guarantee of substitution or analogy, is upset by the parables. Although the parables of Jesus are spoken by the Word, they are not logical. They are not governed, as, say, medieval allegory is said to be, whatever Henry Alford affirms, by the "real analogies impressed by the Creator of all things on his creatures." Or, if they are so governed, they function by a choice of alogical moments in systems of circulation and exchange in the familiar domestic world to indicate the failure of analogy between anything human, including human languages—Aramaic, Greek, Latin, English, or whatever—and the divine Logos, the Word of the kingdom of heaven. If allegory and symbolism in one way or another work by analogy or by correspondence, resonance, or participation between one thing and another thing on a different level, or between one word and another word, as in the proportionalities of metaphor, the parables of Jesus are ana-analogical, or rather, since "ana" is already a double antithetical prefix, which may mean either "according to" or "against," it may simply be said that the parables are "analogical" in the sense of "against logic," "counter to logic." "Paradox": the word means etymologically, "against teaching," or against the received opinion of those in authority. The words or parables of Jesus are a stumbling block to the Greeks because they go against the habits of logical thinking. The Logos in the sense of Jesus as the Word contradicts *logos* in the sense of Greek reason, or reasoned thinking, which is reason as such in the West.

The "literal" language of the parables of Jesus and of his actions themselves as described by the gospel makers is drawn from various realms of domestic economy, production, consumption, and exchange in the family or in the immediate social group such as a household with servants or a farm with hired workers. These various realms include eating, sowing and reaping, fishing, sexual reproduction, the donation and receiving of gifts, the exchange of words, translation from one language to another, counting, and the exchange of money, its use and its usury. In all cases the example chosen breaks down the pattern of a closed circuit of exchange of the same for the same or its equivalent. The fisherman draws fish abundantly from the salt and inhospitable sea. A single seed cast in fertile ground reproduces a hundred, sixty, or thirtyfold, and a tiny mustard seed produces an enormous tree. He who saves his life will lose it. To save it, it must be thrown away, and the same thing may be said of virginity, which is of value or use only if it is given up, just as money has the power of reproducing itself magically but not if it is hoarded, only if it is invested, put out at risk, used. The distinction between male potency and female passive receptivity is broken down in sexual reproduction, since the female must be fertile ground for the seed and thus in a sense already contain its potentiality, as only fertile ground will multiply the seed cast on it and as only those who already have the Word can receive it and multiply it. Although the image Jesus uses in his exegesis of the parable of the sower is that of sexual reproduction, the sexes are strangely reversed, as they are in the image of the soul as the bride of Christ. Jesus speaks of the different persons who receive the seed of the Word always as "he": "But he that received the seed into stony places . . ." and so on, but that fertile ground must in some sense be a feminine matrix, an egg ready to receive the seed. A genuine gift, like the other elements upsetting any domestic economy of equivalence and exchange, is, as Marcel Mauss and Jacques Derrida have in different ways argued, always something incommensurate with any recompense, something suspending the circuit of obligation, of payment and repayment.[7] A true gift can never be returned. It creates an infinite obligation and is not restitution for any claim I have on another. The gift leads to such absurdities as the Northwest American Indian potlatch, in which one man vies with another in destroying great heaps of valuable property.

The power of the gift to break down logical equivalences in social exchange is shown in reverse in what might be called the living parable of the story of the loaves and fishes in Matthew 14. Jesus blesses the bread, breaks it, and gives the five loaves and the two fishes to the disciples. The disciples give them to the multitude. In that double process of giving, the loaves and fishes become multiplied beyond any rational calculation so that there is always enough and some over—twelve baskets of fragments— though about five thousand have been fed. In this case, as in the parables generally, for example the parable of the sower, several different realms, of the ones I have listed, come together: gift giving and receiving, agriculture and fishing in the bread and fishes, and the illogic of an arithmetical sum in which five loaves and two fishes become a countless number with twelve basketsfull left over. In the case of the parable of the sower, sowing and reaping, on the one hand, and sexual reproduction on the other, are used each as a figure for the paradoxes of the other. There is a contamination of the "literal" language of each of the realms, in any vernacular, with figures drawn from others of the realms, as when we speak of "seed money," or of the "dissemination" of the seed in sowing, as well as of the dissemination of doctrine, or of sexual reproduction in terms of "getting" and "spending," and so on, in a perpetual round in which no one set of these terms is the purely literal language that provides figures for the others. Another way to put this is to say that ordinary language, the language Jesus must use to speak to the multitude or to the disciples, is already irremediably parabolic.

The final realm in which rational equivalence and exchange breaks down is then that of language itself, that dissemination of the Word for which all these other realms are not so much figures as living and material hieroglyphs, that is, places where the paradoxes of sign-making and sign-using enter into the actual process of the living together of men and women

---

[7] See Marcel Mauss, *The Gift* (trans. Ian Cunnison; New York: Norton, 1967); the seminars by Jacques Derrida at Yale University in the fall of 1980 focused on Mauss's book.

in family and community, to be incorporated inextricably into that process. In the realm of language, too, the giving of the Word introduces a form of sign into the rational exchanges of word for word in ordinary communication which breaks open that circuit with the alogic of parable. The Word is like a tiny mustard seed, which produces a huge tree, and although it is demonstrably untranslatable, "the propagation of the gospel in foreign lands" depends on its translatability and on the gift of tongues to the apostles and their dissemination, carrying the Word into the four corners of the world. The limitations of a given translation are not contingent but absolute. The failure of translation is not a result of the incompatability of one idiom and another or between a proper original and some improper transfer or *Übersetzung*, as they say in German for translation, "setting over." The failure of translation is the result of the absence of any adequate original in any humanly comprehensible language. When I read the King James Bible today, or some other English Bible, it has behind it the Vulgate, the Greek, the hypothetical Aramaic versions of what Jesus said, language behind language behind language. However, the inadequacy of any translation and the way the propagation of the Gospel is a triumph over its own manifest impossibility lie not in the incorrectness of this or that detail in, say, the King James Bible in relation to the Greek or Aramaic "original" but in the fact that even the words of the parable of the sower, for example, as Jesus originally spoke them, were not an original but already the translation of an untranslatable original Word, which is what Jesus in the parable of the sower "says": "This is why I speak to them in parables, because seeing they do not see, and hearing they do not hear, nor do they understand. With them indeed is fulfilled the prophecy of Isaiah which says: 'You shall indeed hear but never understand, and you shall indeed see but never perceive'" (Matt 13:13–14).

In all these realms the pattern of alogic is "the same." It is analogical, and analogy among ana-analogies or an analogy in one sense among analogies in the antithetical sense. In each case the pattern expresses a strange arithmetic in which one will get you not two but a hundredfold in return, or rather in which something so tiny that it is in effect zero will multiply infinitely, as in that equation Paul Claudel makes among things globular and null or almost null: "*oeuf, semence, bouche ouverte, zéro*," "egg, seed, open mouth, zero," where the open mouth that proffers the word, "Here am I, send me," is equated not only with the egg and seed of sowing and sexual reproduction but also with the zero that divides an infinite number of times even into a single unit, as a single word may be broken, divided, and scattered in all languages to the four winds.[8]

I turn now to modern secular parable, which should in principle, I have suggested, function differently, since a secular parable is not spoken by the

___

[8] Paul Claudel and André Gide, *Correspondance 1899–1926* (Paris: Gallimard, 1949) 91.

Word itself translating itself to human ears and human understanding but is spoken by some all-too-human person casting out figurative language toward something across the border from any direct seeing, hearing, or understanding.

In *Von den Gleichnissen* ("On Parables") Franz Kafka develops a characteristically mind-twisting paradox that turns on the distinction between whether something happens in reality or in parable. It is a triple distinction: a distinction between everyday reality and "some fabulous yonder"; a distinction between the everyday person and that person transfigured; a distinction between literal language and parabolic language:

> When the sage says: "go over," he does not mean that we should cross to some actual place, which we could do anyhow if the labor were worth it; he means some fabulous yonder (*irgendem sagenhaftes Drüben*), something unknown to us (*das wir nicht kennen*), something that he cannot designate more precisely (*von ihm nicht näher zu bezeichnen ist*), and therefore cannot help us there in the very least.[9]

The word "over" (*hinüber*) in parabolic speech refers not to some real place "over there" but to a place out of this world. It is a place, moreover, that cannot be designated more precisely than in topographical terms drawn from the real world and applied figuratively to the place out of the real world. There are no literal terms for the places in parable. They cannot be designated more precisely than by the transferred terms of metaphor or rather of catachresis, which is the proper term for a figure that does not replace any existing proper word. The question posed by Kafka's little text is a double one: What kind of action is performed by the sage when he wrests words from their normal usage and says, "Go over"? What kind of actions should we perform if we wish to obey the sage's injunction?

The answer seems obvious enough. We have only to follow the parables in order to become parables. We would then enter into the realm of parable, and escape cares of real life in the actual place where we are: "Concerning this a man once said: Why such reluctance? If you only followed the parables you yourselves would become parables and with that rid of all your daily cares."[10]

The question about this commentary is also obvious enough. Is the remark by "a man" in itself literal, or is it parabolic? This in turn is a displacement of a more general question. Is Kafka's "On Parables" as a whole literal or is it parabolic? Is it possible to speak of parables literally, or is the language of the commentators on parables always contaminated by what they talk about, subdued to what they work in, so that their language becomes in its turn inevitably parabolic? Would that necessarily be a bad thing? These are the questions raised by the little alternating dialogue that

[9] Franz Kafka, *Parables and Paradoxes*, in German and English (New York: Schocken Books, 1971) 10–11.
[10] Ibid.

ends Kafka's "On Parables." In this dialogue two more voices are heard, and the voice of "Kafka" himself, which spoke at first, as well as the voice of the "man" who said we only need to "follow" the parables, vanishes entirely. The little dialogue has to do with the linguistic status of the exhortation to follow the parables and has to do with winning and losing not in the parables themselves but in the interpreter's stance in relation to them and in his language about them:

> Another said: I bet that is also a parable.
> The first said: You have won.
> The second said: But unfortunately only in parable.
> The first said: No, in reality: in parable you have lost.[11]

The reader (I hope) will be able to follow this somewhat bewildering alternation to the point of blinding clarity it reaches. To say something is a parable can only be done from the point of view of reality and of literal language, since the realm of parable and the language of parable are defined by their difference from the real and the literal. They are a transfer from it, a "going over." To say that by following the parables one becomes a parable is a parable all right, but it is a saying that remains immovably still in the realm of everyday life, which, after all, as "On Parables" says at the beginning, "is the only life we have." One wins the bet ("I bet that is also a parable") but only in reality, which means that one loses in parable. The parables ask to be taken literally. The only way they can become efficacious is for them to become literally true, so that one does literally "go over." As long as they are seen as figures of speech, as merely parabolic, one loses in parable, one has failed to enter into the realm of parable. But they cannot be seen otherwise. They produce neither action nor knowledge. To know that fabulous realm over there is to cross over into it, but the parables merely throw out incomprehensible figures in the direction of the incomprehensible. They are like parables proffered by one of the multitude who hear Jesus speak or at best like a parable given out by one of the disciples. "All these parables really set out to say merely that the incomprehensible is incomprehensible (*unfassbar*), and we know that already."[12]

"On Parables" is a characteristic example of the specifically Kafkan double bind. Either way you have had it. You lose by winning and lose by losing too. If you take the parable literally, then you must understand it as naming some literal crossing over from one place to another in reality, in which case you remain in reality, "the only life we have"; so following the parables does not make anything happen. If you take parable parabolically, then it is seen as merely figurative. In that case neither the parable itself nor following the parable makes anything happen, and so you have lost in parable, since

---

[11] Ibid.
[12] Ibid., p. 258.

winning in parable could only occur if the crossing over promised in the parable were to occur in reality. Either way you lose, since winning in reality is losing in parable, and the one thing needful is to win in parable, to find a joy whose grounds are true.

This may perhaps be made clearer by a return to my comparison with performative language. It would seem at first that two kinds of language, the creative *Fiat lux* of God and statements made by human beings like "I pronounce you husband and wife" are the same. Both are ways of doing things with words. There is, however, an essential difference. The "Let there be light" of God produces the basic condition of visibility and therefore of knowledge. It allows things to stand in the sunlight and be seen. To use the distinction employed also by Nietzsche, as well as by Kafka in the phrase "*das wir nicht kennen*," God's *Fiat lux* leads to an act of knowledge, an *Erkennen*. Human performatives, on the other hand, can never be the object of an epistemological act whereby subject confronts something that has been brought to life and knows it. Human performatives are always from beginning to end baseless positings, acts of *Ersetzen* rather than of *Erkennen*.[13] A secular parable is an *Ersetzen* that must, impossibly, become an *Erkennen*. It must actually create a new realm into which we might cross over. It remains a merely human positing, the making of a realm created by language, existing and sustained only in language. In this it is no different from the complex social world made by promising, contracting, naming, and so on, the "daily life" with all its "cares" "which is the only life we have," and which we would do anything to cross over out of. No speech act, no poetic or parabolic performative can help us one bit to do that. "Over out of": The multiplication of adverbs is meant to mime the repeated unsuccessful attempts to go somewhere with language.

o   o   o   o   o

I shall now attempt to draw such conclusions as I can from my brief side-by-side discussion of sacred parable and secular parable. My primary motivation, it will be remembered, has been to identify distinguishing marks that would allow a firm division between one and the other. I claim to have done this in identifying a different nature and standing place in each case for the speaker or writer of the parable and in identifying a different relation in each case to the distinction between performative and constative language. The latter difference may be phrased by saying that both kinds of parables are catachreses, the throwing out of language toward an "unknown X" which cannot be named in proper or literal language. In the case of secular parable it cannot be known for certain, even by the one who invents the parable, whether or not there is something out there, across the frontier,

---

[13] See Paul de Man's discussion of Nietzsche's use of this distinction in "Rhetoric of Persuasion (Nietzsche)," *Allegories of Reading* (New Haven and London: Yale University, 1979) 119–31.

which pre-exists the language for it. Such language may be a true performative, bringing something into being that exists only in the words or by means of the words. Sacred parable is in principle spoken by someone who has that knowledge to start with, by someone who *is* that knowledge, by someone who is the Logos itself in all the sense of that word: mind, reason, knowledge, speech, measure, ratio, ground of all things.

The distinction seems clear, but the distinction itself involves a double paradox, one on each side of the line separating secular from sacred parable. On the one hand, Christ the Word must in the parables translate the Word into humanly comprehensible language. He is in himself both sides of the dialogue between Jehovah and Isaiah that he says his parables are meant to fulfill. Christ is both the Word of God, "the voice of the Lord" called in vocation or in invocation to Isaiah, "Whom shall I send?" and Isaiah's answering voice in acceptance of vocation, "Here am I! Send me." Christ's words are therefore subject necessarily to the limitations of human language in whatever language they are spoken or into which they might be translated, in spite of the suprahuman standing place from which he speaks. Christ's dissemination of the Word is therefore performed over its logical impossibility, as he says in the parable of the sower. This impossibility may be expressed by saying that the parables of Jesus are not properly performative. They do not in themselves make anything happen, since their auditors must already know the Word to be fertile ground for the Word the parables speak. The parables of Jesus are constative, but they provide knowledge that for many is spoken in a foreign tongue, a tongue that is not going to be understood. The paradox of the parables of the Gospels as at once Word of God and at the same time humanly comprehensible words is "the same as," analogical to in one or the other meaning of the word analogy, the mystery of the Incarnation, in which God and humanity become one across the barrier of the impossibility of their union.

Of another "analogous" problem with the parables in the Gospels I have not even spoken here, and can only indicate a line to be followed. Do the citations of the parables by the authors of the Gospels have the same efficacy as the parables had when they were originally spoken by Jesus to his auditors, or are they only the report of a form of language that has its efficacy elsewhere? Are they still the Word of the kingdom of heaven, the good news itself, or are they only the translation of that Word so it may be disseminated in another tongue? To employ the terminology of the speech-act theorists, are they "use" or only "mention" of Christ's language? These questions, it will be seen, are analogous to, although not quite the same as, the problem of translation on the one hand and the problem of distinguishing sacred from secular parable on the other.[14]

[14] Werner H. Kelber is at work on a study of the parables of the Synoptic Gospels which makes the distinction between citation and original oral utterance suggested in this paragraph.

On the other side of the line separating secular and sacred parable, the paradox is that no purely human parable-maker, even though that person may be someone who, like Kafka, fully accepts the limitations of humanity, can avoid the temerity of at least tentatively, implicitly, or hypothetically putting himself in Christ's place and claiming to serve as an intermediary between this everyday world and the kingdom of heaven on the other side of the frontier of which all parables bring word. Secular parable may be, strictly speaking, a true performative, the creation of something that exists, for humanity at least, only in the words, but this purely performative function is always contaminated by an implicit claim to be based on knowledge and to bring knowledge, even if that knowledge is the negative knowing of the apparent impossibility of "going over." Kafka was fully aware of this danger. It is in fact the fundamental burden of *Von den Gleichnissen*.

Any commentator on parables, secular or sacred, is in the situation of Kafka, or indeed of such a commentator as Henry Alford. One should be anxious to avoid the danger of being parabolic oneself and yet one is unable certainly to do so. The question of the relation between secular and sacred parable is a tiny seed that generates a long line of thought, multiplying itself thirty-, sixty-, or a hundredfold, of which this paper is only a preliminary segment. Such a line of thought is like a parabolic trajectory, sweeping in from an infinite distance and back out again. That my discourse on parable is itself parabolic there can be no doubt, although whether I have been able to keep safely on this side of the line separating secular from sacred parable is not so certain. The uncertainty derives from the difficulty—perhaps the impossibility—in spite of all efforts and in spite of the high stakes involved, of keeping the two kinds of parable absolutely distinct.

V

ANTHROPOLOGICAL APPROACHES TO THE STUDY OF THE BIBLE DURING THE TWENTIETH CENTURY

Edmund Leach

> Old Testament stories were retained and rewritten because a small group of Jews . . . believed themselves to be the sole survivors of the Hebrew people whose glorious traditions ran back into the dim past. They re-used the old stories, adapted them in up-to-date preaching to the needs of their own age. . . . There is a human reason why each story and saying was written and retained when so much was discarded and lost, and it is much more important in biblical study to try to discover why a story was told or a saying recorded than to question its date, origin or historicity.[1]

I had better say right away that my whole contribution will be an exercise in self-justification and that it will be very restricted in scope. I am going to talk about anthropologists who have had the temerity to write about the Bible and *not* to any significant extent about biblical scholars who have in one way or another made use of the writings of anthropologists. Furthermore, I am going to talk almost exclusively about British anthropologists rather than about American or French or Dutch anthropologists or whatever. And finally I am going to take a very narrow view of what constitutes anthropology.

I am adopting this restricted position simply because there is too much ground to cover. I am fully aware that thereby I shall leave out much that some members of my audience may feel is both relevant and important. For example, I shall not be referring to the semiotic studies of biblical texts inspired by Claude Chabrol and Louis Marin,[2] although in fact some of their work comes much closer to my own than does that of any of the British authors whom I shall mention. I shall also be ignoring the American counterpart of these French studies, most of which has appeared in the periodical *Semeia*.[3] My justification is simply that the authors concerned are specialists in semiotics rather than anthropology.

---

[1] J. N. Schofield, *Introducing Old Testament Theology* (London: SCM, 1964) 9–10.

[2] C. Chabrol and L. Marin (*Le récit évangélique* [Paris: Bibliothèque de Sciences Religieuses, 1974] 249–51) have a very valuable bibliography entitled: "Bibliographie sémiotique des textes bibliques." See also the references to A. C. Thiselton, "Structuralism and Biblical Studies: Method or Ideology?" *ExpTim* (1978) 335.

[3] *Semeia* is a publication of the Society of Biblical Literature (Chico, California: Scholars Press).

Those who wish to explore some of the facets of my theme that I myself have neglected may find it useful to take a look at Rogerson.[4] Rogerson is not himself an anthropologist, and his understanding of contemporary anthropological argument is in places decidedly confused. However, he has read quite widely in parts of the relevant anthropological literature that I shall be ignoring in this lecture. Moreover, he makes a serious if not wholly satisfactory attempt to pin down the areas where anthropologists and biblical scholars get into a mutual tangle by using similar terminology to denote quite different ideas. I must confess however that I myself found Rogerson's book somewhat depressing, for, whereas he ends by saying that "some sort of new dialogue between Old Testament experts and anthropologists" is opening up,[5] his book makes it all too clear that so far there has been absolutely no mutual communication between the two sides. Here Rogerson himself is just as much at sea as are those of his theological colleagues whom he is seeking to inform.

My own professional competence is that of a social anthropologist trained in the British functionalist tradition established by Malinowski in the 1920s. As part of that tradition I use the word "myth" to mean "a sacred tale about past events which is used to justify social action in the present."[6] By this definition a myth is "true" for those who believe in it; whether it is also true in a matter-of-fact, empirical sense is irrelevant and would in any case usually be very difficult to demonstrate. Many people, including fellow anthropologists, use the word "myth" in quite a different sense. They assume that the essence of myth is that it is "mythical," that is to say that it is "untrue" in any rational matter-of-fact sense. They therefore restrict the category to stories that contain palpably supernatural happenings: animals who talk, humans who fly like birds, supernatural births and so on. Claude Lévi-Strauss, who has written more about myth than any other living anthropologist, appears to use the word in this way, although I am not aware that he has ever actually said so.

For my present purposes the distinction between the use of myth to mean "a sacred tale" on the one hand and "a fabulous impossible tale" on the other is very important. In the "sacred tale" version, which is my own

[4] J. W. Rogerson, *Anthropology and the Old Testament* (Oxford: Basil Blackwell, 1978).

[5] Ibid., 119.

[6] Malinowski's own references to this topic are numerous but scattered; the most immediately relevant is the following quotation, which comes from *Myth in Primitive Psychology* (New York: W. W. Norton, 1926) [reprinted in B. Malinowski, *Magic, Science and Religion and Other Essays* (Glencoe: Free Press, 1948) 100; and elsewhere]: "Myth . . . is not merely a story told but a reality lived. It is not of the nature of fiction, such as we read today in a novel, but it is a living reality, believed to have once happened in primeval times, and continuing ever since to influence the world and human destinies. . . . Myth is to the savage what, to a fully believing Christian, is the Biblical story of Creation, of the Fall, of the Redemption by Christ's Sacrifice on the Cross. As our sacred story lives in our ritual, in our morality, as it governs our faith and controls our conduct, even so does his myth for the savage."

usage, the whole of the Bible is myth for Christians and the whole of the Hebrew Bible is myth for Jews. In the "fabulous impossible tale" version the scope of biblical myth is not only much more restricted but also open to dispute. Even devout Christians would now presumably agree that the Genesis Garden of Eden story is a myth in this latter, "fabulous-impossible" sense, but there could be wide disagreement even among the faithful over how to classify the New Testament stories of Christ's nativity.

When I declare that "the whole of the Bible is myth" *in the sacred tale sense*, I am merely stating the obvious, but I am also drawing attention to the nature of the canon. The Bible as we have it today is an edited compendium of a great variety of documents of differing origin and differing date. The sacredness of the corpus derives from the fact that it is these documents and these documents alone that the faithful are required to accept. In the process of editorial selection many other similar documents, some of which are known to us, were rejected. In other words, the canon is what it is because the final editors of the period 200 B.C.E. to 200 C.E. felt that these particular documents hang together in some special way. This hanging together is crucial. It is what the books of the Hebrew Bible say as a collectivity that makes it a sacred tale for the Orthodox Jew; it is what both the Old and New Testament say when taken together as a single collectivity that makes the whole Bible a sacred tale for the believing Christian.

Now what these two canons say as collectivities is something very different from what the individual documents contained in the two canons say if they are read piecemeal. As an anthropologist concerned with myth in the "sacred tale" sense, my interest is with the totalities rather than with the component parts of which the totalities are made up. Since a great deal of traditional-style biblical scholarship has precisely the opposite objective of taking the present day collectivity apart in order to demonstrate what were its original component elements, communication between anthropologists of my sort and biblical scholars proper is often very difficult. The difficulties are of many different kinds, but one of them relates to the problem of how we should distinguish between *myth* in the sense that I have defined and *history*.

An infinite number of events have occurred in the historical past. It should be obvious that even in the most favorable circumstances we can only know a tiny fraction of such past events. It should also be obvious that for the most part what we know is a matter of fortuitous accident rather than human planning. But although we may not know much about the past, we can invent a great deal. Down to about 1930 most anthropologists considered that this was their main task; they were pre-historians. Their role was to concoct plausible guesses about how grand-scale history had worked itself out. Some anthropologists still operate within this convention. I myself do not. It seems to me that it is just as difficult to reconstruct the past as it is to predict the future.

Furthermore, since I totally reject all those forms of historicism which assume that the future must necessarily follow the same kind of trajectory that has been patterned by the past, I regard the invention of conjectural history as a total waste of time. The latter part of this personal credo has only an indirect bearing upon what I am going to say, but you need to keep it in mind.

Now if we consider the Bible as a totality, as I urge you to do, it is quite clearly a sacred tale and not a history book. However, if you take the totality to pieces after the fashion of orthodox biblical scholarship, it is equally clear that substantial parts of it are written "as if" they were history, and the majority of biblical scholars seem to have persuaded themselves that these are, in fact, records of "true" history. There is disagreement about just where legend ends and history begins, but mostly it seems to be assumed that Moses (probably) and Saul and David (certainly) were real people who actually existed in the period 1250 to 1000 B.C.E., that is to say five hundred years before the age of Herodotus and Thucydides.[7]

Personally I find this most implausible. There is no archaeological evidence for the existence of these heroes or for the occurrence of any of the events with which they are associated. If it were not for the sacredness of these stories, their historicity would certainly be rejected. Classical scholars do not now believe that the Trojan War as a historical event or that the kind of society depicted in the *Iliad* and the *Odyssey* ever actually existed; still less do they imagine that Achilles and Hector and Agamemnon and the rest were real people of flesh and blood. However, Saul and David were reputedly their contemporaries. In this regard my own position is one of extreme skepticism. If we ignore the rather small number of named biblical characters whose existence is fully vouched for by independent evidence—and by that I mean archaeology rather than Josephus—I regard *all* the personalities of biblical narrative, both in the Old Testament and in the New, as wholly fictional. They are there because they fill a particular role in the totality of the sacred tale and not because they actually existed in history. Moreover, even if a few of them did have some kind of real-life existence, this fact is quite irrelevant. If a named individual X "really existed," so also did thousands of other individuals whose names we do not know. What interests us about X is the role he is made to play in the sacred tale; this interest is not

---

[7] The uncertainty is shared by anthropologists. A striking case is provided by the work of Raphael Patai, who is knowledgeable both as an anthropologist and as a biblical scholar. In *Family, Love and the Bible* (London: Macgibbon and Key, 1960) every incident in the biblical narrative is treated as a record of historical fact and as evidence that "in the days of the Hebrew patriarchs" such and such behavior was "a binding custom." On the other hand, R. Graves and R. Patai (*Hebrew Myths: The Book of Genesis* [London: Cassell, 1964]), who are mainly concerned with noncanonical Hebrew sources, include substantial parts of Genesis under the category "myth." Correspondingly the definition of myth given in *Hebrew Myths* (p. 11) is an uncomfortable compromise between the "sacred tale" and the "impossible tale" view.

affected by the question of historicity. In Tolstoy's novel *War and Peace* quite a number of the characters in the early part of the book are genuine historical personages who played a part in the war of 1812 between the Russians and the French, but the bearing of this fact on the significance of the novel is negligible. The marginal historicity of some features of the Bible story seems to me to be exactly comparable.

However, this distinction between myth and history has another aspect. The view that I adopt—that the biblical narrative is a myth, a sacred tale— implies that I treat the entire text as synchronic. In the story one thing happens after another, because that is the only way you can tell a story. Yet the truth of myth, which is religious truth, is all of a piece. As in a dream, the end is already implicit in the beginning; there is no development, only dialectical inversion. Christ is the second Adam; the Virgin is the second Eve; sinless immortality replaces sinful mortality; and so on.

In contrast, if you adopt a historian's stance, then you must look for diachronic development. The details that come later in the story refer to events that happened later in real time. Furthermore, what comes later is not just a transformation of what came earlier but a complete replacement, an innovation. A recent anthropological advocate for this approach to biblical materials, as against my own, is Professor Julian Pitt-Rivers.[8] Pitt-Rivers is not prepared to defend the strict historicity of the Bible in an unqualified way. He does not, for example, claim that Jacob was a historical personality who lived to be 130 years old. Yet he does argue that because the Genesis story about Dinah comes in chap. 34, while the Genesis story about Abraham's lending his sister-wife Sarah to Pharaoh comes in chap. 12, therefore in real history the morality of the Dinah story, which Pitt-Rivers sees as entailing the principle of Honor that still operates throughout the Mediterranean area, superseded the morality of the wife-lending story, which also has modern analogies but only in what Pitt-Rivers seems to regard as relatively primitive contexts. Comparably he holds that the story of the Levite and his concubine in Judges 19, which is closely modelled on the story of "Lot and the Angels in Sodom" in Genesis 19, represents a progression from the mode of myth to the mode of historical realism. He is prepared to rate the Lot story as myth because it includes palpably supernatural events, but he holds that the Judges story, being cast in "realistic" form, should be treated as a representation of real-life political events.

I find this a most extraordinary view. The Judges story is part of a longer sequence that includes chaps. 20 and 21 just as the Lot-in-Sodom story is a part of a longer sequence that includes the story of Lot's wife and the incest of drunken Lot with his daughters. Structurally the sequences in Genesis and in Judges are permutations of one another, but both are equally remote from "real history."

[8] J. Pitt-Rivers, *The Fate of Shechem: or the Politics of Sex* (Cambridge: Cambridge University, 1977) chap. 7.

I shall presently return to this theme in order to explain my debate with Pitt-Rivers in greater detail, but meanwhile I must fulfill my obligation to give an account of the interactions between anthropologists and biblical scholars during the whole of the twentieth century.

The anthropological study of the Bible did not begin in the year 1900; but, as it happens, that is quite a good point at which to start an account of it. During the eighteenth and nineteenth centuries most of the proto-anthropologists of the period left the Bible alone. The story of the flood, which made Noah the ancestor of all humanity, and the calculations of Bishop Ussher (not to mention those of Sir Isaac Newton), which put the creation of the world only a few thousand years behind the present, could not be easily fitted to the historical fact that the Americas were already inhabited before the arrival of Columbus. In any case, however, prior to the latter part of the eighteenth century hardly anyone had thought of the Bible as a text that might need to take account of materials external to itself. The Bible was the directly revealed word of God; it could be used to throw light on what we know from other sources, but it could not in turn be illuminated by those sources. To suggest otherwise was a dangerous heresy, as Galileo and others discovered to their cost.

Over the centuries the word "religion" had gradually come to embrace other cosmological systems besides that of Judeo-Christianity. The Greeks and the Romans and the Muslims and the Hindus and even the primitive cultures of Africa and the South Seas were all allowed to have "religions" of a sort, but comparative studies that discussed the relations between such systems nearly always managed to leave the Bible out of account. From time to time Christian missionaries had claimed to encounter versions of familiar Bible stories among distant tribes, and this had produced a variety of extraordinary accounts of the wanderings of the Lost Tribes of Israel. Yet systematic attempts to discover the real history of biblical texts only developed in the latter part of the nineteenth century, and the anthropologists only became involved in the game right at the end of it.

As far as Britain is concerned, this development is traceable to a quite specific historical event. In 1881 the erudite polymath William Robertson Smith was dismissed for heresy from his professorial chair of Hebrew and Old Testament at Aberdeen.[9] He was then almost immediately appointed editor of the *Encyclopaedia Britannica* and within a few years was established as Professor of Arabic at Cambridge. He there developed a close friendship with a fellow Scotsman, a young classical scholar named J. G. Frazer. Smith had already endeavored to show that the general anthropological theory of the day had relevance for an understanding of Arabic culture and further that the details of Arabic culture had relevance for our

---

[9] For an account of Robertson Smith's career, see T. O. Beidelman, *W. Robertson Smith and the Sociological Study of Religion* (Chicago: University of Chicago, 1974).

understanding of biblical texts. However, he now commissioned Frazer to write a number of anthropological articles for the encyclopaedia and then went on to persuade Frazer to direct the major part of his academic effort to anthropology rather than to study of the classics.

It was Frazer, as author of *The Golden Bough*, who first made anthropology a fully respectable academic pursuit. In this regard Frazer's present renown is largely undeserved. Most of what he himself contributed to the study of anthropology and comparative religion has proved worthless. On the other hand, almost everything in the whole vast corpus of Frazer's writings that anthropologists continue to value was a direct derivation from the work of his mentor Robertson Smith.

I will not go into details, for it all happened a long time ago; but I can skim over the story. Prior to the 1930s the anthropological discussion of Christianity, considered as a religion comparable with other religions, remained very much hedged about either by reticence or by hostility. Smith and Frazer were among the reticent. Thus, although Smith remained a committed Christian, the first edition of *Lectures on the Religion of the Semites* treated the theme of the slain God of Christianity as comparable with that of earlier Middle Eastern religious systems, but the second edition, completed just before Smith's death in 1894, omits this offending passage.[10]

Similarly, much of the celebrity of Frazer's *The Golden Bough* had originally derived from the notoriety that attached to what he had said in the second edition, of 1900, about the crucifixion of Christ as an example of a dying god sacrifice. However, in the third edition this section is relegated to a hard-to-find appendix,[11] while in the well-known one-volume abridged edition of 1922 it is cut out altogether.

In a very similar way the renowned British folklorist E. S. Hartland had made stories about supernatural birth one of the central themes not only of his three-volume *The Legend of Perseus* but also of the two-volume *Primitive Paternity*.[12] Yet the numerous stories of this genre that appear in the Bible receive scarcely any attention in either publication. On the other hand there was, at this same period, another class of scholar (of whom J. M. Robertson[13] was a notable example) who rewrote the works of Smith and Frazer with the quite explicit intention of exhibiting parallels between biblical

[10] The passage in question came at p. 393 of W. R. Smith, *Lectures on the Religion of the Semites*, 1st ed. (London: A. & C. Black, 1889; 2d ed., 1894; 3d ed. S. A. Cook, 1927). It is quoted at length in Beidelman, *Smith and Sociological Study*, 57.

[11] J. G. Frazer, *The Golden Bough* (2d ed; London: Macmillan, 1900) 3. 186–96; reprinted in 3d ed. of 1913 as a "Note" at pp. 412–23 of Pt. 6, "The Scapegoat."

[12] E. S. Hartland, *The Legend of Perseus* (3 vols.; London: D. Nutt, 1894–96); *Primitive Paternity: The Myth of Supernatural Birth in Relation to the History of the Family* (2 vols.; London: D. Nutt, 1909).

[13] J. M. Robertson, *Pagan Christs: Studies in Comparative Hierology* (2d ed.; London: Watts, 1911).

Christianity and heathen religions. Their express purpose was to display Judeo-Christianity as a form of archaic superstition.

Even by the 1920s there was scarcely any *positive* interaction between biblical scholars and anthropologists. Frazer's massive three-volume *Folklore in the Old Testament* was published in 1918, but it retained the convention of reticence.[14] Frazer here explored the folktales of the whole world to find parallels for details of content in the Old Testament stories. However, the details he considered were not such as might be likely to arouse passionate debate among theologians, either Jewish or Christian. Thus Part I, Chapter 4 is a 250-page monograph entitled "The Great Flood." Fewer than twenty pages are devoted to the Bible story, and these simply repeat the textual criticism that was generally accepted by orthodox biblical scholars of the day. The rest of the chapter is a compendium of flood stories from all over the world. They are presented as a long list of separate items with little attempt at generalization. Frazer notes that these stories of a universal flood cannot represent the folk memory of a historical event since they are contradicted by geological evidence. However, he offers no explanation of why stories of this kind should be so widespread or why they should be concentrated in some parts of the map rather than in others.

Even today there is no general agreement among anthropologists about such matters, yet there are a number of specifically anthropological observations of a structuralist kind that might have a bearing on the Genesis story. For example, it is a characteristic of flood stories that the survivors become the ancestors of all humankind. These survivors are related to one another in a variety of ways: sometimes, although rather rarely, as mother and child or as brother and sister; sometimes as two orphans brought together by chance; sometimes, as in the Bible, as husband and wife and their married offspring. What is common to almost all the stories is that the survivors are ordinary human beings who have been born in an ordinary way. They are thus quite unlike the first parents in the first creation, who belong, like Adam and Eve, to some kind of other world paradise and who have come into being in some spontaneous irregular fashion.

Although these mysterious original first parents engage in sex relations in some fashion and thereby have offspring, it is a union that is contaminated with the sin of abnormality. The function of flood stories is to destroy this first creation and its ambiguities and to start again. The end of the flood marks the beginning of true time. The intermediate period between the first creation and the flood is a kind of betwixt and between, an other time fitted to an other world inhabited by other creatures who are not altogether humans. The offspring of the Garden of Eden first parents and the offspring

---

[14] J. G. Frazer, *Folklore in the Old Testament: Studies in Comparative Religion, Legend, and Law* (3 vols.; London: Macmillan, 1918).

of the Flood Survivor first human ancestors are contrasted as abnormal versus normal, sinful versus legitimate.

In the case of Noah, the survivors are legitimately married husbands and wives, so their offspring are in no way contaminated by similarity to the strange creatures of Genesis 6 who were the product of sexual cohabitation between the sons of God and the daughters of humans. However, Frazer discusses flood stories and first creation stories in quite different chapters and fails to recognize that they are in any way connected. This comment could be applied to the whole of Frazer's immense exercise. Most of the biblical details he chooses to discuss seem trivial; yet if they were to be treated in a different anthropological style they could appear interesting.

Here is a case in point that is relevant to what I shall be saying later. Chapter 1 of Volume 3 is entitled "Keepers of the Threshold." It runs for eighteen pages. The biblical reference is minimal—although, such as it is, it is consistent with the proposition that an aura of sanctity of some special kind attached to the threshold of the Temple at Jerusalem. Frazer makes that point and then rambles around the world giving instances of ritual practices that suggest that thresholds are frequently sacred-tabooed localities. However, the best that he can manage by way of an explanation is to say that "all these various customs are intelligible if the threshold is believed to be haunted by spirits."[15] Perhaps so; but Frazer offers no suggestion of why thresholds should be haunted by spirits! Yet here again we are concerned with the ambiguities of betwixt and between.

Even before 1910[16] the associates of Emile Durkheim had already developed a sophisticated theory that explains in a very convincing way just why intermediate places and intermediate social conditions are likely to be treated as sacred and therefore subject to "taboo." Fined down to its essentials the argument runs something like this. Uncertainty generates anxiety, so we avoid it if we can. The categories of language cut up the world into unambiguous blocks. The individual is either a human or a beast; either a child or an adult; either married or unmarried; either alive or dead. In relation to any building I am either inside or outside. However, to move from one such clear-cut state to its opposite entails passing through an ambiguous "threshold," a state of uncertainty where roles are confused and even reversed. This marginal position is regularly hedged about by taboo. This finding clearly has an important bearing on my general topic of the relevance of anthropology to biblical studies. For, after all, mediation between opposites is precisely what religious thinking is all about.

[15] Ibid., 3. 18.

[16] I have in mind R. Hertz, "Contribution à une étude sur la représentation collective de la mort," Année Sociologique 10 (1907) 48–137; and A. Van Gennep, Les rites de passage (Paris, 1909) (English ed., The Rites of Passage [London: Routledge & Kegan Paul, 1960]). Hertz was Durkheim's pupil. Van Gennep was not actually a member of Durkheim's group, but his intellectual stance was very similar.

Thresholds, both physical and social, are a focus of taboo for the same reason that in the Bible inspired sacred persons, who converse face to face with God or who in themselves have attributes that are partly those of mortal humans and partly those of immortal God, almost always experience their inspiration in a "betwixt and between" locality, described as "in the wilderness," which is neither fully in this world nor in the other. Frazer understood none of this, but I have given it emphasis here because the sacredness that attaches to entities that are ambiguous or intermediate is a key theme that links together the otherwise disparate approaches to the interpretation of religious symbolism that are to be found in the work of such contemporary British social anthropologists as Mary Douglas, Victor Turner, D. F. Pocock, and myself.

After Frazer, the next initiative for an interaction between biblical scholarship and anthropology came from the side of biblical scholars. In 1933 there appeared two books with rather similar titles: E. O. James's *Christian Myth and Ritual*[17] and a collection of essays edited by S. H. Hooke, *Myth and Ritual: Essays on the Myth and Ritual of the Hebrews in Relation to the Culture Pattern of the Ancient East.*[18] Further exercises of the same sort appeared in later years, and the production as a whole came to be known as the work of "the Myth and Ritual School." James was Professor of Philosophy and History of Religions at Leeds; Hooke was Professor of Old Testament Studies in the University of London. Both had had some training in academic anthropology and were influenced not only by Frazer but also by an intellectually more distinguished contemporary, A. M. Hocart. Hocart rejected the item-by-item style of ethnographic comparison favored by Frazer and adopted a semi-functionalist form of argument which held that social institutions need to be considered as constituent wholes that correspond to a limited number of ideal types. Thus he maintained that the rituals surrounding kingship and the annual celebration of the New Year always have the same specifiable set of component parts.[19]

It was from Hocart rather than from Frazer that Hooke and his associates picked up the idea that ancient Babylonia, ancient Egypt, and the Kingdom States of the Old Testament all conformed to a single "culture pattern." Taking this notion as axiomatic, they then proceeded on the assumption that gaps in the sociological records of the Old Testament can be filled in by interpolating bits and pieces from the surviving documentary and archaeological records of other ancient Middle Eastern societies. The outcome of this exercise was conjectural history of a very farfetched sort.

---

[17] E. O. James, *Christian Myth and Ritual: A Historical Study* (London: John Murray, 1933).

[18] S. H. Hooke, ed., *Myth and Ritual: Essays on the Myth and Ritual of the Hebrews in Relation to the Culture Pattern of the Ancient East* (London: Oxford University, 1933).

[19] A. M. Hocart, *Kingship* (London: Oxford University, 1927); and *Kings and Councillors: An Essay in the Comparative Anatomy of Human Society* (Cairo: Paul Barbey, 1936), reprinted, ed. by R. Needham (Chicago: University of Chicago, 1970).

However, the theologians in Hooke's company had the further objective of showing that the Christianity of the first century C.E. represented an evolved and ethically sophisticated version of this same ancient (hypothetical) pattern.

In matters of biblical exegesis the recent work of Julian Pitt-Rivers to which I referred earlier has much in common with this latter aspect of the work of the Myth and Ritual School. My own very different position is that there was no such ancient common pattern. The imaginary historical past from which early Christian society is supposed to have evolved through the processes of history is, for the most part, simply the mythical projection of their own past which was believed by Jews and Christians alike in the era of Josephus. Oddly enough the relationship between biblical texts and nonbiblical materials that was assumed by the various Christian apologists of the Myth and Ritual School was often very similar to that which had been proposed by J. M. Robertson a generation earlier in his efforts to exhibit Christianity as a tissue of antique superstitions.

Despite Hocart's explicit repudiation of the Frazerian method of cultural comparison, the *content* of much of the argument presented by these various essayists was a fairly direct borrowing from what Frazer had written about divine kingship and dying gods in the pages of *The Golden Bough*. However, the *form* of the argument derived from an earlier generalization by Robertson Smith concerning the intimate interdependence of myth and ritual. Smith had maintained that the heart of religion is to be found in religious practice (ritual) rather than in the verbal formulas of belief (myth) that are supposed to be expressed through ritual. The ritual is fixed and obligatory; what is believed varies from one worshiper to another and is inaccessible to the outside observer except insofar as it is enshrined in a dogmatic creed. In Smith's words, "it may be affirmed with confidence that in almost every case the myth was derived from the ritual and not the ritual from the myth."[20] Years later a rather similar point was made by the anthropologist Malinowski who wrote of myth as a "charter for social action."[21] Broadly speaking it is a position with which I agree. Hooke and his colleagues seem likewise to have accepted this general proposition, but they then went on to make the entirely unwarrantable assumption that the interdependence of myth and ritual is so close that if you know the myth you can infer the ritual from which it was derived. Their claim to have demonstrated that throughout the ancient Middle Eastern world there had once been a unified system of ritual practice that was centrally concerned with divine kingship, sun worship, and the cycle of the agricultural calendar has a certain plausibility, but it is not based on any genuine evidence. Strictly speaking it rates no better than a guess.

[20] *Lectures*, 3d ed., 18.
[21] See n. 6 above.

A reassessment of the whole enterprise was published in 1958 in a further collection of essays entitled *Myth, Ritual, and Kingship*.[22] Hooke was again the editor, but this time round the remaining contributors were philologists and historians rather than anthropologists or theologians. The general view, which was much influenced by the arguments of Henri Frankfort,[23] was thoroughly skeptical. The ancient states of the Middle East had been nothing like so similar as Frazer and Hocart had suggested. Kingship is not a single unified institution. Hence we cannot infer anything about kingship in Israel and Judah from a consideration of kingship in Egypt or kingship in Babylonia, or wherever. And here again I agree. History cannot be reconstructed on the bases of homology. The only way we can learn anything about what happened in the past is by gaining access to contemporary evidence, either from documentary records written at the same time as the events they purport to record or from the evidence of archaeology. Legends and oral traditions of various kinds can be very interesting, but they are not history.

In the case of biblical materials few scholars would now want to maintain that any of the documents other than some of the letters of St. Paul are strictly contemporaneous with the events they purport to record. Anyone who asserts that, even so, these documents do represent an approximation of historical fact needs to demonstrate that they are in accord with what archaeology has to tell us. Yet in fact, despite a vast amount of research, archaeology tells us very little; furthermore, what little it does tell us is nearly always in radical disagreement with the biblical record. I should perhaps add that, on this side of the Atlantic, the E. O. James/S. H. Hooke technique for the blending of anthropology and the history of religions was given a new lease on life by the arrival of Mircea Eliade in Chicago in 1956. Eliade's best book, *The Myth of the Eternal Return*,[24] which dates from 1949, ranges far beyond the geographical limits of the ancient Middle East, but his assumptions about how cross-cultural comparison may be considered to throw light on biblical materials are markedly similar to those of the Myth and Ritual School. However, the Eliade manner in the field of comparative religion does not really fall within my brief. The *Festschrift*[25] in his honor, published in 1969, included articles by twenty-nine contributors, but none of them was an anthropologist and only two of them wrote on biblical themes.

[22] S. H. Hooke, ed., *Myth, Ritual and Kingship: Essays on the Theory and Practice of Kingship in the Ancient Near East and in Israel* (Oxford: Clarendon, 1958).

[23] H. Frankfort, *The Problem of Similarity in Ancient Near Eastern Religions* (Frazer Lecture for 1951; London: Williams and Norgate, 1951).

[24] M. Eliade, *The Myth of the Eternal Return* (London: Routledge & Kegan Paul, 1955); French original, 1949.

[25] J. M. Kitagawa and C. H. Long, eds., *Myths and Symbols: Studies in Honor of Mircea Eliade* (Chicago: University of Chicago, 1969).

So let me now turn to the work of some anthropologists whose style of argument is of a more modern sort. The first occasion on which a British social anthropologist applied his skills to an interpretation of a biblical text was in October 1954 when Isaac Schapera gave his Frazer Lecture, which was entitled "The Sin of Cain."[26] The focus of Schapera's attention was the detail of the Cain and Abel story by which, although Cain was driven out into the wilderness as a punishment for his act of fratricide, he was nevertheless thereafter marked by God as a protected person. The gist of Schapera's argument is that there are many biblical texts that support the view that homicide among the ancient Hebrews was considered to be a private delict; that is to say, responsibility for reprisal did not lie with the state but with the near kin of the deceased. Homicide created a situation of feud that was resolved on an "eye for an eye, a tooth for a tooth" basis.

Now there are many still existing societies in which the general custom of feud vengeance of this kind still prevails, but it is very common to find that the offenses of patricide and fratricide provide "exceptions to the rule." A blood feud calls for vengeance by the kin of the deceased against the kin of the assassin; but, if the deceased and the assassin are immediate kin, feud vengeance is impossible, and the destiny of the assassin, either for glory or oblivion, then becomes the direct responsibility of God. So, in Schapera's view, Cain was the beneficiary of divine protection because he was a fratricide as well as a murderer.

Schapera's essay deserves your attention, but I myself feel that he largely missed the point. Cain was not only a murderer and a protected wanderer; he was the creator of civilization, the founding ancestor who built the first city (Gen 4:17). In one sense the killing of his brother is a mythical prototype of "murder," but it is also the prototype of "sacrifice." By killing Abel, Cain replaces him, while at the same time he makes himself sacred. However, this is not an appropriate occasion for the elaboration of that theme. In any case, as I shall indicate presently, I do not myself believe that biblical texts can ever be illuminated by direct comparisons with modern ethnographic evidence.

Before I go further perhaps I should consider an issue of principle. What could anthropologists be expected to contribute to the study of the Bible? I am in difficulty here because the various fellow anthropologists whom I have mentioned as having certain points in common with myself would certainly not give the same sort of answer to that question that I might give myself. Yet if I indicate some of the areas where we are in disagreement, my own views will become apparent.

One widely held assumption is that anthropologists can illuminate biblical texts by drawing attention to ethnographic phenomena that are

[26] I. Schapera, "The Sin of Cain" (Frazer Lecture in Social Anthropology, 1954), *Journal of the Royal Anthropological Institute* 85 (1955) 33–43.

superficially similar to matters reported in the Bible. This was the basis of Frazer's approach and of works such as Morgenstern produced. Morgenstern in fact writes:

> The monuments of ancient Semitic cultures unearthed in excavations, the Bible and other ancient Semitic writings, and the records of classical and mediaeval authors, are supplemented by the varied and informative accounts of observant travelers and ethnologists of modern times. Hence, our knowledge from these varied sources is sufficient to permit far-reaching conclusions.[27]

My own view is that the observations of the "travelers and ethnologists of modern times" cannot help us at all. My fellow anthropologists do not share this negative attitude to cross-cultural comparison.

Pitt-Rivers has expert knowledge of the social values of the contemporary peoples of the Mediterranean area, and he believes that there has been a historical continuity between the cultural system recorded in the Bible and that with which he is himself familiar. This is perfectly possible, but there seems no good reason to believe it. Pitt-Rivers seems to be thinking of a time span covering about three thousand years. We know for certain that vast political upheavals have occurred during that period, but we cannot possibly know whether any features of general culture have persisted throughout. There can be no case for reading biblical texts as if they were a record of remote history which, by some happy accident, becomes more intelligible if referred to the present!

My complaint against Mary Douglas is similar. Her well-known discussion of the abominations in Leviticus 11,[28] in which she maintains that the prohibited animals are all in some way anomalous and that the system as a whole is designed to exhibit God's approval of order and completeness, was an adaptation of her theories concerning the classification of animals among the Lele, a Central African people whom she herself had studied.[29] Insofar as it concerns Leviticus Douglas's essay is of considerable interest, but whenever she tries to strengthen her argument by resort to ethnographic comparison she is led into writing nonsense. For example, it is quite clear that all the books of the Old Testament are addressed to a population of urbanized agriculturalists. Their imagined ancestors, the Israelites of the Pentateuch who wander in the never-never land of the sacred wilderness, are pastoralists only as ideal types. Moreover, not only were the Israelites of real history agriculturalists rather than pastoralists but also, as archaeology clearly demonstrates, they were at all times very much mixed up with their non-Israelite neighbors. So it is wholly inappropriate that Douglas should try to

---

[27] J. Morgenstern, *Rites of Birth, Marriage, Death and Kindred Occasions among the Semites* (Cincinnati: Hebrew Union College, 1966) 6.

[28] M. Douglas, *Purity and Danger: An Analysis of Concepts of Pollution and Taboo* (London: Routledge & Kegan Paul, 1966) chap. 3.

[29] M. Douglas, "Animals in Lele Religious Symbolism," *Africa* 24 (1957) 214–19.

support her Leviticus arguments by references to present-day practices among the Nuer, a pastoralist people of the Southern Sudan.[30] As for the following argument about the pig, it seems to me totally absurd:

> As the pig does not yield milk, hide nor wool, there is no other reason for keeping it except for its flesh. And if the Israelites did not keep pig they would not be familiar with its habits. I suggest that originally the sole reason for its being counted as unclean is its failure as a wild boar to get into the antelope class, and that it is on the same footing as the camel and the hyrax, exactly as stated in the book.[31]

If anthropologists are to be taken seriously by other kinds of biblical scholars, they have got to do better than that.[32]

So let me try to give you my own answer to the question: What might anthropology be expected to contribute to biblical studies? I hold that anthropologists first need to make a case for saying that no part of the Bible is a record of history as it actually happened. Then, on the positive side, they can show that the whole of the Bible has the characteristics of mytho-history of the sort that anthropologists regularly encounter when they engage in present-day field research. The similarity is a matter of structure not of content. Finally, they can show that if biblical texts are treated as mytho-history of this kind, then the techniques that modern anthropologists employ for the interpretation of myth can very properly be applied to biblical materials. If this is done, then some parts of the text will appear in a new light or at any rate in a light that has not been generally familiar to Bible readers during the past four centuries. This new-old way of looking at things is not necessarily better than currently more conventional ways of looking at things, but it deserves consideration.

These are large claims; I have time only to indicate how they might be substantiated. First of all I must emphasize that I completely reject Lévi-Strauss's view that a radical distinction can be drawn between what he calls "hot" and "cold" societies.[33] "Hot" societies are sophisticated social systems with a literary tradition whose members are fully aware that they are caught up in a historical process of change and development; "cold" societies

[30] *Purity*, 54.
[31] Ibid., 55.
[32] I have not considered in this paper the nature of my disagreement with D. E. Pocock, "North and South in the Book of Genesis," in J. H. M. Beattie and R. G. Lienhardt, eds., *Studies in Social Anthropology: Essays in Memory of E. E. Evans-Pritchard by his Former Oxford Colleagues* (Oxford: Clarendon, 1975) 273–84. I share Pocock's view that the geography of the Pentateuch has symbolic significance, but I do not agree with him that this can be consistently linked with the "real" cardinal directions of north, south, east, west. It would take up too much space if I were to comment on Pocock's argument in detail. Some of the issues will be independently considered in my Huxley Lecture for 1980, which will eventually be published through the Royal Anthropological Institute under the title "Why did Moses Have a Sister?"
[33] C. Lévi-Strauss, *Conversations with Claude Lévi-Strauss*, ed. G. Charbonnier (London: Cape, 1969).

are the primitive societies of anthropological literature in which there is no literary tradition and no sense of historical progression. In "cold" societies, so it is said, everyone behaves as if social life as it is now had been like that since the beginning of time and will continue like that forevermore. Lévi-Strauss considers that his own theories have only marginal application to the culture of "hot" societies. In particular, he holds that since the Bible is the product of a "hot" society, it is quite inappropriate to attempt to apply to the study of biblical materials any kind of modified version of his own procedures for the study of myth.

For many years I have adopted a precisely opposite stance. It is true that societies with a tradition of literacy differ in important ways from societies that lack such a tradition, but the differences are not, in my view, of the kind Lévi-Strauss suggests. All peoples everywhere imagine that they know quite a lot about their own history. That "history" may be stored in traditional sagas memorized by a few experts, or it may be recorded in books; but, in any social system, there is always someone around who is eager to tell the visiting stranger just how it all began and how things came to be as they are now.

Now "history" of this sort, which explains how things now are, may or may not be true as a record of *actual* history. But the general probability is that it is not true in any matter-of-fact sense. I can illustrate why this is so from my own experience. When I was engaged in anthropological fieldwork in North Burma in 1940 I was given, in great detail, three entirely different accounts of an inter-village war that was supposed to have taken place only forty years previously. I also, as it happened, had access to a contemporary account of the same matter written by the British colonial administrator who was in charge of the area at the time. This last version, dating from 1900, was quite incompatible with any of the three oral versions given to me in 1940. However, since the administrator in question clearly did not understand what was going on, his factual statement was no better as history than were the others. What was at issue was a matter of political rivalry and rights over land. I got three different versions because, in 1940, there were three different factions each with its own version of how things had come to be as they were. Even now I do not know what really went on around 1900, but in order to understand the rivalries of 1940 it was quite essential that I should take account of all the different versions of the "history" of the 1900 period.

I would claim that, in a backhand sort of way, this case history has relevance for our understanding of the Bible. For example, it is now fairly generally agreed that the earliest of our present Gospel texts could not have been put together before the destruction of Jerusalem by the Romans in 70 C.E. If so, then, at the very earliest, the Gospels were written forty years after the events they are supposed to record. Orthodox biblical scholars have usually overcome this difficulty by making two assumptions. First, they assume that forty years is not a very long time, so that an oral tradition could survive such a period without much distortion. Second, they assume that the discrepancies between the different Gospel stories are minor and are to be explained by the circumstances of this period of oral tradition. If we put the Gospel stories together we have, at the core, a record of events that really happened in a historical sense.

I do not know how many members of this distinguished audience still take that kind of view; my anthropological experience leads me to assert categorically that it is absolutely unjustified. Real history *may* be embedded in oral tradition, but where oral tradition is concerned it is impossible to distinguish the factually true from the factually false. Furthermore, if we cannot be sure that any particular part of the New Testament is true as history, how much less confident can we be about the Old! And yet most Old Testament scholars continue to write as if substantial parts of our modern text were a record of events that actually happened. They assume not only that the authors concerned had a serious interest in recording history in this factual, archival sense, but also that they had the technical resources to make such records.

However, in the second millennium B.C.E. the past was not viewed as a sequential chronology. The archival records of the ancient civilizations consist of lists of various kinds, including lists of the names of kings. But when we encounter narratives they are "mythical" sagas such as the Gilgamesh epic. The written versions of such narratives, which are all we now have, can only have been intended for the eyes of fellow scribes and schoolboys since no one else could read.[34] Not only that, but the Old Testament stories that scholars now rate as history—the saga of Saul and David, for example— are nearly all of the intimate but self-contradictory mytho-historical kind anthopologists encounter in their present-day fieldwork. The North Burma stories to which I referred just now are a case in point.[35]

If the Bible is not true as history, it still remains a sacred tale, and there remains the problem of interpretation. Here the crucial anthropological point is one that would presumably be accepted by all but the most fundamentalist theologians. There is a theological meaning (or perhaps several theological meanings) other than the manifest meaning of the narrative as such. The meaning of the narrative as such appears to be plain. How can we progress from this superficial sense to the other (postulated) subliminal sense? At the heart of the method I advocate, which is a direct borrowing from a principle that Lévi-Strauss has used in other contexts, is the insistence that the really significant elements in biblical narrative are the contradictions.

---

[34] J. Goody, *The Domestication of the Savage Mind* (Cambridge: Cambridge University, 1977), especially p. 152.

[35] E. R. Leach, *Political Systems of Highland Burma* (London: Bell, 1954) 89–100 [later editions Athlone Press].

Orthodox biblical scholarship of the nineteenth-century sort disposed of the inconsistencies in the text by a careful process of unscrambling the omelette. It was shown that the text, as we now have it, is an edited compendium of a variety of distinct "original" documents. However, the main purpose of this scholarly endeavor was directed toward the reconstruction of the original documents; relatively little attention was paid to the problem of why the final editorial compilers of the canon should have acted as they did, passing on to posterity composite texts full of palpable inconsistency and transformed repetitions. Why is the Adam of Genesis 1 given dominion over the whole earth, but the Adam of Genesis 3 is condemned to a life of permanent toil and sweat? Why is Moses the adopted son of Pharaoh's daughter at the beginning of Exodus 2, a prince among princes, but the son-in-law of a shepherd priest in the backside of the desert by the end of it? Why do we have four contradictory Gospels when one would have been so much less confusing? And so on.

The anthropologist Victor Turner has not, so far as I know, made any specific reference in his writings to such biblical contradictions, but what he has written about structure and anti-structure in his book *The Ritual Process*[36] provides the beginnings of an answer to my question. Turner's arguments, which derive fairly directly from what Van Gennep wrote about rites of passage at the beginning of the century, depend upon the view that what is valued in religious and para-religious experience is a sense of *communitas*, a feeling of intense social togetherness in which all the barriers of hierarchy that prevail in the rational secular affairs of everyday life are temporarily abandoned or even directly reversed. This sense of *communitas* is associated with a state of liminality, of being betwixt and between, neither in this world nor in any other. It is a mystical state to which the rules of strict logic do not apply.

Now in ritual performance the symbolization of such intermediate states is fairly straightforward; the actors do exactly the opposite of what they would do in normal secular life. Those who normally wear very grand clothing go around naked or in rags; those who normally wear common clothing dress up in splendor. Hierarchies are reversed; masters wait on their servants; children give orders to their elders. Taboos on food and sex are either enormously intensified or abandoned altogether; transvestite behavior is common. . . . Anthropologists can provide thousands of examples of this kind of symbolic coding. The life style of contemporary hippies, who whatever their limitations certainly put strong emphasis on the values of *communitas*, provides a good example of what I mean.

However, while confusion and inversion are readily employed in ritual action, they become self-defeating if they are employed in narrative. If

[36] V. W. Turner, *The Ritual Process: Structure and Anti-Structure* (London: Routledge & Kegan Paul, 1969).

narrative mytho-history is to serve as a charter for present-day religious and para-religious behavior, it cannot be gibberish. It must appear to make sense. Indeed, that is how mythologies are presented. They do not exist as single stories but as clusters of stories that are variations around a theme. Each individual story seems to make sense by itself. However, if we take all the stories together and assert, as a matter of dogma, that they are all "true" at the same time, then we arrive at a nonsense because, in detail, the collectivity of stories is self-contradictory. Yet according to the liminality, betwixt-and-between, *communitas* argument, it is precisely the self-contradictions that carry religious significance. The analyst therefore must find some way of discovering the sense behind the non-sense.

In a lecture such as this, which is designed as a large-scale survey, it is hardly possible to give a satisfactory illustration of what is involved because, as in all forms of structuralist analysis, demonstration calls for the close comparison of a number of different texts in considerable detail. However, I can perhaps show you the general idea by making brief reference to several well-known and seemingly unedifying Old Testament stories. Since Pitt-Rivers used two of these stories in his purported demonstration that my methodology is wholly misplaced, it may be appropriate if I now show that in fact they fit much better with my thesis than with his.

As I indicated much earlier on, the crux of the issue between us is that Pitt-Rivers holds that a clear-cut distinction can be drawn between the mythical supernatural style of narrative that characterizes the early chapters of Genesis, in which chronology does not really matter, and the historical realistic mode of later parts of the Bible, in which progression from earlier to later is an essential part of the message. I myself cannot discern any such distinction. God converses face to face with Samuel just as he does with Abraham and Moses. The Acts of the Apostles, despite a superficially realistic form, is almost as full of supernatural events as the book of Genesis. Angels come to the aid of Peter in prison (Acts 5:12) just as they come to the aid of Lot in Sodom (Gen 19:10–17). Moreover, the transformation of Lot in the Sodom story into the Levite in the Gibeah story (Judg 19:22–30), which Pitt-Rivers uses as the paradigm for his contrast between myth and realism, entirely fails to support his thesis. I will now try to demonstrate this.

As I have indicated, I hold that the whole of the Bible is mythical and that all the individual stories in the total corpus need to be read as if they were synchronous. So let us start at the end and work backwards. In the New Testament Bethlehem is the birthplace of Jesus Christ, the Messiah who is born to be king but who is also born to die as a sacrifice for the remission of sins. Bethlehem is given this distinction because of the prophecy in Micah 5:1 (Eng. 5:2): "But you, O Bethlehem Ephrathah, who are little to be among the clans of Judah, from you shall come forth for me one who is to be ruler in Israel." Micah's prophecy is also a retrospective observation concerning "history." The Ephrathites from Bethlehem included the lineage of Elimelech, the husband of Naomi and father-in-law of the Moabite Ruth from whom was descended David, son of Jesse. The Ruth reference, like the Micah reference, puts Bethlehem in Judah (Ruth 1:1–2; 4:18–22). However, the first reference to Bethlehem in the Old Testament is at Gen 35:16–20 where it is declared to be "but a little way" from the birthplace of Benjamin and the deathplace of Rachel, who died in childbirth. This is consistent with 1 Samuel 10, which declares that the tomb of Rachel is in the territory of Benjamin. The context of this latter statement is the summoning of Saul to the kingship. So Bethlehem-Ephrathah seems to be a betwixt-and-between sort of place, between death and birth, between lowliness and kingship, between Saul and David, a threshold to the new life. However, everything that happens there seems to be consistently associated with sinless virtue.

Just the opposite is the case with Gibeah, which is the locality where the horrid events of Judges 19 take place. Gibeah provides us with a paradigm of sin; the men of Gibeah behave like the men of Sodom. Its position is unambiguous. It is in Benjaminite territory and is the home of Saul (1 Sam 10:20–26; 11:4). Where Bethlehem stands for *communitas*, Gibeah stands for factional strife. It is thus appropriate that the Levite's concubine, who is destined to die on a threshold and to be sacrificially dismembered into separate pieces in Gibeah, should originally have come from Bethlehem, where the story starts (Judg 19:1–5). Also it is appropriate that her death, which is the direct consequence of the sin of the men of Gibeah, should be followed by a holocaust of dissension and civil war which is not finally worked out until the bones of Saul and his sons are returned to the land of their fathers at 2 Sam 21:14. Nevertheless, the sins of the men of Gibeah are eventually remitted. The sacrifice is not in vain.

However, there is much more to it than that, for the story of Gibeah, like the story of Sodom and the story of Noah, is a story about the survival of the virtuous few elected from among the sinful many. Although this is an audience of Bible readers, I had best remind you of the relevant details. In the first part of the Gibeah story a male traveler, the Levite, is offered hospitality by a local citizen, whose house is then surrounded by a mob. This croud demands that the guest be handed over to them for purposes of homosexual rape, whereupon the host offers instead the sexual services of his virgin daughter. All this is a direct copy of the story of Lot in Sodom (Genesis 19). The only difference is that in the latter there are two travelers, who turn out to be angels, and two virgin daughters. In the Sodom story the daughters are saved because the angels strike the mobsters with blindness; in the Gibeah story the daughter is saved because the traveler offers his concubine as a sacrificial substitute.

Yet that is not the end of the matter. Sodom is destroyed by God, and Lot and his daughters are the sole survivors. The problem of how the race shall be perpetuated is solved by having the daughters commit incest with their drunken father. From this intercourse are descended the Moabites and the Ammonites. Gibeah is likewise destroyed along with the whole tribe of Benjamin except for six hundred male survivors. The destruction in this case is by human agency. Nevertheless, there is again a problem of the survival of the race since their fellow Israelites have bound themselves by oath not to marry their daughters to any Benjaminite (Judg 21:1). What follows is highly complex. Incest is not involved, but the solution entails an irregular form of marriage and the introduction of a further collective mythological entity, "the people of Jabesh-Gilead," whose only function in the biblical texts is to play a punctuating role with respect to the career of Saul. The people of Jabesh-Gilead are first exterminated so that their surviving virgins shall provide spouses for the surviving Benjaminites (Judg 21:12–14). The descendants of this union are the elect of God who provide the first king, Saul (1 Sam 10:21). Immediately before Saul's final investiture the rehabilitated people of Jabesh-Gilead are besieged by the Ammonites. At the last minute they are rescued by Saul, who has mustered his troops by first cutting his plough oxen into pieces and distributing the portions in direct imitation of the Levite's treatment of his dead concubine (1 Sam 11:7–15).

Finally the men of Jabesh-Gilead recover the dead body of Saul from the Philistines, thereby earning David's commendation (1 Sam 31:11–13; 2 Sam 2:4–7). The bones remain in limbo in their charge until the lineage of Saul (with David's collaboration) has been exterminated by the Gideonites and the feud thus brought to an end (2 Sam 21:14). Overall, the men of Jabesh-Gilead play a complementary role to the Levite's concubine. The latter takes the story away from Bethlehem in a context of faction and fragmentation; the former brings it back again in a context of reunification. So it is structurally most significant that, whereas the story of David's relationship with Saul starts out with David, "the son of Jesse of Bethlehem" (1 Sam 17:58), killing the Philistine giant Goliath and then being prevented by Saul from returning to Bethlehem (1 Sam 18:1–2), the whole complex of stories should end by coming back to just the same point. No sooner have we been told of David's recovery of the bones of Saul and Jonathan from the men of Jabesh-Gilead than we get a listing of the heroic deeds of David and his men. This time it is Elhanan, "son of Jair of Bethlehem," who is credited with the death of Goliath, but it is the Bethlehem reference that is significant: *communitas* has been restored (2 Sam 21:14–22).

There are many other structuralist points that might be made about this group of stories, and I am well aware that I have left all sorts of loose ends hanging in the air. Yet to tie in all these bits and pieces we should need to consider many additional stories. Here is one example: The wives who are eventually found for the bereaved Benjaminites are proper members of the Israelite population, but the procedures by which the marriages take place fall outside the ordinary rules (Judges 21). However, in the counterpart story of Ruth, which immediately follows in the Alexandrian canon, Ruth's marriage to Boaz (which provides heirs to the lineage of Elimelech) exploits to the full the subtleties of the Israelite law of levirate marriage. Despite its abnormality it is a marriage that falls within the normal rules. Yet Ruth herself, being a Moabite, ought to be excluded from the congregation (Deut 23:3), and because she is a foreigner her marriage is against the rules anyway (Neh 13:25). However, it is David and Solomon, the descendants of Ruth, rather than Saul, the descendant of the bereaved Benjaminites, who ultimately serve as the paradigm of kingly virtue. Once again we have an association between sacredness and ambiguous marginality.

Please do not misunderstand me. I am not trying to teach the historians their proper business. I have no idea which incidents in the biblical narrative, if any, have some basis in history as it actually happened, and frankly I personally am not greatly interested in this issue. However, I insist very strongly that, if we are to get at the subliminal, religious meaning of biblical stories, then they all need to be considered at the same time without consideration of the order in which they appear. They are there in the Bible as we have it today because they were felt to make sense by editors who were sympathetic to Nehemiah's diatribe against the marriage of strange wives (Neh 13:23–31). Yet these same editors were also very sensitive to the close interrelationship between sin and salvation, purity and danger. The religious state of *communitas* lies right on the edge between the permissible and the impermissible. That is what these stories, taken collectively, are really all about.

It is not for me to preach to theologians on such matters, but I do seriously suggest that if you would all forget the purportedly historical frame in which the Bible stories are set you would find that much that is incomprehensible (the story of the massacre of the Benjaminites, for example) would begin to make religious sense. In the Middle Ages Christians took one story with another without worrying about chronology or about so-called realism. I believe we should do the same.

VI

IS HISTORICAL ANTHROPOLOGY POSSIBLE?

The Case of the Runaway Slave

Gillian Feeley-Harnik

If you have a servant, treat him as a brother,
for as your own soul you will need him.
If you ill-treat him, and he leaves and runs away,
which way will you go to seek him?

Sir 33:31

What Is the Question?[1]

I have been asked to speak to you on the topic, "Is Historical Anthropology Possible?" Let me start by admitting to a divided mind. As an anthropologist interested in the Bible and the work of biblical scholars, I am struck by the fact that we often ask very different questions. Actually this is the common experience of those who enter another field, whether in print or in the farthest recesses of another continent. As Wilson discovered, biblical scholars interested in ancient Israelite prophecy have concentrated on the issue of ecstasy, whereas anthropologists interested in divine-human intermediaries seldom use the word "ecstasy" in their work.[2] One of the problems in cross-disciplinary as in cross-cultural research has always been to establish common ground.

So it is with the issue of history. If I asked you, "Is *comparative* anthropology possible?", you would probably perceive it as a contradiction in terms. Anthropology *is* the comparative study of human behavior. That is how we anthropologists see it for all our differences. Most anthropologists

[1] A shorter version of this paper was delivered as a plenary address that formed part of a program on "Approaches to the Bible through Social Analysis" at the Centennial Meeting of the Society of Biblical Literature in Dallas, Texas, 5–9 November 1980. I am grateful to Professors T. O. Beidelman, Glenn Jacobson, and Norman R. Petersen for their very helpful discussions with me concerning the paper and to Professors W. Malcolm Clark, Leander E. Keck, David L. Petersen, and Robert R. Wilson for their critical comments as co-participants in an interdisciplinary panel on the topic "Is Historical Anthropology Possible?".

[2] R. R. Wilson, "Prophecy and Ecstasy: A Reexamination," *JBL* 98 (1979) 324; see also R. R. Wilson, *Prophecy and Society in Ancient Israel* (Philadelphia: Fortress, 1980) 21–32.

would see the historical question in the same way. Historical societies are simply among those included within the comparison. In fact, if they are historically earlier forms of societies also known ethnographically, they may provide the most closely controlled comparison.[3]

Nineteenth-century evolutionists, even if we now disagree with their methods, were simply taking the anthropological mission seriously: to study human behavior in all times and places in order to determine the limitations and potential of the species. If they were Americans, they included not only archaeology in this venture, that is the study of *pre*-historic communities, but also human and eventually primate evolution. Today most anthropologists would take as their domain not merely the world but a time span of some seventy million years.

Naturally there have been some controversies concerning the best way to handle this vast reservoir of human and near-human affairs. Social and cultural anthropologists in the 1930s, 1940s, and 1950s reacted against what they considered their predecessors' casual ways with the evidence. Impelled by philosophical and political ambitions of their own, they tended to put history aside on the grounds that there was little evidence for it under most field conditions, especially if anthropology aspired to be a science.

This trend was particularly marked among British social anthropologists working in little known areas of Africa.[4] It was more difficult to maintain in areas with indisputably ancient traditions of literacy, for example, India, Southeast Asia, China, and Madagascar. Yet even British Africanists were not united among themselves on the issue. E. E. Evans-Pritchard, best known for his work on the Azande and the Nuer of the Sudan, argued in 1950 that anthropology was closer to certain kinds of history than to the natural sciences, and it was in fact "a kind of historiography."[5] He developed this argument in a famous lecture delivered in 1961 entitled "Anthropology and History," in which he concluded by reversing Maitland's famous dictum that anthropology must choose between being history and being nothing. Evans-Pritchard would accept Maitland's statement only if its

[3] See E. E. Evans-Pritchard, *Social Anthropology and Other Essays* (New York: Free Press, 1962) 60; I. M. Lewis, "Introduction" in *History and Social Anthropology* (ed. I. M. Lewis; London: Tavistock, 1968) xix–xx. In this case, the ethnography itself constitutes a historical record (see M. G. Smith, "History and Social Anthropology," *Journal of the Royal Anthropological Institute* 92 [1962] 74).

[4] The anti-historicism of African ethnography during this period had less to do with Africa than with the attitude of scholars like A. R. Radcliffe-Brown, chief advocate of the structural-functional approach, toward the "conjectural history" of his predecessors and the attitudes of some British colonial administrators toward their subjects (see, for example, A. R. Radcliffe-Brown, "Introduction" in *Structure and Function in Primitive Society: Essays and Addresses* [New York: Free Press, 1952]; *Anthropology and the Colonial Encounter* [ed. T. Asad; New York: Humanities Press, 1973]).

[5] Evans-Pritchard, *Social Anthropology*, 152; see pp. 146–54.

opposite were also true: "history must choose between being social anthropology or being nothing."[6]

Anthropologists working in Africa and elsewhere began to return to the subject of history in the 1950s and 1960s. Furthermore, owing to their brush with eternity, if only in the present tense, they developed a sensitivity to questions concerning the relationships between oral tradition, genealogy, myth, history, and the influence of writing and other media on the transmission of these forms, which scholars in other fields have also found useful.[7] The 1970s have seen the publication of the kind of "how-to" books that commonly mark the establishment of a new orthodoxy.[8]

The question, then, is not whether anthropological methods and theories can be applied to historical societies for which we have no face-to-face

[6] Evans-Pritchard, *Social Anthropology*, 190. Lewis ("Introduction," xiii) argues that Evans-Pritchard wrote in 1950 and 1961 as if he were presenting a novel and controversial point of view, thus promoting the opinion, at least among outsiders, that British social anthropology had turned its back on history, whereas in fact most of the monographs in the structural-functional tradition included "some excursions into history however unsophisticated or unsystematic these may seem to the orthodox historian." He cites the work of I. Schapera ("Should Anthropologists be Historians?" *Journal of the Royal Anthropological Institute* 92 [1962] 143–56) and others to support his observation that the number of "essentially and explicitly" historical anthropological studies from this period is much larger than usually recognized and that historical research was "by no means a fringe activity but an integral part of the mainstream of British social anthropology" ("Introduction," xiv).

Nevertheless, Schapera himself notes that Evans-Pritchard's article of 1950 "aroused considerable interest and led to a lively controversy in the pages of *Man* [the major journal in British social anthropology] and elsewhere" (Schapera, "Should Anthropologists be Historians?" 143). His own essay and those of M. G. Smith ("History and Social Anthropology," *Journal of the Royal Anthropological Institute* 92 [1962] 73–85) and K. Thomas ("History and Anthropology," *Past and Present* 24 [1963] 3–24), a social historian, were written as responses to Evans-Pritchard's second essay of 1961. It seems clear that even if British social anthropologists had not totally ignored history, nevertheless the effect of Evans-Pritchard's articles, combined with the social and political-economic changes in Africa following the Second World War and culminating in independence movements, inspired them to examine the nature of their efforts more closely.

[7] See, for example, G. M. Berg, "The Myth of Racial Strife and Merina Kinglists: The Transformation of Texts," *History in Africa* 4 (1977) 1–30; L. Bohannan, "A Genealogical Charter," *Africa* 22 (1952) 301–15; G. Feeley-Harnik, "Divine Kingship and the Meaning of History Among the Sakalava of Madagascar," *Man* n.s. 13 (1978) 402–17; *Literacy in Traditional Societies* (ed. J. Goody; Cambridge: Cambridge University, 1968); J. Middleton, "Myth, History and Mourning Taboos in Lugbara," *Uganda Journal* 19 (1955) 194–203; E. Peters, "The Proliferation of Segments in the Lineage of the Bedouin of Cyrenaica," *Journal of the Royal Anthropological Institute* 90 (1960) 29–53; M. Southwold, "The History of a History: Royal Succession in Buganda," in *History and Social Anthropology* (ed. I. M. Lewis; London: Tavistock, 1968) 127–51; J. Vansina, *Oral Tradition: A Study in Historical Methodology* (London: Routledge & Kegan Paul, 1965); R. R. Wilson, *Genealogy and History in the Biblical World* (New Haven: Yale University, 1977).

[8] A. Macfarlane in collaboration with S. Harrison and C. Jardine, *Reconstructing Historical Communities* (Cambridge: Cambridge University, 1977); D. C. Pitt, *Using Historical Sources in Anthropology and Sociology* (New York: Holt, Rinehart & Winston, 1972).

evidence. Obviously they can, within the constraints of the comparative method, in virtually any context. It would be a positivistic conceit to assert otherwise. Historical data may be limited, but contemporary data are not substantially different. As Marc Bloch once said, "A document is a witness; and like most witnesses, it does not say much except under cross-examination. The real difficulty lies in putting the right questions."[9] Precisely the same is true of ethnographic research, where the laconic reply is usually, "It's custom." Ethnography may be biased and selective often in ways we do not completely understand precisely because of our lack of historical perspective on the questioner. We construct hypotheses concerning "structure" on the basis of limited evidence in either case.

A more useful question, at the moment anyway, is whether anthropological methods and theories can contribute to our understanding of historical development and change. The structure is only half the answer. We have to know how it was used, manipulated, interpreted, and reinterpreted, not only by different persons or groups in relation to one another but also by the same persons or groups in different times and places. Indeed, we are compelled to recognize that there is no one structure to the social life of any people but rather as many structures as there are groups and individuals to construct them, differing according to their changing perspectives in patterned, planned, unexpected, and frequently contradictory ways.

The appropriate unit of study according to this approach is not a "society" in the ethnographic present but rather a "social field" over time, the limits of which are determined according to the problem. The fundamental assumption is that culture is not simply a product of social organization or vice versa. Each may influence the other, but both are also subject to the effects of ecology, human physiology, demography, and other factors that constantly alter them, not always congruently. To use words that seem current among biblical scholars, map is not territory, territory is not map. One cannot be deduced from the other, as Morgan derived primitive promiscuity from Hawaiian kinship terminology. Rather we labor daily to achieve a livable congruence between them, or as Lévi-Strauss once put it, "Every day is a pretext for negotiation with the universe."

The problem then is not to understand how a system works but rather how it is worked by the individuals and groups involved in such a way as to achieve their goals, which may or may not be in harmony with the goals of those around them.[10] This is the crux of the matter for biblical scholars concerned with developing a truly substantive understanding of the *Sitz im Leben* of religious belief.[11] There simply is not the evidence to achieve that

---

[9] M. Bloch, *Land and Work in Medieval Europe* (Berkeley: University of California, 1967) 48.

[10] See Lewis, "Introduction," xxii.

[11] J. Z. Smith, "The Social Description of Early Christianity," *RelSRev* 1 (1975) 19.

kind of detailed picture of historical times. Thus, Smith criticizes Gager's recent effort at reconstructing the social world of early Christianity[12] by saying:

> Gager exhibits in a more elegant form the sort of difficulties that have plagued New Testament and early Christian historians as they have attempted to take seriously anthropological and sociological perspectives on their subject matters . . . a refusal to accept the consequences of concreteness; that is, at the present stage of research we cannot conduct the enterprise on the New Testament.[13]

My response to this objection is twofold. First of all, the presence of the living flesh no more guarantees an appreciation of the subtlety and variability of human life in the ethnographer than it guarantees loquaciousness in his subject. It is perfectly possible to write an ethnography that reads like a law code. Indeed, it is not only possible but positively encouraged by the conditions under which anthropologists normally do field work.[14] The second point is that there is never enough evidence, precisely because the questions change, provoking the search for more.[15] As Lewis puts it, historians appear to have the advantage of hindsight.[16] Knowing how events ended, they are in a better position to interpret how they began and developed. But of course they recognize that events never end in the sense that subsequent developments must always suggest new interpretations of the past. This is the basis of E. H. Carr's contention that it is only through the ever-widening horizons of the future that we may approach "ultimate objectivity" in historical studies.[17]

Anthropology might serve to widen horizons for biblical scholars provided they are willing to admit ethnography into their domain, that is, to become students of comparative religion with a focus on the Bible and related material, as opposed simply to raiding the anthropological camp for models while leaving the "savages" safely behind. The purpose of cross-cultural comparison—by which anthropologists, like biblical scholars,[18]

---

[12] J. G. Gager, *Kingdom and Community: The Social World of Early Christianity* (Englewood Cliffs, NJ: Prentice-Hall, 1975).

[13] J. Z. Smith, "Too Much Kingdom, Too Little Community," *Zygon* 13 (1978) 129; see W. A. Meeks, "The Image of the Androgyne: Some Uses of a Symbol in Earliest Christianity," *HR* 13 (1974) 179–80.

[14] T. O. Beidelman, "Some Sociological Implications of Culture," in *Theoretical Sociology* (ed. J. McKinney and E. A. Tiryakian; New York: Appleton-Century-Crofts, 1968) 500–27.

[15] This is clearly illustrated in the recent foundation of the working group of the American Academy of Religion and the Society of Biblical Literature, chaired by Leander E. Keck and Wayne A. Meeks, to explore "the social world of Christianity," focusing initially on Syrian Antioch (W. A. Meeks, "The Social World of Early Christianity," *BCSR* 6 [1975] 1, 4–5).

[16] Lewis, "Introduction," x.

[17] E. H. Carr, *What Is History?* (Harmondsworth: Penguin, 1964) 123.

[18] E.g., J. Neusner, "Map Without Territory: Mishnah's System of Sacrifice and Sanctuary," *HR* 19 (1979) 103; J. Z. Smith, *Map is Not Territory: Studies in the History of Religions* (Leiden: Brill, 1978) ix.

legal metaphors of the redemption in legal terms have been very few."[27] D. Daube is one exception, yet even he attributes the primacy of salvation/redemption ideology in the Passover to the fact that God redeemed Israel out of Egypt.[28] Bartchy's discussion of slavery in 1 Cor 7:21 is another outstanding exception.[29] Unfortunately (from my perspective), he treats the passage as if Paul's advice were primarily a response to a largely Greco-Roman audience having no deep roots in his own Jewish heritage.

Daube includes slavery together with monarchy, polygamy, and sale of the paternal estate as an example of the way in which Israelite jurists consciously built into the law principles and institutions that were in conflict with the "ideal order." He notes that the concept in Jewish law of an institution "fully valid yet wrong" is extremely ancient, reaching "far back into Old Testament times."[30] Much the same disjunction between theology and social organization seems to be involved in slavery in the Christian context. Early Christianity appears to have been a religion calling for equal rights for all persons, at least in the eyes of God. Yet it remains agonizingly unclear, even to this day, whether Paul or any other early Christian actually called for the abolition of slavery—or perhaps I should say, agonizingly clear that they did not. They seem able to have developed a theology or theologies that emphasized equality, while being perfectly content to retain what was considered an injustice not only from our own perspective but also, the evidence suggests, from their own (e.g., 1 Tim 1:9-10; Rev 18:13; see also *Jub.* 11:2 and Philo's remarks on the Essenes in *Every Good Man is Free* xii, 79, and on the Therapeutae in *On the Contemplative Life*, ix, 70).

This is essentially the question from both a substantive and a theoretical point of view. Slavery in Palestine presents us with a situation, paralleled elsewhere, in which ambiguity and contradiction were not isolated by ritual

---

Historical and Critical Study (2d ed.; London: Oxford, 1963); J. B. Segal, *The Hebrew Passover from the Earliest Times to A.D. 70* (London Oriental Series, 12; London: Oxford, 1963); W. Zimmerli and J. Jeremias, *The Servant of God* (SBT 20; London: SCM, 1957).

[27] "The Trial of Jesus and the Doctrine of the Redemption," in *Law in the New Testament* (London: Darton, Longman and Todd, 1970) 401-2.

[28] D. Daube, "Law in the Narratives," *Studies in Biblical Law* (Cambridge: Cambridge University, 1947) 1-73.

[29] Bartchy, ΜΑΛΛΟΝ ΧΡΗΣΑΙ.

[30] D. Daube, "Concessions to Sinfulness in Jewish Law," *JJS* 10 (1959) 1-13. He compares Jewish slave legislation with Roman law, in which a slave was defined as someone subject to the *dominium* of another *contra naturem*. According to M. I. Finley ("A Peculiar Institution?" *Times Literary Supplement* 3877 [1976] 820), this is the only instance in all of Roman law in which jurists acknowledged that their law violated the law of nature. Yet they drew from it no practical or moral conclusions whatsoever. He interprets the Roman definition as putting "the seal of finality" on the failure of Greeks and Romans to resolve the ambiguity in slavery as they practiced it and comments on "the fallacy . . . that a society cannot long survive if it contains contradictions and ambiguities in fundamental institutions." Slavery appears to have been a "peculiar institution" virtually everywhere it has been found (Finley, "A Peculiar Institution?" 821).

or otherwise shoved to the margins of life but were central, even fundamental, to the way it operated. How did it work, or rather how was it
worked, and what implications does this case have for our understanding of
the structure of belief and the nature of social change?

Slavery in the Judaic Tradition

A great deal has been written on the subject of slavery in Palestine and
neighboring countries. I have depended primarily on Mendelsohn, Urbach,
and Zeitlin in interpreting the biblical slave legislation recorded in Exodus
20, Leviticus 25, Deuteronomy 15, and in the Aramaic Papyri, the Mishnah,
and the Talmud, and on Finley and Bartchy for the Greco-Roman law and
custom that may relate to early Christian texts.[31]

The Hebrew term for "slave" ('ebed) derives from the verb "to work"
('bd).[32] Mendelsohn argues that Hebrews acquired their slaves in the same
way as surrounding groups, that is, primarily as prisoners of war (Num
31:26–27, Deut 20:10–11), although trade, for which there is less evidence
(Lev 25:44–45), was probably also involved, the slave trade being fundamental to commercial life in the ancient Near East.[33] Mendelsohn is relatively unhistorical in his account, arguing that the similarities in neighboring
groups derive from the fact that "slavery was part of an economic pattern
which remained constant through the ages."[34] Urbach, concerned to explain
the existence of Hebrew slaves following the restoration, is more historically
minded. He distinguishes three different periods: (1) the pre-Maccabean
period, in which Judea was politically too weak and economically too poor
to acquire foreign slaves in sufficient numbers to restrict internal slavery,
primarily of fellow Jews; (2) the Maccabean period, in which Gentile slaves
predominated owing to the wars of the Maccabees and the economic and
political strength of the Hasmonean dynasty; (3) the period following the
destruction of the Temple in 70 C.E. to the fourth century, in which the
enslavement of Jews increased again, owing to the weakness of their position
and their suspicion of outsiders.[35]

Slavery in Palestine took very different forms at different periods. The
feature common to all of them is the intimate connection between slavery as

---

[31] Mendelsohn, *Slavery in the Ancient Near East*; Mendelsohn, "Slavery in the Old Testa-
ment"; Urbach, "Laws Regarding Slavery"; Zeitlin, "Slavery During the Second Common-
wealth"; M. I. Finley, "Between Slavery and Freedom," *Comparative Studies in Society and
History* 6 (1964) 233–49; Finley, "Masters and Slaves," in *The Ancient Economy* (Berkeley:
University of California, 1973) 62–94; Finley, "A Peculiar Institution?"; Bartchy, ΜΑΛΛΟΝ
ΧΡΗΣΑΙ.

[32] *EncJud* 14. 1655.

[33] Mendelsohn, "Slavery in the Old Testament," 384, 389, 390.

[34] Mendelsohn, *Slavery in the Ancient Near East*, 121.

[35] Urbach, "Laws Regarding Slavery," 3–93.

an institution and reigning social and political conditions.[36] In other words, slavery within Palestine has to be understood in a regional context.

Hebrew Slaves

Slaves were ideally aliens, which fits in well with comparative anthropological and historical evidence suggesting that "outsiderness" is one of the chief qualities distinguishing slaves from other kinds of dependent laborers.[37] Yet in Palestine as elsewhere,[38] modes of enslavement ranged from the compulsory to the voluntary and affected those within the group as well as those outside it, although the biblical legislation appears to have been unique in the ancient Near East in mentioning the case of self-sale or voluntary slavery.[39]

Major causes of self-enslavement included poverty and debt. The impoverished or the debtor unable to pay his debts would sell himself or minor members of his family into slavery (Exod 21:5–6; Lev 25:39–55; Deut 15:16–17; Prov 22:7; 2 Kgs 4:1; Isa 50:1; Amos 2:6; 8:6).[40] The sale of daughters was especially frequent (Exod 21:7–11).[41] Members of families were dedicated to temples, forming hereditary castes.[42] Defaulting debtors also were enslaved by the court, not as punishment but by way of compensation (Exod 22:2).[43] On the other hand, anyone caught "stealing" a fellow Israelite for the purpose of enslaving or selling him was subject to the death penalty (Deut 24:7; see Exod 21:16). Self-enslavement and debt bondage were not meant to be equivalent to the enslavement of aliens. The legislation in Lev 25:44–46 is particularly clear on that point:

> *As for your male and female slaves whom you may have: you may buy male and female slaves from among the nations that are round about you. You may also buy from among the strangers who sojourn with you and their families that are with you, who have been born in your land; and they may be your property. You may bequeath them to your sons after you, to inherit as a possession for ever; you may make slaves of them, but over your brethren the people of Israel you shall not rule, over one another, with harshness.

Hebrew slaves might be acquired with their families, for whose maintenance their masters were then responsible (Lev 25:41). They were not supposed to be worked too hard or at servile tasks (Lev 25:39–40, 43, 46, 53;

---

[36] Urbach, "Laws Regarding Slavery," 93.

[37] P. Bohannan, *Social Anthropology* (New York: Holt, Rinehart & Winston, 1963); Finley, "A Peculiar Institution?"; Kopytoff and Miers, "African 'slavery'"; Watson, "Slavery as an Institution."

[38] See Kopytoff and Miers, "African 'slavery,'" 12–14.

[39] Mendelsohn, "Slavery in the Old Testament," 384.

[40] Mendelsohn, "Slavery in the Old Testament," 385; Urbach, "Laws Regarding Slavery," 18.

[41] Urbach, "Laws Regarding Slavery," 16.

[42] Mendelsohn, *Slavery in the Ancient Near East*, 105.

[43] Urbach, "Laws Regarding Slavery," 18, 21.

Deut 23:17).[44] The daughter sold into slavery on condition that she be married on coming of age had to be manumitted if she were not (Exod 21:7–11).[45]

In contrast to aliens, no Jew could be enslaved permanently.[46] He had to be released if not after six years of servitude (Exod 21:2–4; Deut 15:12–17) then in the jubilee year (Lev 25:39–55), according to laws that Mendelsohn describes as unparalleled in the slave legislation of the ancient Near East and Greece.[47] Furthermore Hebrew slaves were supposed to be released with some kind of compensation, as opposed to the alien, who got nothing when manumitted. Yet scholars uniformly question whether either the six-year law or the jubilee law was ever observed.[48] Indeed, there are strong passages in Jeremiah (34:8–22) and Nehemiah (5:1–13) that suggest that they were not. On the other hand, the Hebrew slave might refuse manumission, in which case his master should pierce his ear with an awl against the door post of the house, making him a slave for life (Exod 21:5–6; Deut 15:15–17). Yet in so doing, both of them violated the sacred bond uniting the Israelites with their God, who had redeemed them from Egypt in order to make them his slaves. The passage in Deuteronomy makes this clear. The rabbis confirmed it, prompting Daube to comment on the "astonishing" extent to which ancient Israelite attitudes toward slavery survived in rabbinism.[49] Paul echoes the same sentiments (1 Cor 7:22–23): "For he who was called in the Lord as a slave is a freedman of the Lord. Likewise he who was free when called is a slave of Christ. You were bought with a price; do not become slaves of men."

The practice of self-enslavement, including debt bondage, resulted in a category of persons distinguished as "Hebrew slaves," a distinction unique in the ancient world despite the fact that the practice of debt bondage was ubiquitous.[50] Urbach argues that the existence of this category, which Jews regarded with ambivalence then as now, was motivated partly by the religious obligation and desire to maintain separation between Jews and Gentiles by preventing the sale of Jews across national and ethnic boundaries.[51] In other words, it was preferable to have Hebrews enslaved to others within

---

[44] Mendelsohn, *Slavery in the Ancient Near East*, 49–50, 85; Urbach, "Laws Regarding Slavery," 25–26.

[45] Mendelsohn, "Slavery in the Old Testament," 385; Urbach, "Laws Regarding Slavery," 16–17.

[46] Finley ("A Peculiar Institution?" 819) argues that the permanence of the condition of slavery is another feature that distinguishes it from other forms of dependent labor.

[47] Mendelsohn, "Slavery in the Old Testament," 388.

[48] Mendelsohn, *Slavery in the Ancient Near East*, 88–91; "Slavery in the Old Testament," 385; Urbach, "Laws Regarding Slavery," 29; *EncJud* 14. 1657.

[49] Daube, "Concessions to Sinfulness in Jewish Law," 4.

[50] Mendelsohn, "Slavery in the Old Testament," 383–84.

[51] Urbach, "Laws Regarding Slavery," 15.

the group than to have them enslaved to outsiders.[52] Yet there seem to have been many inconsistencies in the way the law was practiced. Hebrew slaves did not invariably enjoy the rights to which they were entitled. Although Jews, they could be treated as aliens. The ambiguities in their status were more than matched by the ambiguities in the status of Gentile slaves, outsiders treated as insiders.

Mosaic law required that the Gentile slave participate in the religious observances of his master, including circumcision (Gen 17:12–13, 17), the sabbath (Exod 20:10; 23:12; Deut 5:14–15), Passover (Exod 12:44), and other ceremonies (Deut 12:12, 18; 16:11–14). These rules were apparently motivated by the need to avoid defilement, but they brought the enslavement of aliens curiously close to the process of proselytization in the view of both insiders and outsiders alike: "The very fact that a slave entered a Jewish household in a servile position implied something of the process by which proselytes were accepted, since circumcision and ritual immersion were involved."[53] From then on, according to Talmudic law, the slave became subject to the "yoke of the Commandments" and was therefore reckoned as his master's "brother in the Commandments," liable to all the penalties prescribed in the biblical law. In fact, he seems to have been subject to all the penalties but only those positive commandments that women were allowed to observe.[54] Furthermore, they did not bring him close enough to full Jewish status to be manumitted. Converted slaves could not be sold, but they were not freed either. On the contrary, they were inherited. In other words, the Gentile slave was converted sufficiently to make his presence unpolluting, and probably in order to control him better, but not enough to make him a full-fledged member of the Jewish community. Like the Hebrew slave, he was maintained in an ambiguous status, neither fish nor fowl. As J. Jeremias explains it:

> The equivocal position of the Gentile slave is explained by the fact that though circumcised he was still in slavery. By circumcision he had become "a son of the covenant" (Mek. Ex. 20.10, 26b.51 L II,255), but at the same time, since he was not a freedman he could not belong to the community of Israel (b.B.K.88a). He had "lost the status of a heathen, but . . . not yet attained that of a Jew" (b. Sanh. 58b). This equivocal position determined both his religious duties and his rights, and both were limited by consideration of the rights of his owner.[55]

Slaves could accumulate property with which they could redeem themselves (2 Sam 9:10; 16:4; 19:18, 30; Lev 25:29). Urbach argues that freed

---

[52] Urbach, "Laws Regarding Slavery," 49. He does not neglect economic factors. Compare also his reasons for why the enslavement of compatriots was never officially prohibited as it was ultimately in Greece and Rome (p. 49).

[53] Urbach, "Laws Regarding Slavery," 40–41, 42.

[54] Urbach, "Laws Regarding Slavery," 42, 43.

[55] J. Jeremias, *Jerusalem in the Time of Jesus: An Investigation into Economic and Social Conditions During the New Testament Period* (Philadelphia: Fortress, 1969) 349.

slaves were easily assimilated into Jewish society because they were already familiar with Jewish customs and were used to fulfilling the command-ments.[56] But according to Jeremias, they were treated with disdain: "it showed a very deep popular contempt that the members of the Herodian royal family were reckoned among them."[57] He is confirmed by the rabbis, who argued that despite having grown up in a Jewish environment ex-slaves would always rank lower than proselytes because they had fallen into the category of the cursed (Gen 9:25) and, in the case of females, into the cate-gory of the promiscuous as well, whence their inferior value on the marriage market (*t. Hor.* 2.10).[58]

These conflicting ideas and practices raise many questions concerning the identity of the slave. Is the slave a Jew or a Gentile? If he is a Gentile and has been circumcised and trained to the commandments, is he now a Jew? If he is a Jew and has been enslaved by another Jew, has he not been transformed into something other than a Jew?

Some anthropologists working in Africa would argue that these kinds of questions are answered in the course of time.[59] Slavery—at least in Africa—must be seen as a historical process by which outsiders are gradually trans-formed into insiders like everyone else, the more or less forceful absorption of strangers being a way of acquiring members for one's group that may be as important as marriage or childbirth. Other Africanists, primarily French ethnologists writing from a Marxist perspective, emphasize the ways in which slaves are prevented from becoming incorporated into the social sys-tem, even after manumission.[60] Still others, anthropologists and historians expanding the range of comparison to include Asia and Southeast Asia, argue that it depends on the kinship system.[61] In societies with "open" kin-ship systems that display a wide variety of ways of incorporating strangers, probably because labor is more valuable than land, slaves are more likely to be incorporated, too. In societies with "closed" kinship systems in which the ways of incorporating strangers are extremely limited, probably because land rather than labor is the scarce resource, slaves are more likely to be shut out altogether, remaining in their servile condition for generations.

The Palestinian situation in OT and intertestamental times does not seem to match any of these hypotheses, although I am not well enough acquainted with land tenure and related issues to be sure. I would agree that slavery must be seen in historical perspective in terms of changing or unchanging statuses over time, but I would also argue that, despite the movement of some persons absolutely into or out of the system, in this case

---

[56] Urbach, "Laws Regarding Slavery," 48.
[57] Jeremias, *Jerusalem in the Time of Jesus*, 337; see p. 331, n. 76.
[58] Cited by Urbach, "Laws Regarding Slavery," 48–49.
[59] S. Miers and I. Kopytoff, eds., *Slavery in Africa*.
[60] *L'esclavage en afrique précoloniale*, ed. C. Meillassoux.
[61] *Asian and African Systems of Slavery*, ed. J. L. Watson.

the category remained essentially a category of persons who were both and neither insiders and outsiders, familiar yet alien, perpetual transgressors of national, religious, and familial boundaries. The essence of the category seems to be the questions it poses concerning identity, allegiance, and authority.[62] Let me explain by going further into the evidence.

Kinship

The essentially ambiguous character of Palestinian slavery is seen particularly clearly in the case of kinship, the primary means of incorporating strangers and the primary area in which they worked. Mendelsohn emphasizes that slavery had relatively little significance in agriculture, trades, or industry. The number of slaves owned by private families ranged from one to four.[63] The slave was treated as a member, "albeit inferior," of a large household.[64]

What did this mean exactly? On the one hand, slavery was the antithesis of kinship. A slave was an outsider who had no kin, totally without the social ties to family, community, and nation that normally served to identify a person in Palestinian society. Or he was a Hebrew who had been sold by his kin or who had enslaved himself as a result of poverty or debt, a process that usually involved the destruction of kinship bonds, as the prophets especially make clear (Neh 5:5; Isa 50:1; Amos 2:6; 8:6). Although "Hebrew slaves" were meant to be freed in six years, aliens could be inherited indefinitely like other property (Lev 25:46).[65] Even the children of a Hebrew slave, if they were born of a wife given him by his master, belonged to the master

[62] This is essentially what Kopytoff and Miers ("African 'slavery'") mean by "the institutionalization of marginality." It seems to me that they move more quickly from the institutionalization of marginality (which involves "rehumanization," as they rightly point out, but not necessarily in a way that contributes to being a full or proper human being as indigenously defined) to the incorporation of aliens than either their own arguments or their data warrant. In many of the cases described in their volume (as in Meillassoux ["Introduction"], in which the "humanization" of the slave tends to be underemphasized), slaves seem to constitute a useful pool of persons in perpetual limbo that can be drawn out or pushed back in as politicaleconomic considerations warrant, much in the same way as F. F. Piven and R. A. Cloward (*Regulating the Poor: The Functions of Public Welfare* [New York: Vintage Books, 1971]) have argued concerning the welfare system in the United States. Those cases of incorporation that they discuss seem best explained in terms of the politics of slavery within and between lineages in which some persons may see an advantage in absorbing a particular stranger while others will not, and their disagreements are not forgotten but are perpetuated over generations in accusations and counter-accusations when the need arises.

[63] Mendelsohn, *Slavery in the Ancient Near East*, 92–120, 121; see Urbach, "Laws Regarding Slavery," 31–32.

[64] Mendelsohn, "Slavery in the Old Testament," 387.

[65] Unfortunately there is no evidence concerning the legal and social status of slaves of the second and subsequent generations, except the existence of the Hebrew terms "houseborn slave," "those born in the house," or "a son of the house" versus "those bought with money from a foreigner" (e.g., Gen 18:27). See Mendelsohn, *Slavery in the Ancient Near East*, 58; *EncJud* 14. 1656.

together with their mother (Exod 21:4). On the other hand, slaves were more than kin, precisely because of the fact that they were slaves, by definition bereft of conflicting social ties. A good example is Abraham's nameless slave, who was nevertheless "the oldest of his house, who had charge of all that he had . . ." (Gen 24:2), whom Abraham charged with the exceedingly delicate task of finding a wife for Isaac, progenitor of the people of Israel.

Slaves could be incorporated into the kinship structure. Fathers sold their daughters on condition that they be married to their masters or masters' sons once they came of age or be otherwise manumitted. Slave owners might cohabit with alien female slaves in order to produce a needed heir. Cohabitation did not necessarily lead to freedom for the mother (Genesis 16, 21, 29, 30), although marriage did or should (Deut 21:10–14).[66] The owner could adopt an alien slave as his heir directly. According to Prov 17:2, "A slave who deals wisely will rule over a son who acts shamefully, and will share the inheritance as one of the brothers."[67] He could also marry one of his daughters to an alien slave, taking the children as his own. There is only one biblical example of a male slave married to a freeborn woman, a practice that was common elsewhere.[68] Sheshan, "who had no sons, only daughters," married Jarha, his Egyptian slave, to one of his daughters who bore the son needed to carry on his line (1 Chr 2:34–41). Comparative evidence from Babylonia and Sumeria suggests that Jarha was almost certainly manumitted and adopted before the marriage was consummated.[69]

Nevertheless, choices like these seem to have been made reluctantly and only when some pressing need arose relating to production or reproduction. Abraham was reluctant at the prospect of adopting even his trusted Eliezar (Gen 15:2–4). The whole story of Abraham and Sarah, Hagar, Ishmael, and Isaac reinforces the sense of ambiguity surrounding the issue, especially as it related to the issues of election and inheritance. Philo asks the obvious question: "Who *is* the heir of divine things?" He finds a solution in the "division of equals and opposites" on the basis of his faith. But the substance of the story is doubt, the gnawing doubt that prompted his own musings even centuries later.

Production

These same conflicts and ambiguities are reflected in slave labor in other contexts. As Finley points out, the most striking feature of slavery in classical antiquity is the variety of kinds of work involved, so many that it is

[66] The story of Abraham, Sarah, and Hagar also indicates, as Mendelsohn notes, that slaves could have different, even conflicting, statuses in relation to different members of the same family.

[67] The letter to the Galatians depicts Christians as former slaves whom Christ redeemed in order to adopt them as sons and heirs (Gal 4:1–7).

[68] Mendelsohn, *Slavery in the Ancient Near East*, 55.

[69] Mendelsohn, "Slavery in the Old Testament," 386.

sometimes very difficult to distinguish slavery from other kinds of dependent labor:

> The word *latris* (hired man, servant, slave) upsets modern lexicographers and legal
> historians, but the historical situation behind the lexical "confusion" is surely that in
> earlier Greece, as in other societies, "service" and "servitude" did in fact merge into
> each other.[70]

The same is true in the biblical case. In theory, slaves were confined to the lowest kinds of work. They were not merely agents of production; they were kinds of tools or instruments and should be handled accordingly (Exod 21:21; Sir 33:24–29). Mendelsohn is unequivocal on this point:

> Legally the slave was a chattel. He was a commodity that could be sold, bought,
> leased, exchanged, or inherited. In sharp contrast to the free man, his father's name
> was never mentioned; he had no genealogy, being a man without a name. As a piece
> of property the slave was usually, though not universally, marked with a visible sign,
> just as an animal was by a tag or a brand.[71]

During the period of the monarchy, slaves were used in corvée labor and in the mines of Elat. They were also employed in the Temple and in some industries.[72]

At the same time, Mosaic law recognized that the slave was also a person. Mendelsohn continues: "Although theoretically the slave was considered a mere chattel and classed with moveable property, both law and society could not disregard the fact that he was human."[73] He could and did occupy the highest positions of trust. As Philo observed, many slaves "pursue the occupations of the free" (*Every Good Man is Free*, 11.35). Joseph's rise to power, set in Egypt, is described in unusual detail (Genesis 37, 39–50). The counterpart of Eliezar and Abraham at the highest level is the relationship of Moses to God: "If there is a prophet among you, I the Lord make myself known to him in a vision, I speak with him in a dream. Not so with my servant Moses; he is entrusted with my house. With him I speak mouth to mouth, clearly, and not in dark speech; and he beholds the form of the Lord" (Num 12:6–8). Slaves in New Testament times were put in charge of estates (Matt 24:45–51; Luke 12:42–46), appointed stewards of their masters' accounts (Luke 16:1–7), entrusted with capital to be invested on their masters' behalf (Matt 25:14–30; Luke 19:12–27), and charged with the supervision of other slaves (Luke 12:45).

As Mendelsohn concludes, "We thus have the highly contradictory situation in which, on the one hand, the slave was recognized as possessing the qualities of a human being, while on the other hand, he was considered as

---

[70] Finley, "Between Slavery and Freedom," 234.
[71] Mendelsohn, "Slavery in the Old Testament," 385.
[72] Mendelsohn, *Slavery in the Ancient Near East*, 95–98, 100, 105, 106, 112, 116–17.
[73] Mendelsohn, "Slavery in the Old Testament," 386.

being void of these and was treated as a 'thing'."[74] In other words, slavery in Judaism stumbles over the same paradoxical association of person and thing that anthropologists and historians have encountered elsewhere. There were sound practical reasons for recognizing that a slave was not merely a tool but a "living tool," to use Aristotle's famous phrase. Social advancement and manumission encouraged slaves to work harder. Urbach points out that the money slaves paid for their freedom was often higher than the price of slaves on the market, so that manumission could be a lucrative business for the master.[75] Furthermore, anthropologists have noted that high rates of manumission are usually associated with a thriving slave trade because of the need to replenish bodies.[76]

Allegiance and Authority

The main factor in the social mobility of the slave in the production as in reproduction was clearly allegiance. From the slave's perspective, he was bereft of the group ties that could provide him with alternative sources of strength and therefore was totally dependent on his master for security and livelihood. From his master's perspective, he was bereft of conflicting loyalties and therefore totally devoted. Like an "empty vessel" (Phil 2:7), he could be turned to any use that would advance his master's goals. Allegiance is in turn the key to the ambiguities in authority that seem inevitably to be associated with slavery. At one level, slavery in Palestine as elsewhere was virtually a metaphor for hierarchy, ordered relations of authority. Freeborn and slaves stood for the division into equals and opposites, even as in Philo's essay on the question *Who is the Heir of Divine Things?* (see Matt 10:24). Slaves may have been found at every level of society, but this fact did not indicate the existence of a continuum between slave and free[77] but rather the usefulness of undivided loyalty in a variety of situations, in which the master generally retained the power to bend the slave to his will.[78]

Yet from another perspective, slavery appears to have been associated with equality and the ambiguity of authority. The counterpart of the domestic and eschatological question "Who is the heir?" was, as Jesus Christ put it, "Which is the greater, one who sits at table, or one who serves?" (Luke 22:27). The ambiguity is clearly expressed in relation to Hebrew slaves. The strictures governing their treatment, specifically the law requiring their release after six years of service, provoked these comments from the rabbis:

[74] Mendelsohn, "Slavery in the Old Testament," 386; see Urbach, "Laws Regarding Slavery," 94, n. 213.
[75] Urbach, "Laws Regarding Slavery," 47.
[76] J. Goody, "Slavery in Time and Space," in *Asian and African Systems of Slavery* (ed. J. L. Watson; Berkeley: University of California, 1980) 41.
[77] Finley, "Between Slavery and Freedom."
[78] Finley, "A Peculiar Institution?".

> For it is well for him with thee [the preposition could also carry the nuance *like thee*]—like thee in food, like thee in drink; you are not yourself to be eating fine white bread while he eats black, you drinking vintage wine while he drinks unmatured, you sleeping on flock while he sleeps on straw. That is why it has been said, "whenever one acquires a Hebrew slave he acquires a boss." (*Qidd.* 22a)[79]

Temple slaves in high positions could achieve such eminence that they fell into the category of those to whom the saying was applied "the King's slave is as the King" (*Šebu.* 47b).[80] Urbach points out that, although in theory a slave's peculium belonged to his master, self-interest and the desire to retain the slave's loyalty made his master hesitant to contest his rights. Acquisition of wealth could thus result in a condition of "partial manumission" unrecognized in Roman law.[81] So Sirach counsels masters: "Do not abuse a servant who performs his work faithfully, or a hired laborer who devotes himself to you. Let your soul love (like yourself) an intelligent servant; do not withhold from him his freedom" (7:20–21, following advice on wives and preceding advice on cattle, children, and daughters). And the first letter to Timothy counsels slaves: "Let all who are under the yoke of slavery regard their masters as worthy of all honor, so that the name of God and the teaching may not be defamed. Those who have believing masters must not be disrespectful on the ground that they are brethren; rather they must serve all the better since those who benefit by their service are believers and beloved" (1 Tim 6:1–2).

This ambiguity seems to lie behind Mendelsohn's very interesting qualification of the person/thing dichotomy of slave status as articulated in Palestine:

> The slave's status as a chattel, deprived of any rights, is clearly emphasized in his relation to a third party. . . . Although both the Mesopotamian and the biblical laws treat the slave in relation to a third party as a "thing," there is a fundamental difference in the attitude of these two legislations in regard to the status of the slave in relation to his own master. Mesopotamian law does not consider the latter aspect at all—the slave's fate is in fact, if perhaps not in theory, at the mercy of his owner. The biblical legislation, on the contrary, recognizes the humanity of the slave by restricting the master's power over him.[82]

The special character of the relationship between master and slave seems to be the source of what other writers have frequently distinguished

[79] Baraita on Deut 15:16, cited by Urbach, "Laws Regarding Slavery," 49–50.
[80] Cited by Urbach, "Laws Regarding Slavery," 32–33.
[81] Urbach, "Laws Regarding Slavery," 34–36.
[82] Mendelsohn, "Slavery in the Old Testament," 386–87. Finley notes the existence of such distinctions in a court decision rendered by an Alabama judge in 1861, commenting: "I leave it to those more qualified to uncover the logic in the propositon that my slave is a thing while he is filling my purse with the profits from his labour, a person when he steals my purse" ("A Peculiar Institution?" 821).

as the "humaneness" of Jewish legislation pertaining to slaves.[83] It is exemplified in the wisdom literature in the book of Job (31:13–15; see Joel 2:29):

> If I have rejected the cause of my manservant or my maidservant,
>   when they brought a complaint against me;
> What then shall I do when God rises up?
>   When he makes inquiry, what shall I answer him?
> Did not he who made me in the womb make him?
>   And did not one fashion us in the womb?

and in the words of the same Ben Sira who assured us that slaves could be inhumanely treated (Sir 33:30–31):

> If you have a servant, let him be as yourself,
>   because you have bought him with blood.
> If you have a servant, treat him as a brother,
>   for as your own soul you will need him.
> If you ill-treat him, and he leaves and runs away,
>   which way will you go to seek him?

It was expressed in the legislation stipulating that the murder of a slave was punishable in the same way as that of any freeman, even if the act were committed by his master (Exod 21:20). Urbach emphasizes that "this absolute equality of slave and free man in all matters regarding the judicial safeguarding of their lives has no parallel in either Greek or Roman law."[84]

It was expressed above all in the identification of the Jewish people as slaves of Egypt whom God redeemed for the purpose of making his slaves his "peculiar people," absolutely bound by the terms of his law, owing him total allegiance (Lev 25:55; Deut 15:15; 16:12), a concept of salvation that seems to have been unique to Judaism.[85] The Passover served as a permanent reminder, commemorated annually, of Israel's liberation from namelessness and dispersal in Egypt into a reunited community based on kinship

---

[83] Mendelsohn, *Slavery in the Ancient Near East*, 122–23; Urbach, "Laws Regarding Slavery," 93. For now, I am treating this "humaneness" as a persistent strain in Jewish thought of the biblical and intertestamental periods. But I would hope that eventually it might be understood in the historical detail that Urbach suggests when he says in summary, "A humane concern for the lot of the slave was occasionally aroused but only after the economic situation had brought about a continual deterioration of his legal and social status" ("Laws Regarding Slavery," 94).

[84] Urbach, "Laws Regarding Slavery," 39–40, see pp. 38, 93; Mendelsohn, "Slavery in the Old Testament," 388.

[85] Daube emphasizes that, although concepts of salvation were widespread in the ancient world, "yet that peculiar element from the legal-social sphere, the idea of salvation by means of 'red-emption,' as far as I know, occurs in no other system. (It) is a distinctive mark of the Jewish-Christian edifice" ("Law in the Narratives," 61). Bartchy makes the same point about Paul. Arguing that Paul did not rely on Delphic manumission customs in expressing his doctrine of redemption or his doctrine of calling in 1 Cor 7:22–23, he cites Bömer's observation that "no Greek would ever ask another Greek to become a 'slave of a god'; to describe 'freedom' in such terms would have been unthinkable for a Greek" (ΜΑΛΛΟΝ ΧΡΗΣΑΙ, 125).

with a clear identity as the chosen servants of God. At the same time, the Passover is an outstanding example of the defense against enslavement through the celebration of family ties, suggesting that divine servitude is the condition of the greatest freedom, the ultimate source of strength and power.

Early Christian writers used Jesus' slave-like status to express the divine and mysterious origin of his absolute power, his claim to be "the head of all rule and authority" (Col 2:10) in the complete absence of any formal authorative office. It is spelled out in the most unequivocal terms in Paul's letter to the Philippians:

> Have this mind among yourselves, which is yours in Christ Jesus, who, though he was in the form of God, did not count equality with God a thing to be grasped, but emptied himself, taking the form of a slave, being born in the likeness of men. And being found in human form he humbled himself and became obedient unto death, even death on a cross. Therefore God has highly exalted him and bestowed on him the name which is above every name, that at the name of Jesus every knee should bow, in heaven and on earth and under the earth, and every tongue confess that Jesus Christ is Lord, to the glory of God the Father. (Phil 2:5–11)

Both Luke and John raise the issue in the very context of the last supper (Luke 22:24–27; John 13:1–20). Indeed, it is one of the most fundamental organizing principles of the Gospels as a whole. In addition to the other varieties of structure they exhibit, the Gospels may be analyzed as falling into two parts: a first part in which Jesus is portrayed as slave to both humanity and God, working, yet with mysterious power, and a second half in which he is portrayed as "King of the Jews," cast down, despised, beaten, utterly subject to the will of others, including the inexorable and most punishing will of God, to which he is "obedient unto death, even death on the cross" (Phil 2:8), the ultimate degradation which is his exaltation. The turning point in this complex inversion, according to Matt 26:49 and Mark 14:45, comes precisely at that moment of betrayal when Judas calls him "master" and kisses him. In Luke 22:48 and John 18:4–8, Jesus identifies himself.

Questions

We know from comparative evidence that Jews, including early Christians, were not unique in describing themselves as slaves of their God. The Akkadian and Ugaritic terms for "slave" were also used to designate the inferior status of a freeborn person in relation to a king or deity.[86] Yet the self-description of the pious Jew as a slave of God is distinguished from them by its "total claim."[87] Furthermore, the idea experienced an unusually rich development in Judaism, with several very distinctive features, as we

---

[86] Mendelsohn, "Slavery in the Old Testament," 383.
[87] Zimmerli and Jeremias, *The Servant of God*, 15.

have already seen. We might even paraphrase Buckland's observation about the place of slavery in Roman law and say: "there is scarcely a problem which can present itself in any branch of [theology or law], the solution of which may not be affected by the fact that one of the parties to the transaction is a slave [of God]."[88]

The question is: Why? The central position of slavery in Hebrew scripture is clearly related in some way to enduring questions of monotheism or allegiance, election, equality with or knowledge of God, authority, community, and above all, identity, the identity of God's suffering servants, including Jesus Christ himself about whom we still know almost nothing despite intensive historical research. The power of the symbolism, its effectiveness, must have been rooted in some way in the political, economic, and social realities of Jewish life in the Middle East during the Old Testament and intertestamental periods. Yet the association cannot have been simple, because Jews were not simply victims of Egyptians, Assyrians, Babylonians, and Romans, but also themselves actively enslaved, subjugated, intermarried, and proselytized. Furthermore, the centrality of this complex and ambiguous imagery has persisted under very different cultural and social circumstances.

As an anthropologist, I would ask not only about the thousand years or so before the common era but about the centuries that came after. In what way is this ideology of freedom in slavery related to the way in which Jews were exploited and resisted exploitation as instruments in the transformation of cultural and social relations in a wide variety of contexts, e.g., as agents of economic reform in Baroque Germany,[89] as agents of citizenship in revolutionary France,[90] as agents of modernism in Europe.[91] Finally, I would ask how and why this complex of ideas changed with early Christians, who, although they continued to use many of them in a variety of forms, nevertheless advocated a radically different kind of community, based essentially on the denial of family and kin ties.[92] I would like to conclude by trying to answer this question as expressed on a much smaller scale in Paul's letter to Philemon.[93]

[88] Cited by Finley, "A Peculiar Institution?" 819.

[89] L. Coser, "The Alien as a Servant of Power: Court Jews and Christian Renegades," in *Greedy Institutions: Patterns of Undivided Commitment* (New York: Free Press, 1974) 32–46.

[90] F. Malino, "Ethnicity or Citizenship? Attitudes Toward Jewish Communal Autonomy in Pre-Revolutionary and Revolutionary France," (Bunting Institute Working Paper; Cambridge, MA, 1980); F. Malino, *Jewish Autonomy and Citizenship in 18th Century France* (New York: SUNY, forthcoming).

[91] P. Gay, *Freud, Jews and Other Germans: Masters and Victims in Modernist Culture* (New York: Oxford University, 1978).

[92] G. Feeley-Harnik, *The Lord's Table: Eucharist and Passover in Early Christianity* (Philadelphia: University of Pennsylvania, 1981).

[93] I am making the assumption that Paul was writing as a Jew—formerly a Pharisee, now a follower of Christ—in an effort to convert others to beliefs and practices he regarded as the

Paul's Letter to Philemon

The Letter

I mentioned earlier that slavery in the NT posed problems for Christians, since it suggested that a universalistic religion promising equality for all in Christ could nevertheless perpetuate old hierarchies, ignoring social reform. The tension is most acute in Paul's letter to Philemon in which he returns a runaway slave to his master instead of seizing the opportunity (as we might see it) to free him, perhaps making his manumission the prototype for the abolition of slavery as a whole.

To begin with, the abolition of slavery does not seem to have been the issue. Christianity is not incompatible with slavery, as history has proved. Indeed, it has frequently been used to justify it.[94] The abolition of slavery does not seem to be Paul's intent in his other letters (1 Cor 7:21-23; Eph 6:5-9; Col 3:22-4:1) nor that of other early Christian writers (1 Tim 6:1-2; Titus 2:9-10; 1 Pet 2:18-25; *Barn.* 19:7; *Did.* 4:10-11).[95] The power and efficacy of Paul's "slave in Christ" ("slave of God") symbolism are rooted in political-economic realities that included the practice of slavery; Paul may simply have intended Philemon to transfer ownership in Onesimus to himself or make them co-owners. Even if Paul intended Philemon to manumit Onesimus so that Onesimus could serve the gospel as a freeman, the manumission of individual slaves had nothing necessarily to do with the abolition of slavery. Philemon, deprived of a slave in this way, was likely to replace him with another.

Most biblical scholars would now agree in general, if not with these points specifically.[96] Yet they are left with the problem of what Paul meant to accomplish by making a public issue of returning a slave to his owner in view of the fact that all are one in Christ (1 Cor 12:13; Gal 3:26-29; Col 3:11). Various solutions to this problem have been suggested: (1) to portray Onesimus as a "shrewd and peculating slave" and Paul as his dupe;[97] (2) to portray Paul as socially ethical despite his disinterest in abolition and perhaps also manumission, indeed ethical according to two different criteria in

---

only true expression of Judaism, and that he therefore relied on the law and narrative contained in Jewish scripture and on Jewish custom for many of his arguments, even if he did not always refer to these sources explicitly. I recognize that Judaism was strongly influenced by "Hellenism" during the periods of Greek, Hasmonean, and Roman rule (and vice versa, see M. Hengel, *Judaism and Hellenism: Studies in Their Encounter in Palestine during the Early Hellenistic Period* [Philadelphia: Fortress, 1974]). The extent to which Jewish legislation, ideology, and practice relating to slaves were affected by this interaction is an area for further research.

[94] See Finley, "Masters and Slaves"; "A Peculiar Institution?".

[95] See H. Bellen, *Studien zur Sklavenflucht im römischen Kaiserreich* (Wiesbaden: Franz Steiner, 1971) 78-82.

[96] See E. Lohse, *Colossians and Philemon* (Philadelphia: Fortress, 1971) 205-6; Bartchy, ΜΑΛΛΟΝ ΧΡΗΣΑΙ.

[97] E. R. Goodenough, "Paul and Onesimus," *HTR* 22 (1929) 181-83.

the philosophy of ethics;[98] (3) to argue that Paul returned Onesimus to Philemon on condition that Philemon free Onesimus and return him to Paul as
an evangelist for the church, who eventually became a bishop;[99] (4) to argue
that Paul, like Jesus Christ, did not care about worldly statuses, which were
short-lived anyway, in real or eschatological terms, that the important issue
was to continue living according to God's call regardless of where it came.[100]

All of these arguments are not only plausible, they could all be true.
There is no reason to assume that the parties to this affair had identical
opinions or desires, and we have no knowledge of the outcome, given that
the identity of Onesimus the slave and Bishop Onesimus remains unproven.

I would differ less on the immediate purpose of the letter than on its
ultimate purpose, which must be related to the fact that it was a public
rather than private communication as has sometimes been suggested.[101] The
fundamental assumption of all these arguments seems to be that although
Paul had no interest in abolition he was ultimately using this slave to abolish
relations of hierarchy and to establish a community based on "love." Essentially I will be arguing the opposite, that whatever the immediate purpose of
the letter and its outcome he was ultimately using the slave to establish his
authority, to establish a way of making Philemon obey him and making his
obedience permanent.

Evidently Paul took slavery for granted. However, to acknowledge that
he accepted the institution of slavery is not to say that he accepted a rigid
and unchanging hierarchy, but rather that he accepted ideas and practices
about social order that were fraught with the complex and ambiguous contradictions I have tired to describe. I would infer from the frequent references to the subject that the letter of Philemon has less to do with Onesimus
than with Philemon himself: "the sharing of (his) faith (that) may promote
the knowledge of all the good that is ours in Christ" (v 6) which is the subject of the prayer with which Paul opens his request.[102] Essentially Paul
wants Philemon to obey him in acting like a Christian and actively spread-
ing the faith. Onesimus is the means by which he seeks to achieve this end.

---

[98] W. J. Richardson, "Principle and Context in the Ethics of the Epistle to Philemon," *Int* 22
(1968) 301–16.

[99] J. Knox, *Philemon Among the Letters of Paul* (rev. ed.; Nashville: Abingdon, 1959);
P. N. Harrison, "Onesimus and Philemon," *ATR* 32 (1950) 268–94; F. F. Bruce, "St. Paul in
Rome. 2. The Epistle to Philemon," *BJRL* 48 (1965–66) 81–97.

[100] Lohse, *Colossians and Philemon*, 203; Bartchy, ΜΑΛΛΟΝ ΧΡΗΣΑΙ.

[101] T. Preiss, "Life in Christ and Social Ethics in the Epistle to Philemon," in *Life in Christ*
(ed. T. Preiss; London: SCM, 1954) 33; C. F. D. Moule, *The Epistles of Paul the Apostle to the
Colossians and to Philemon* (Cambridge: Cambridge University, 1957) 18–19, n. 6; Lohse,
Colossians and Philemon, 187.

[102] Moule notes that v 6 is "notoriously the most obscure verse in this letter" and that an
important part of the problem concerns "who is to attain to the 'recognition' or 'knowlege' in
question—Philemon himself, or those who notice and profit from his 'fellowship of faith?'"
(Moule, *The Epistles of Paul to the Colossians and to Philemon*, 142, 143).

As he says in his letter to the Romans, "For as by one man's disobedience many were made sinners, so by one man's obedience many will be made righteous" (Rom 5:19).

Why does he not simply order Philemon, head of one of his house churches, to spread the gospel? He is "bold enough in Christ" to do so, yet "for love's sake" he prefers to appeal at length to Philemon for his consent (vv 8–9).[103] As Church observes (and this is the implicit assumption of many other commentators[104]), "Paul has seized the opportunity to instruct an entire community in the principle of practical Christian love." Why must we "invent a hidden agenda to follow his argument," he asks, alluding to Knox,[105] when "it accords with the common-sense logic of contemporary rhetorical practice"?[106] We must because rhetoric is not enough. It is precisely in practice that the commandment to love, "the Christian case for love and real equality between persons, be they slave or free,"[107] must be imposed with authority, and who, after all, is Paul to impose it? By his own admission, he is merely "an ambassador/old man and now a prisoner also for Christ Jesus" (v 9b, repeating in part the self-description with which he opened his letter). In other words, his status is quite ambiguous. Having no personal power whatsoever, it is not only his mission to the Gentiles that is mysterious (emphasized especially in the letters to the Ephesians and Colossians) but also "the divine office which was given to me for you, to make the word of God fully known" (Col 1:25; see Col 1:1; Eph 1:1).

The evidence suggests that Philemon is indeed his ally not his subordinate, his "beloved fellow worker," "brother," "partner," as Paul repeatedly puts it (vv 1, 7, 17).[108] Paul converted Philemon to Christianity during

---

[103] Many authors have commented on the unusual length and obliqueness of Paul's request. It is so long and circuitous that it has proved very difficult to determine precisely what he is requesting. See, for example, Knox, *Philemon Among the Letters of Paul*, 7; Harrison, "Onesimus and Philemon," 275; F. F. Church, "Rhetorical Structure and Design in Paul's Letter to Philemon," *HTR* 71 (1978) 25.

Lohse argues that Paul uses the words "entreat" or "request" when the question of authority does not present a problem (*Colossians and Philemon*, 198, n. 12). I would agree with Church, however, who identifies the phrase in Paul's letter to Philemon as a common rhetorical device designed to influence an outcome that is *not* certain (Church, "Rhetorical Structure," 25–26, see also pp. 30–31 concerning the parallel case in v 21). In just those passages that Lohse (*Colossians and Philemon*, 198, n. 10) adduces as evidence of Paul's apostolic authority to command, Paul is equally careful to dissociate *God's* commands from his own role as intermediary of those commands and from his own opinion (Rom 16:26; 1 Cor 7:6, 25; 2 Cor 8:8; see also 1 Cor 14:37–38).

[104] E.g., Lohse, *Colossians and Philemon*; Bruce, "St. Paul in Rome"; Preiss, "Life in Christ."

[105] *Philemon Among the Letters of Paul.*

[106] Church, "Rhetorical Structure," 32–33.

[107] Church, "Rhetorical Structure," 32.

[108] Meeks suggests that the heads of Paul's house churches became his "patrons" informally, if not legally, that they probably provided material and financial assistance in addition to the use of their houses, and that "in return, they undoubtedly expected to receive honor and recognition,

the one time they seem to have met.[109] Philemon responded by offering his house to the church as a meeting place. Paul had power over the Christian Philemon to the degree that Philemon was still Christian, i.e., accepted the reality of that divine power, but Paul had no formal authority. His authority came solely from the recognition of the people: "Am I not free? Am I not an apostle? Have I not seen Jesus our Lord? Are not you my workmanship in the Lord? If to others I am not an apostle, at least I am to you; for you are the seal of my apostleship in the Lord" (1 Cor 9:1–2). He had to reestablish that authority with each new church. Philemon's church was the one he was preparing to visit shortly (v 22). This letter constituted part of his preparation (see 2 Cor 10:10). Yet he had to acquire the recognition of Philemon and the members of his community for his holy office without appearing to seek it for himself personally. As he expressed it in the first letter to Thessalonians without, however, altering his "hidden agenda": "Nor did we seek glory from men, whether from you or from others, though we might have made demands as apostles of Christ. But we were gentle among you, like a nurse taking care of her children" (1 Thess 2:6–7; see 2 Cor 10:1–13:10; Gal 1:10).

Paul's problem of getting his equals to carry out the Christian mission, of which he claims to be merely the intermediary, is a problem that is very familiar to anthropologists working in small-scale societies: How do you persuade people to do what you want when you have no formal office of authority or means of force at your disposal? To restate the problem in Weberian terms: How do you persuade people that you have power when you have no authority? How do you transform that power into authority they would concede as being rightfully yours? One of the most common solutions to this problem is "the gift," brilliantly analyzed from a comparative perspective by the French sociologist Marcel Mauss.[110]

---

and to exercise some special influence in the decisions of the group," as was common practice in the "private clubs" of Paul's time and place. The Christian communities differed, however, not only in the countervailing authority of charismatic leaders within the congregation but also in the countervailing authority of the apostles and their itinerant "fellow workers" (Meeks, "The Social World of Pauline Christianity," to appear in *Aufstieg und Niedergang der römischen Welt*, II/27 [Berlin/New York: de Gruyter]; see also E. A. Judge, "The Early Christians as a Scholastic Community," *JRH* 1 [1960–61] 130; A. J. Malherbe, "House Churches and Their Problems," in *Social Aspects of Early Christianity* [Baton Rouge, LA: Louisiana State University, 1977] 75–76; G. Theissen, *Sociology of Early Palestinian Christianity* [Philadelphia: Fortress, 1978]). Although Philemon probably ranked higher than the other members of his house church, it is unclear where he stood in relation to Paul: whether he was Paul's equal, as Paul seems to insist (preparatory to subordinating him), or whether he was socially his superior.

[109] See Bruce, "St. Paul in Rome," 96; Lohse, *Colossians and Philemon*, 192–93, n. 9.

[110] M. Mauss, "Essai sur le don," *Année sociologique* n.s. 1 (1925) 30–186; translated by I. Cunnison as *The Gift* (London: Routledge & Kegan Paul, 1954). Anthropologists tend to regard gift exchange as a universal human practice, expressed differently in different contexts. J. Pedersen (*Israel: Its Life and Culture* [London: Oxford University, Geoffrey Cumberlege, 1926, 1940]) refers to aspects of the gift in ancient Israel. Paul's awareness of the significance of the gift in

The Gift

Paul, having some power but no formal authority, has to act adroitly to persuade his ally to consent to do what he wants him to do, what he perceives as God's will. So he uses the coercive power of the gift. Paul gives every impression that he is *giving* Onesimus back to Philemon, in order that he may extract a counter-gift from Philemon, "not . . . by compulsion but of (his) own free will" (v 14), which is perfectly in keeping with the spontaneous yet calculating nature of the gift.

Is Onesimus Paul's to give? The laws conflicted. According to Deuteronomic legislation, "You shall not deliver a slave unto his master who escaped to you from his master" (Deut 23:16). This is another piece of slave legislation that Mendelsohn finds unique to Jewish law. Yet noting that its application would have spelled the end of slavery in Palestine, he is forced to conclude that it was not always observed, or when observed may have involved the fugitive's reenslavement at the hands of the person to whom he had escaped.[111]

According to the Greco-Roman law to which Paul was also—perhaps primarily—bound, a fugitive slave might seek asylum with a third party, but that party was obliged to return him to his master, otherwise to sell him in the market and return the money he got for him.[112] However, Moule cites contemporary documents indicating that third parties received rewards for returning slaves, which suggests that their compliance with the law was not automatic in this case either.[113] Daube's description of the operations of the "professional *fugitivarius*" tends to confirm that impression.[114]

In other words, Paul seems to be in a position of considerable strength in relation to Philemon. Although by rights he should be obligated to return Philemon's valuable slave, in practice the burden seems to have been on the master to get his property back.[115] Paul himself suggests as much when he

---

mediating spiritual and social relations is revealed in such passages as Rom 11:34–36, referring to Job 35:7, 41:11.

[111] Mendelsohn, "Slavery in the Old Testament," 384, see 386, 388–89; Urbach, "Laws Regarding Slavery," 76–78.

[112] Commentators on Philemon assume that this is the law that Paul was obliged to obey (see Preiss, "Life in Christ," 35; Knox, *Philemon Among the Letters of Paul*, 54; Goodenough, "Paul and Onesimus"; Moule, *The Epistles of Paul to the Colossians and to Philemon*, 19–20; Lohse, *Colossians and Philemon*, 296ff., 201). Goodenough ("Paul and Onesimus," 182) quotes Philo, who attempted to harmonize the two legislations. Lohse (*Colossians and Philemon*, 296ff., 201) is the only other major commentator who draws attention to the existence of the Jewish law.

[113] Moule, *The Epistles of Paul to the Colossians and to Philemon*, 34–37.

[114] Daube, "Slave-Catching," *Juridical Review* 64 (1952) 12–28.

[115] Moule makes the same point in observing that, however Onesimus happened to come into contact with Paul, "St. Paul is now in a position to make big demands on Philemon, and he might have taken advantage of this to keep Onesimus with him (v. 13)," despite the fact that "strictly speaking, it was defrauding a master to retain his runaway slave" (*The Epistles of Paul to the Colossians and to Philemon*, 20). Moule argues that Paul would have felt obligated to return Onesimus not only because holding him was against Roman law, but also because "the

says: "I would have been glad to keep him with me, in order that he might serve me on your behalf during my imprisonment for the gospel; but I *pre-ferred* to do nothing without your consent . . ." (vv 13–14, my emphasis). And in fact, he returns Onesimus to Philemon only *after* he has made him his own, following both laws in the breach and in the observance.

Paul makes Onesimus his own in precisely what sense? There are various possibilities here: (1) Paul has made Onesimus his own by enslaving him. The use of "child," "son," or "daughter" to refer to a slave is extremely common cross-culturally. It is possible that Paul was using the terms in that sense here.[116] (2) Paul has made Onesimus his by converting him to Christianity. The use of the same terms to refer to converts was common in Palestine (1 Cor 4:15–17; Gal 4:19; 1 Pet 1:3; 2:2; Jas 1:18; John 3:3–8). Whether either or both were the case, since it was common for Jews to convert their slaves, Paul identifies himself as Onesimus's "father," i.e., as the person in charge of him, the one who "owns" him, even as a father owned the minor members of his lineage in the sense that they belonged to as well as in it, and he could dispose of them as he wished.[117]

Paul's offer to pay Onesimus's debts, presented with unusual emphasis in vv 18–19, is either a further indication that he, as his owner or father in Christ, is master over Onesimus, or an additional ploy (since it is unclear whether there actually are any debts—Onesimus may have run away because Philemon mistreated him) to get Philemon to agree to Paul's position. If Philemon agrees to let Paul pay Onesimus's debts, if only the loss in service he has suffered, then Philemon must acknowledge that Paul "owns" Onesimus in some way, either as Christian convert or as slave or both, that they are in some sense now "partners" in Onesimus, even as they have been partners in the faith (v 17).

What is this gift then? Mauss has shown that whenever people use gifts for strategic purposes, they choose the gifts extremely carefully to express exactly what they want to say in terms they think will be unmistakable to the recipient.[118] To understand what Paul is saying to Philemon in the language of the gift, we must therefore place his gift in its culturally specific

---

Christian view of a proper relation between persons required that the breach between master and slave should not be acquiesced in but repaired by bravely grasping the nettle of repentance and forgiveness" (*The Epistles of Paul to the Colossians and to Philemon*, 20–21). It is not clear why this should be so, since Christians, then Jews, might have felt obligated to observe the Deuteronomic law on fugitive slaves. Furthermore, there is no mention whatsoever of repentance and forgiveness (in contrast to Pliny the Younger's letter on behalf of Sabinianus's runaway slave).

[116] The objection that Paul could not have enslaved Onesimus because he was a prisoner himself cannot be sustained. Commentators have been unable to determine on the basis of available evidence whether Paul was actually in prison or whether he was speaking metaphorically here as elsewhere. Bruce ("St. Paul in Rome," 88) even suggests the possibility of "house arrest."

[117] See Kopytoff and Miers, "African 'slavery,'" 10, and above.

[118] Mauss, "Essai sur le don."

context. Paul is giving Philemon a slave that was Philemon's but is now also Paul's. The choice of a slave as the gift turns on the person/thing ambiguity in slavery that expresses itself differently in Judaism depending on whether a two-party or three-party relationship is concerned. Paul is playing on the fact that, between master and slave, the slave is a kind of person, indeed, a kind of alter ego. He is a thing only in relation to a third party. Thus the relationship of Onesimus to Paul and Philemon respectively is that of person. But in terms of their relationship to one another, he is a thing, to be used as an instrument of God's larger design (v 15). Onesimus is useful to Paul's theological and social strategy precisely because he is a slave. Paul's pointed designation of Onesimus, meaning "useful" (see v 11), makes this perfectly clear. Like God, Paul was faced with the problem of establishing and maintaining the authority of Christ in many different places at once. Letters were not always a sufficiently authoritative means of communication as they themselves show. Human agents were also required. Onesimus, his "living tool," was useful to Paul in acting as his means of reaching and transforming Philemon.

From another perspective, however, in terms of his own relationship to each one of his masters, Onesimus is the substance Paul is intent on transforming. Onesimus is useful to Paul in his earthly designs precisely because he is beneficial in the spiritual sense (v 20). Through God's design, Philemon lost his soul. But that which was lost has been found and is being returned to him in a new form. Having received and converted Philemon's soul, Paul has made it his own. He has chosen to return it to Philemon in the form of Onesimus as a means of reminding Philemon that he is indebted to Paul for "even (his) own self" (v 19), that Paul is co-owner, partner with him in the soul that constitutes his whole being.

Having transformed Onesimus, Philemon's soul, into his own, whether by enslavement, conversion, or both simultaneously, Paul can then say that he is sending his heart, and add: "So if you consider me your partner, receive him as you would receive me," affirming by continuing, "If he has wronged you . . . ," that Onesimus is indeed Paul. If Philemon recognizes Paul in Onesimus, he is bound to receive the gift and to acknowledge the obligations that the gift entails to make Paul's mission his own.[119]

This interpretation helps to make sense of the otherwise rather difficult sequence: "I, Paul, write this with my own hand, I will repay it—to say nothing of your owing me even your own self. Yes, brother, I want some benefit [possibly another play on Onesimus's name] from you in the Lord. Refresh my heart in Christ" (vv 19–20), which is immediately followed by "Confident of your obedience . . ." (v 21a). Paul is saying to Philemon with Onesimus: you must obey me because your soul is my slave. Onesimus is the

---

[119] Paul advocates a comparable exchange of material and spiritual "gifts" in several other letters (e.g., Rom 15:25–27; 1 Cor 9:11; 16:1–14; 2 Corinthians 8–9).

means by which Paul seeks to bind Philemon, to "enslave" him to the work of the church, as he has enslaved his soul. Thus I would argue that when he continues by writing, "Knowing that you will do even more than I say" (v 21b), he is referring not to Onesimus and the possibility of manumission, but to Philemon and the fulfillment of his efforts "to promote the knowledge of the good that is ours in Christ" (v 6), the subject with which he began his letter.

Paul's letter to Philemon could thus be described as a classic case of the "slave" as an instrument of the Lord, used to achieve something of God's purpose. Paul is using Onesimus as a tool to bring Philemon into line exactly as God is alleged to have used the prophets, including Jesus. Paul is following totally in the footsteps of God—as he himself suggests elsewhere: "Therefore be imitators of God, as beloved children" (Eph 5:1)—God, who conventionally used his slaves as the means of establishing new relations among persons, agents in the transformation of political, social, and economic structures, instruments of submission.

Having united the souls of his two masters, Jew and Gentile, in one flesh, Onesimus has served as the agent of their reconciliation, even as Jesus Christ, by "creating in himself one new man in the place of the two," has brought aliens and foreigners together as "fellow citizens" of the ordered household in which they must be "subject to one another out of reverence for Christ" (Eph 2:11–22; 5:21).

But why a runaway slave? God's slaves were typically very obedient. The striking exception is Jonah. Like Paul's letter to Philemon, the book of Jonah is the story of an escaped slave, and apparently unique among the prophetic books in telling the story of a disobedient servant who tried to run away from God rather than obey his orders. In this case, even a disobedient, contrary, sullen slave is shown to be a missionary *malgré lui*, an instrument of God's will, useful in converting not merely a shipload of heathen sailors but an entire city of Gentiles, "an exceedingly great city, three days' journey in length" (Jonah 3:3). The context is strikingly similar in both cases: the mission to the Gentiles, which was Paul's overwhelming concern. As Jonah was the unwilling tool in the hands of God to be used for the conversion of the Gentiles, so Onesimus is the unwitting tool in the hands of Paul to be used for the same purpose and by God's design (v 15). Neither had any choice in the matter.

Does Philemon himself have any choice? The parallel with Jonah, who was a Jew, raises the possibility that the real fugitive is not Onesimus but Philemon whose soul he represents. Philemon, the Christian, may be the real escapee from the house of God and Onesimus merely the agent of his return—a critical element like the sailors, the whale, or the castor-oil plant, perhaps even converted like the sailors, in the process—but not the main character.

Slaves were expressive not only of the ambiguity of authority but also of the ambiguity of identity, of affiliation. The circumstances of Jonah's flight force him to identify himself and declare his allegiance, to identify himself by declaring the identity of his master. This point is raised early on when the sailors question him: "'Tell us, on whose account this evil has come upon us? What is your occupation? And whence do you come? What is your country? And of what people are you?' And he said to them, 'I am a Hebrew; and I fear the Lord, the God of heaven, who made the sea and the dry land'" (Jonah 1:8–9).

Like the book of Jonah, which has often been interpreted as a brief interlude of fantasy in the prophetic storm of chaos and recrimination, Paul's letter to Philemon has frequently been interpreted as one of his few letters written "in a situation which involved no doctrinal or ecclesiastical dispute," a calm moment of private loving-kindness.[120] Yet it is possible that the runaway Onesimus is an allusion to the fact that Philemon himself was thinking of "running away," that his disobedience or potential disobedience was the occasion for the letter. The time factor is perhaps a point in favor of this argument. Paul does not seem to have felt compelled to return Onesimus immediately. He kept Onesimus long enough possibly to convert him. Clearly he has chosen the moment of Onesimus's return carefully, and his reasons seem to have less to do with the laws involved than with his mission to the Gentiles.

Paul does not have the whales or castor-oil plants at his command, but Paul is the one who has caught Philemon's runaway soul. Like the sailors, he may be commanding Philemon: "Declare yourself! Who are you working for? Are you working for me to spread the Christian gospel, or are you working for someone else, which will mean our ruin?" Philemon must declare his identity by identifying his "Master in heaven" (Eph 6:9; Col 4:1), Jesus Christ as represented in his ambassador, Paul.

But how can Paul be sure that his tactic is going to work, that Philemon will understand the request he is making of him? This is the perennial problem of Paul's chosen mission which required him to deal cross-culturally with all kinds of foreigners in far-flung churches:

> . . . from Jerusalem and as far round as Illyricum I have fully preached the gospel of Christ, thus making it my ambition to preach the gospel, not where Christ has already been named, lest I build on another man's foundation, but as it is written [Isa 52:15], "They shall see who have never been told of him, and they shall understand who have never heard of him." (Rom 15:19–21)

Here we encounter questions that are as yet unanswerable. Who is Philemon? What does it mean to be a resident probably of Colossae with a Greek name? Probably it means that Philemon is not a Jew of any persuasion, but is he then a "Greek"? And if so, what kind of "Greek"? It could still be argued that Paul would not use the strategy (that I have attributed to him)

---

[120] H. G. May and B. M. Metzger, *The New Oxford Annotated Bible with the Apocrypha: Revised Standard Version* (New York: Oxford University, 1977) 1453.

unless he were fairly certain of its success. Furthermore, he could be reason-ably sure of its success not only because he skillfully employed "the basic tactics of persuasion taught and widely practiced in his day"[121] but also because the subject of his rhetoric—the fugitive slave—was a subject that was well understood across social, cultural, and national borders.

This brings us back to the factor of regionalism with which I began. Slavery was not simply a matter of slippery, ambiguous concepts, constantly crossing boundaries and constantly being whipped back into place. It was literally a regional phenomenon, requiring cooperation across cultural and national boundaries that had long brought people of different groups together in cross-cultural communication.[122]

Paul's mission was to establish Christianity in social worlds in which its authority was as yet unrecognized, to transform relations of "love" into the "varieties of working" God had allotted to the members of Christ's body that constituted the church: "first apostles, second prophets, third teachers, then workers of miracles, then healers, helpers, administrators, speakers in various kinds of tongues" (1 Cor 12:6, 27–28; see Rom 12:6–8; Eph 4:11–16). To transform the child into the man, as he puts it in precisely this context, he had to use the tools and materials that were available to him. Providentially, Onesimus fell into his hands.

Conclusion

How does all this relate to the original problem: that of devising concep-tual systems that will enable us to understand variation and change over time? I have argued that the slave-master relationship in Old Testament and intertestamental Judaism was not a simple matter of exploitation and domi-nation but rather that it embodied profound contradictions and ambiguities in authority, allegiance, and identity.

Paul's imagery was rooted in these ambiguities. Paul used the image of the slave to express the power of one who had no formal authority. But he used it not merely as a means of expression but also as a means of trans-forming the power of God's slaves into the earthly varieties of service appro-priate to their spiritual gifts. He used an image that embodied the deep ambiguity of authority relations—their changeableness, subtle reversals, myriad variations—to create new authority relations, new allegiances, new identities. Moreover, he may have depended on the essentially regional or international character of slavery to get his point across, given the essentially cross-cultural nature of his chosen mission.

We too are recipients of Paul's letter, many centuries later. How can we be sure that we have got it right? We cannot. But I hope, by looking at the

---

[121] Church, "Rhetorical Structure," 17.
[122] See J. Goody, "Slavery in Time and Space," 18.

subject matter from a comparative perspective, I have indicated some of the ways in which anthropology may contribute to our understanding of the particular problems it presents. We are not simply dealing with "models" derived from other cultures but rather with the assumption that the beliefs and practices of all human beings are fundamentally comparable. As my colleague, Edmund Leach, said many years ago, St. Matthew's Gospel has to be treated on a par with Roth's Bulletin No. 5 on the North Queensland Aborigines as a record of theological doctrine.[123] It is only by continuing to refine our view of the particulars through comparison that we may ever come to appreciate the universal in human behavior, if not the transcendent.

[123] E. R. Leach, "Virgin Birth," *Proceedings of the Royal Anthropological Institute of Great Britain and Ireland for 1966* (London: Royal Anthropological Institute of Great Britain and Ireland, Richard Madley, 1967) 39–49.

VII

TREATY AND OATH IN THE ANCIENT NEAR EAST
A Historian's Approach

Hayim Tadmor

Elias Bickerman, in memoriam
Obit 29. VIII. 1981

The study of the covenant in the Bible has become a major topic of biblical scholarship during the last two or three decades. An inherent feature of this area of study is its comparative character: covenant formulations in the Bible are constantly being compared with treaties of the ancient Near East, the latter viewed as a constant, an Archimedian point, upon which the biblical evidence rests or around which it sometimes moves in orbit. I therefore wish to express my gratitude to the organizers of the SBL Centennial Meeting for having given me the opportunity to present the point of view of a historian and an Assyriologist, who is nevertheless no outsider to biblical scholarship. I hope that this inquiry into certain aspects of treaty and oath in the ancient Near East will serve biblical scholars in their studies of the covenant idea, form, and practice.

The following problems will be considered, though not necessarily in this sequence: for the second millennium, the geographic distribution of Akkadian terms for alliance and treaty making; the specific West Semitic terminology and its relationship to biblical Hebrew (כרת ברית "cut a covenant"); for the first millennium, the Assyrian loyalty oath—the adê, often referred to as "vassal treaty"; and, finally, forms of political dependence in the Assyrian empire, especially in regard to the kings of Israel and Judah. Our emphasis is on the multiplicity of forms and their diversity, despite the obvious similarities that have been underlined by the comparativists. In addition, I hesitate to accept unchallenged the assumption, implicit in most works on treaty and covenant, that the flow of influence in terminology and formulas was from Mesopotamia westward, since the Mesopotamian experience has always been, it is claimed, more ancient and dominant. Obviously this is so; but is it not possible that the flow was occasionally in both directions?

Before we proceed, let me mention briefly some seminal studies on treaty and covenant, mainly those devoted to the comparative aspects. The first insight into the comparative trend, which stressed the classical material, was provided by E. J. Bickerman in 1950,[1] but at the time it made little impact on biblical scholarship. It was the work of G. E. Mendenhall in 1955,[2] followed in Germany by that of K. Baltzer in 1960,[3] that inaugurated a new stage in covenant research in biblical scholarship. The cardinal issue at that stage was the structure of biblical covenants and their comparison with Hittite treaties of the second millennium B.C.E. The publication of the vassal treaties of Esarhaddon by D. J. Wiseman in 1958[4] and the obvious similarity between certain of its maledictions and those in the book of Deuteronomy introduced yet another element: a possible dependence of the biblical treaty formulation upon that of the Assyrian vassal treaties, as exemplified by those of Esarhaddon. This view was presented in 1965 independently by R. Frankena[5] and by my Jerusalem colleague Moshe Weinfeld, who subsequently expanded it in his comprehensive book on Deuteronomy.[6] About the same time (1963) an exhaustive and detailed analysis of the ancient Near Eastern and biblical treaties was offered by D. J. McCarthy, revised fifteen years later.[7] Some of what is presented below has been anticipated—though in a different form—in McCarthy's 1978 edition of his study.[8]

[1] E. Bickerman, "Couper une alliance," *Archive d'histoire du droit oriental* 5 (1950–51) 133–56; reprinted and updated in his *Studies in Jewish and Christian History* (Leiden: Brill, 1976) 1. 1–32.

[2] G. E. Mendenhall, "Law and Covenant in Israel and the Ancient Near East," *BA* 17 (1954) 26–46; 50–76 (= *BAR* 3. 3–53).

[3] K. Baltzer, *Das Bundesformular* (WMANT 4; Neukirchen: Neukirchener Verlag, 1960 [2d ed., 1964]).

[4] D. J. Wiseman, *The Vassal-Treaties of Esarhaddon* (London: British School of Archaeology in Iraq, 1958 [= *Iraq* 20]), now in a revised translation by E. Reiner in *ANET*[3], 534–41. Note also the review articles by I. J. Gelb (*BO* 19 [1962] 160–62) and R. Borger (*ZA* 54 [1961] 173–96).

[5] R. Frankena, "The Vassal-Treaties of Esarhaddon and the Dating of Deuteronomy," *OTS* 14 (1965) 122–54.

[6] M. Weinfeld, "Traces of Assyrian Formulae in Deuteronomy," *Bib* 46 (1965) 417–27; *Deuteronomy and the Deuteronomic School* (Oxford: Clarendon, 1972) 59–157.

[7] D. J. McCarthy, *Treaty and Covenant* (AnBib 21; Rome: Pontifical Biblical Institute, 1963; new edition, completely rewritten [AnBib 21a], 1974).

[8] Of the numerous studies on various aspects of treaty and covenant in the Bible I should mention those which, in addition to the formative works quoted above, were consulted in preparing the present paper: M. Tsevat, "The Neo-Assyrian and Neo-Babylonian Vassal Oaths and the Prophet Ezekiel," *JBL* 78 (1959) 199–204; A. Jepsen, "Berith: Ein Beitrag zur Theologie der Exilzeit," *Verbannung und Heimkehr*, Festschrift Wilhelm Rudolph (ed. A. Kuschke; Tübingen: Mohr, 1961); F. C. Fensham, "Maledictions and Benedictions in Ancient Near Eastern Vassal-Treaties and the Old Testament," *ZAW* 74 (1962) 1–19; W. L. Moran, "The Ancient Near Eastern Background of the Love of God in Deuteronomy," *CBQ* 25 (1963) 77–87; D. R. Hillers, *Treaty Curses in the Old Testament Prophets* (BibOr 16; Rome: Pontifical Biblical Institute, 1964); E. Gerstenberger, "Covenant and Commandment," *JBL* 84 (1965) 38–51; H. B. Huffmon, "The Exodus, Sinai and the Credo," *CBQ* 27 (1965) 101–13; G. M. Tucker, "Covenant Forms and Contract Forms," *VT* 15 (1965) 487–503; P. J. Calderone, *Dynastic Oracle and Suzerainty Treaty* (Manila: Loyola House, 1966); J. Muffs, *Studies in the Aramaic Legal Papyri from Elephantine* (Leiden: Brill, 1969) 116–41; R. Polzin, "*HWQY* and the Covenantal

The discussion at present takes place mostly on biblical ground; few students of the Mesopotamian or Hittite cultures have contributed to that inquiry. Notable exceptions are the works of V. Korošec, E. von Schuler, and more recently that of G. Kestemont on the Hittite vassal treaties,[9] and M. Munn-Rankin's study of diplomatic terminology in Babylonia during the Mari period, which has not received the attention it deserves.[10]

Other significant contributions to the study of the vassal treaties, such as those of W. L. Moran,[11] R. Frankena,[12] and M. Cogan,[13] have been directed primarily at the biblical audience. My presentation is no exception; though dealing essentially with Near Eastern material, it is offered not to orientalists but to biblical scholars, on the occasion of a festive biblical convention.

The Second Millennium

Two periods of international diplomatic activity—in extensive treaty making—are attested in the second millennium. These are (1) the First International Period, the age of Hammurabi and Shamshi-Adad—often referred to as the Mari Period—the nineteenth to eighteenth centuries B.C.E.; and (2) the Second International Period—the age of the Egyptian, Hittite, and Hurrian empires—the fifteenth to thirteenth centuries, elsewhere referred to as the Club of the Great Powers, in which also Babylonia, and

---

Institutions in Early Israel," *HTR* 62 (1969) 226–40; M. Weinfeld, "The Covenant of Grant in Old Testament and Ancient Near East," *JAOS* 90 (1970) 184–203; F. M. Cross, *Canaanite Myth and Hebrew Epic* (Cambridge: Harvard University, 1973) 265–73; E. Kutsch, *Verheissung und Gesetz* (Berlin: de Gruyter, 1973); M. Weinfeld, "Covenant Terminology in the Ancient Near East and its Significance in the West," *JAOS* 93 (1973) 191–99; "*Bᵉrît*-Covenant vs. Obligation," *Bib* 56 (1975) 120–28; "Loyalty Oath in the Ancient Near East," *UF* 8 (1976) 379–414; T. Mettinger, *King and Messiah* (ConBOT 8; Lund: Gleerup, 1976) 301–4; J. Barr, "Some Semantic Notes on the Covenant," *Beiträge zur alttestamentlichen Theologie* (ed. H. Donner, R. Hanhart, and R. Smend [Festschrift Zimmerli]; Göttingen: Vandenhoeck und Ruprecht, 1977) 23–38; K. A. Kitchen, "Egypt, Ugarit, Qatna and Covenant," *UF* 11 (1979) 453–64.

[9] V. Korošec, *Hethitische Staatsvertäge* (Leipziger rechtswissenschaftliche Studien 60; Leipzig: Weicher, 1931); E. von Schuler, "Staatsverträge und Dokumente hethitischen Rechts," *Neuere Hethiterforschung* (ed. G. Walser; Wiesbaden: F. Steiner, 1964 [= *Historia*, Einzelschriften, Heft 7] 34–54); "Sonderformen Hethitischer Staatsverträge," *Anadolu Arastirmalari* (= *Jahrbuch für Kleinasiatische Forschung* 2/1–2 [In Memoriam H. Bossert; Istanbul, 1955]) 445–641; G. Kestemont, *Diplomatique et droit international en Asie occidentale (1600–1200 av. J. C.)* (Publication de l'Institute Orientaliste de Louvain 9; Louvain-la-Neuve: Université Catholique, 1974).

[10] J. M. Munn-Rankin, "Diplomacy in Western Asia in the Early Second Millennium B.C.," *Iraq* 18 (1956) 68–110.

[11] W. L. Moran, "A Note on the Treaty Terminology of the Sefire Stelas," *JNES* 22 (1963) 173–76.

[12] See above, n. 5.

[13] M. Cogan, *Imperialism and Religion: Assyria, Judah and Israel in the Eighth and Seventh Centuries B.C.E* (SBLMS 19; Missoula: Scholars Press, 1974).

somewhat later Assyria, were active participants.[14] The first period has been illuminated by the archives of Mari, Shemshara, and Tell al-Rimah. Its last part is attested in documents from Alalakh, level VII. The second period is documented by the rich finds from the state archives of Boghazkoy, the capital of Hatti, from el-Amarna in Egypt, from Ras Shamra-Ugarit, and from Alalakh, level IV.

It is noteworthy that all these archives come from the west, i.e., west of the Euphrates; consequently, our knowledge of the treaty documents themselves as well as of the western procedures of treaty making is far greater than our knowledge of such procedures and documents from Mesopotamia proper. Likewise, the diplomatic relations and alliances between the kings of Egypt and Hatti and those of Babylonia and Assyria are reflected extensively in the political correspondence of that period, although but for one— the treaty between Rameses II and Mattusili III—the actual treaty documents have not been preserved.

In the First International Period the struggle for dominion encompassed the area from Elam in the east to Aleppo in the west, the major powers being Elam, Babylon, Larsa, Eshnunna, Ashur, and (in Syria) Yamhad/ Aleppo. The multiplicity of states, mostly equal in status and power, resulted in a multiplicity and complexity of political relations: oaths between kings were sworn and broken, wars declared, peace established, new oaths sworn, and treaties concluded. That some cases were extreme can be illustrated by a letter of Shamshi-Adad of Assyria, from the Shemshara Archives, relating the case of a certain Yashub-Addu, a minor king in the eastern Zagros.[15] "He becomes the ally of a king and swears an oath, (then) he becomes the ally of a(nother) king and swears an oath, while becoming an enemy of the first king with whom he was allied. His alliance with and then hostility to the king he is allied with [take place] within two months!" The necessity to cope with a variety of complex ethnopolitical situations is reflected in rich treaty terminology, varied in spite of the seemingly uniform clichés and formulas. It is submitted that a difference in the distribution of terminology should be distinguished between the east—Babylonia proper—and the west; moreover, this distinction did not always include Assyria and its colonies in Anatolia. Thus we shall see that some terms are general, i.e., common to all the cuneiform-writing civilizations; others are specific, typical either of eastern or western usage. Yet others may be defined as West Semitic isoglosses, distinct from all the rest.

Let us then review in brief that terminology, placing emphasis on the

---

[14] For this terminology see H. Tadmor, "The Decline of Empires in Western Asia ca. 1200 B.C.E.," *Symposia Celebrating the Seventy-fifth Anniversary of the Founding of the American Schools of Oriental Research (1900–1975)* (ed. F. M. Cross; Cambridge: American Schools of Oriental Research, 1979) 3–4.

[15] J. Læssøe, *Det første assyriske Imperium* (København, 1966) 83–87; quoted here in W. L. Moran's translation, *ANET³*, 628.

specific Assyrian and West Akkadian usage, as distinct from that of Mesopotamia proper. The two main phrases expressing alliance that were commonly used in the second millennium and are found in both east and west are: (1) "peace, reconciliation, friendship," *salīmum*, and its later by-forms: *sullumû, šalāmu*, and *šulmu*,[16] confined mostly to the Assyrian and western usage; and (2) "brotherhood," *athūtum*—the usual form in the Mari Age—or *ahhūtum*—the somewhat later form which prevailed.[17] *salīmum* denoted not only the covenantal relationship between kings of equal rank, who addressed each other as "brothers," but also the relations between sovereign kings and their minor dependents, who addressed each other—again in kinship terms—as "father" and "son" or in social terms as "master" and "slave."[18] *ahhūtum* expressed the nature of the *salīmum* and referred both to the cordial relationship that preceded or is claimed to have preceded the alliance, and specifically to the newly formed relationship resultant from this *salīmum*.

To the same semantic sphere of "friendship and brotherhood" belong *damqātum* (literally "good things," "good relations") current in the Mari documents and its later synonyms: *ṭabūtu* and *ṭubtu*,[19] common in the Neo-Assyrian sources. However, *atterūtu* ("friendship") and *ra'amūtu*[20] ("love,"

---

[16] For the ample lexical evidence see now the current Akkadian dictionaries: *The Chicago Assyrian Dictionary* (= CAD) and W. von Soden's *Akkadisches Handwörterbuch* (= AHW), *sub voce*. Note, however, that the use of *šulmu* ("health," "well-being") for "peace" in the political sense (*AHW* 1269ᵃ[6]) is rather exceptional and so is that of *šalāmu* for *salīmu* (*AHW* 1143ᵃ[1]). The few occurrences of these terms in texts from the second millennium (all from the west!) are: *riksu u šalāmu* (hendiadys, "peace," hence "allegiance, fidelity," *PRU* 4, 36: 19,23) and *šulmu epēšu* ("to make peace," ibid., 180: 11,16).

[17] The antonym of *ahhūtum* was *(w)ardūtum* ("vassalage") e.g. in *ARM* 2 No. 49: 6–11; more in *CAD* vol. A II 252ᵇ. In the Amarna period the usual form is *ahhūtu*; *athūtu* is seldom used, e.g., *athūti ṭabti* ("good brotherly relations") *EAT* No. 1:64 (a letter of the Egyptian Pharaoh to the King of Babylonia).

[18] For the evidence see Munn-Rankin, "Diplomacy," 80–84, and more in *CAD* vol. A I 71ᵇ; 200ᵇ–201ᵃ; vol. A II 248; vol. M I 314.

[19] Very little can be added to the evidence adduced by W. L. Moran in his brief but seminal paper on treaty terminology (see above, n. 11) 174–76. Note especially the hendiadys constructions *ṭubtu u sullumû*, said of the peace effected by treaty (current in Babylonian Chronicles and some Assyrian Royal Inscriptions) ibid., 174, and *ṭubtu u sullumû gamru* ("total peace"), describing the relationship between Assyria and Babylonia in the twelfth to ninth centuries: A. K. Grayson, *Assyrian and Babylonian Chronicles* (TCS 5; Locust Valley, NY: Augustin, 1975) 162:1; 166:18; 167:24.

[20] *atterūtu*—a word of unknown derivation—is used only in texts from the Hittite–Hurrian area: *CAD* vol A II 371; vol. E 204. *ra'amūtu* (literally "love," a western form of the Old Babylonian *ra'imūtu* "friendship") is found exclusively in the correspondence between kings of Mitanni and Egypt from el-Amarna: *EAT*, 2 p. 1494 (and see W. L. Moran, *CBQ* 25 [1963] 77–87). Another rare term, specific for the usage of North Syria in the second millennium, is *manahāte*, which occurs three times in the inscription of Idrimi of Alalakh (Smith, *Idrimi*, ll. 47, 51–52, 54). A. Goetze's translation, "Treaty Stipulations" (*JCS* 4 [1950] 228), is preferable to "vassal service" of *CAD* M II 206ᵇ; see also in E. L. Greenstein and D. Marcus, "The Akkadian Inscription of Idrimi," *JANESCU* 8 (1976) 81–84.

hence "faithfulness"), which were restricted to the diplomatic parlance of the west in the Second International Period, became obsolete in the first millennium. The treaty, *riksātum*,[21] or the later forms—in the singular—*riksu, rikiltu* (= *rikištu*)[22] (literally "bond"), was solemnized and sanctioned—as it should be—by an oath *niš ilī* ("oath (sworn by) the life of the gods"),[23] which usually contained an imprecation, *mamītum*.[24] Here, the hendiadys form was common: *riksu u mamītu*, which was replaced in the eighth century by the Neo-Assyrian terms *adê (u) mamītu* and *adê niš ilāni* ("loyalty oaths")[25] (see below on the first millennium). As *pars pro toto*, "oath" or "imprecation" would often stand for the whole phrase and imply "treaty," "covenant," "allegiance." Similarly, *ṭuppi niš ilī* ("tablet of the oath") and especially *ṭuppi mamīti* ("tablet of the imprecation") could stand for *ṭuppi riksi u mamīti* or *ṭuppu ša rikilti u ša mamīti*.[26]

The close resemblance among all these terms and their biblical counterparts *bĕrît, 'ālâ, šĕbu'â*, and especially the hendiadys constructions *'ālôt habbĕrît, hā'ālâ wĕhaššĕbū'â*, was well noted in modern research and hardly needs repeating.[27] Also, the significance of the oath containing the self-curse

[21] On *riksātum*, the Old Babylonian term for contract, pact, and especially a marriage contract, see B. Landsberger's comments in *Symbolae iuridicae et historiae Martino David dedicatae*, 2 (Leiden: Brill, 1968) 89ff.

[22] The term *rikiltu, rikištu*, does not occur in the Old Babylonian period. Could it be a back formation of *riksātum*? (See W. S. Greengus, *JAOS* 89 [1969] 506, n. 9.) An early occurrence of *riksu* for "treaty" is attested in Alalakh: Wiseman, *AT* No. 3 obv. 1 (treaty between Alalakh and Kizzuwatna), where it is written in western orthography: *ṭuppi rikši* (see Greenstein and Marcus, "Idrimi," 60–61).

[23] Oaths were "given" (*nadānu*), "placed" (*šakānu*), "imposed" (*šuzkuru; tummû*), "sworn" (*tamû*), "uttered" (*zakāru*), etc. A "definitive oath" (*niš ili gamrum*), i.e., a binding treaty, is mentioned in a letter from Shemshara (J. Læssøe, *The Shemshara Tablets* [Arkaeol. Kunsthist. Medd. Dan. Vid. Selsk. 4 No. 3; København, 1959] 77–78; 10, 26). Another Old Babylonian Text, a letter of Anam of Uruk to Sin-muballit of Babylon (nineteenth century), relates that in order to safeguard the treaty it was advisable that the oath be repeated every year: *ema salimim u damqātim niš ilim innērišu adi napištim la(!)-pa-a-tim* (so: *CAD* L 84[b]) *libbum la iqqippu u ša šattišu niš ilim uteddišu*, "Whenever 'peace and friendship' (exist) an oath is required; (but) not until the 'touching of the throat' is performed and the oath is renewed every year—could one be trusted" (A. Falkenstein, *Baghdader Mitteilungen* 2 [1963] 59, Col. IV: 17–19).

[24] See the lexical evidence in *CAD* A 131[b]-132; M I 191[a]-192[b]; vol. N I 292[b]-293[a].

[25] Like *niš ilim* so *mamītum* is "placed" (*šakānu*), "sworn" (*tamû*) or "imposed" (*tummû*). It is also "made" (*epēšu*) or "taken" (*ṣabātu*), i.e., put into effect, concluded. On the specific Sumerian idiom "to cut an oath," nam-erim TAR (= ku₅) see the recent discussion of D. O. Edzard, "Zum sumerischen Eid," *Sumerological Studies in Honor of Thorkild Jacobsen* (Assyriological Studies 20; Chicago: University of Chicago, 1974) 63–94; for the etymology see p. 77.

[26] See Korošec, *Staatsverträge*, 21–22; I. J. Gelb, *BO* 19 (1962) 61–62; see also *CAD* M I 190–91, N I 292[b]-293[a].

[27] E. A. Speiser, "An Angelic 'Curse': Exodus 19:20," *JAOS* (1960) 198 n. 1; H. C. Brichto, *The Problem of Curse in the Hebrew Bible* (SBLMS 13; Philadelphia: SBL, 1963) 45–59; Weinfeld, *Deuteronomy*, 63, 67, 107.

as the essential—if not the most potent—component of the treaty has been recognized long ago[28] and needs no further comment. Yet, the distinction in the geographical distribution between the two main Akkadian terms for oath cannot be overlooked. Whereas *niš ili*—said of treaty making—was commonly used in Mesopotamia and the west throughout the second millennium, *mamītu* was mostly prevalent in Assyria and west of the Euphrates. Taking the *mamītu* (*mamītam laqā'um*) was the usual procedure in the Assyrian colonies in Cappadocia in the nineteenth and eighteenth centuries. The *kārum*—the "colony"—swore an oath of allegiance to the local Anatolian ruler upon his accession before the sacred symbol of the god Aššur.[29] In anticipation of our discussion below, it should be remarked here that the practice of swearing allegiance to the king—though usual in Anatolia and apparently also in Syria—was not current in Assyria proper (nor in Babylonia) before the days of Esarhaddon.

Some two hundred years later, i.e., in the fifteenth to fourteenth centuries, *mamītu* became the customary term for a treaty in Hatti and North Syria. One of its earliest attestations is the inscription of Idrimi, King of Alalakh, incised upon his statue, which refers to a treaty between his ancestors and the former kings of the Hurrians: "They made a binding treaty (*mamīta danna*, literally, 'mighty oath') between them."[30] A *mamītu* is regularly referred to in the treaties and charters from Ugarit[31] and is common in the Amarna letters from Canaan, e.g.: "King X made a treaty (*mamīta ētepuš*) with men of Byblos"; "The King of Sidon and Aziru of Amurru and the people of Arwad have taken the oath (*itmûni*) and repeated the oath (*mamīta*) between them."[32]

Also the kings of Assyria, at least from the fourteenth century onward,[33] speak of imposing a *mamītu* upon their vassals. So does for example Tiglath-pileser I to the defeated kings of Na'iri: "I made them swear (*utammišunūti*) by my great gods an oath (*mamītu*) of eternal vassaldom."[34] An Assyrian chronicle reports that when border disputes between Assyria and Babylonia were settled, the two kings—Aššur-bēl-nišēšu and Karaindaš—concluded a treaty between them (*riksāni ina biritišunu ana aḫameš urakkisu*) and "took

[28] Already in the classical study of Johs. Pedersen, *Der Eid bei den Semiten* (Strassbourg: Trubner, 1914) 70, 82, 108–14.

[29] I have followed the interpretation of K. Balkan, *Observations on the Chronological Problems of the Kārum Kaniš* (Ankara: Türk Tarih Kurumu, 1966) 73–75. For a different view on *mamītam laqā'um* see J. Lewy, *Or* 26 (1957) 28 n. 5, and see also P. Garelli, *Les Assyriens en Cappadoce* (Paris: Maisonneuve, 1963) 234; L. L. Orlin, *Assyrian Colonies in Cappadocia* (The Hague: Mouton, 1970) 129.

[30] Smith, *Idrimi*, 50–51; Greenstein and Marcus, "Idrimi," 83.

[31] E.g., *PRU* 4, 122:12; 156:22; 284:4–5.

[32] *EAT*, No. 67:13 and No. 149:60.

[33] A. K. Grayson, *Assyrian Royal Inscriptions* 1 (Wiesbaden: Harrassowitz, 1972) §360, last line.

[34] See below, n. 108.

an oath" (*mamīta iddinu*) concerning the boundary between the two
countries.[35] If this preference of *mamītu* to *niš ilī* in the passages quoted
above does not result from a dialectical distribution, we are entitled to
conclude that in Assyria as well as in the lands west of the Euphrates, the
imprecation element of the treaty-oath played a major role, whereas in
Babylonia, so it seems, curses were not invoked. There, an oath sworn by the
life of the gods, although followed by certain symbolic actions, was sufficient
to guarantee the implementation of the treaty.

The exact contents of the *mamītu* oaths are not stated in any document,
but it was obviously a solemn self-curse, powerful enough, so it seemed, to
prevent any transgression. No symbolic actions accompanying the taking of
the *mamītu* are attested. However, symbolic actions very frequently accompanied treaty making in Babylonia of the Mari Age, a society ruled by
princes of Amorite descent. Most common was the "touching of the throat,"
napištam lapātum. This symbolic act could be either a knife or finger
drawn across the throats of both parties or a euphemism for sacrificing an
animal[36] (and so already in Sumerian texts: "he touched the kid's throat, he
shed his blood").[37] Other symbolic acts, pertaining to the treaty ceremony in
the Mari letters, are "seizing the hem of the garment," *sissiktam ṣabātum*,
qarnam ṣabātum, expressing submission, or "binding the hem of a garment,"
qannu rakāsu; breaking the treaty is "to relinquish the hem."[38] None of these
customs is attested in the Assyrian colonies in Cappadocia, and they do not
figure in Hittite treaty terminology.

At this stage another symbolic act that accompanied treaty making should
be considered: the sacrificial rite. It is attested in Alalakh, in Northern Syria, in
the Mari area—mainly in tribal West Semitic society—and in the Habur
region on the Upper Tigris, but again, not among the urban Babylonian
centers or among the Assyrian colonists and their Anatolian overlords. We
have here yet another feature specific to the West Semitic treaty practice, as
distinct from those current in Mesopotamia of the Old Babylonian period. The
sacrificial rite consists of "killing a donkey," *hayāram qaṭālum*,[39] or, as stated
in one case, "killing a donkey of peace," *hayāram ša salīmim qaṭālum*,
followed by taking an oath, *niš ilāni*.[40] By "killing a donkey" peace was

---

[35] A. K. Grayson, *Assyrian and Babylonian Chronicles* (TCS 5; Locust Valley, NY: Augustin,
1975) 158 I:1′–4′.

[36] Munn-Rankin, "Diplomacy," 85, 89, see also *CAD* L 84^b–85^a, 201^b.

[37] A. Falkenstein, *BO* 11 (1954) 114; Munn-Rankin, "Diplomacy," 90.

[38] Munn-Rankin, "Diplomacy," 91–92; see also *CAD* Ṣ 17^b, 223^b.

[39] M. Held, "Philological Notes on the Mari Covenant Rituals," *BASOR* 200 (1970) 32–37; add
now: *hayārī i niqṭul [ni]š ilē ina birīni i niškun* = "let us kill donkey foals, let us make an
oath—(sworn) by the life of the gods—between us" (S. Dalley, in *The Old Babylonian Tablets
from Tell al Rimah* [London: British School of Archaeology in Iraq, 1976] No. 1: 11–12; see also
lines 39–40).

[40] G. Dossin, "Les archives épistolaires du palais de Mari," *Syria* 49 (1938) 108:19–21.

established between the two parties concerned, one of them usually a West Semitic tribe, like the Haneans or the "Yaminites."

On another occasion[41] the animals sacrificed are a young dog, *mīrānum*, and she-goat, *hazzum* (not "lettuce," חסה, as previously translated[42]). Indeed, both the killing of a goat and the swearing of an oath are components of the treaty ceremony between Aban of Aleppo and Yarim-Lim of Alalakh, as described in the only treaty that has survived from the late eighteenth century: "Aban cut the neck of a sheep, saying (I swear that I will not) take back that which I gave thee," *niš ilāni zakir u kišad imēram iṭbuḫ.*[43] Another Alalakh document—not a treaty but a sale document that records the king of Alalakh's purchase of a village from another prince—reads "the neck of the sacrificial (or, literally 'a tabooed') lamb was cut."[44]

In contrast to these practices none of the treaty documents of the following centuries (i.e., the Second International Period) attests to a symbolic sacrificial ritual accompanying a treaty. Neither the Hittite treaties nor those from Ugarit or Alalakh mention a sacrifice. The lists of curses and divine witnesses were regarded as sufficiently powerful means to ensure the enforcement of the treaty. Nevertheless, there can be little doubt that some such practice as the symbolic killing of an animal during a treaty ceremony must have continued among the western Semites as part of their traditional tribal heritage. Thus, we find it in Arpad in northern Syria almost a thousand years later. In the treaty of Ashur-nirari V with Mati-ilu of Arpad (ca. 750 B.C.E.), the Assyrian overlord resorted to dramatic and extreme means—a vassal oath reinforced by powerful curses and an apotropaic ceremony. The following passage quoted in E. Reiner's masterful translation illustrates that ceremony.

> This spring lamb has been brought from its fold not for sacrifice, not for a banquet, not for a purchase, not for (divination concerning) a sick man, not to be slaughtered for [. . .]: it has been brought to sanction the treaty (*adê*) between Ashurnirari and Mati'ilu. If Mati'ilu sins against (this) treaty made under oath by the gods (*adê tamîti ilāni*) then, just as this spring lamb, brought from its fold, will not return to its fold, will not behold its fold again, alas, Mati'ilu, together with his sons, daughters, officials, and the people of his land [will be ousted] from his country, will not return to his country, and not behold his country again. This head is not the head of a lamb, it is the head of Mati'ilu, it is the head of his sons, his officials, and the people of his land. If Mati'ilu sins against this treaty, so may, just as the head of this spring lamb is torn off, and its knuckle placed in its mouth, [. . .], the head of Mati'ilu be torn off, and his sons [. . .]. This shoulder is not the shoulder of a spring lamb, it is the shoulder of Mati'ilu, it is the shoulder of his sons, his officials, and the people of his land be torn out. . . .[45]

[41] ARM 2 No. 37: 5; and cf. Held, "Philological Notes," 39–40.

[42] So G. E. Mendenhall, "Puppy and Lettuce in Northwest-Semitic Covenant Making," *BASOR* 133 (1954) 26–30; W. F. Albright in *ANET*³, 482.

[43] D. J. Wiseman, "Aban and Alalakh," *JCS* 12 (1958) 126:40–43.

[44] Wiseman, *AT* No. 54:16–18, so read by A. K. Draffkorn in *JCS* 13 (1959) 95 n. 11.

[45] *ANET*³, 532ᵃ–533ᵇ (= E. Weidner, "Der Staatsvertrag Aššurnirâris VI. von Assyrien mit Mati'ilu von Bît-Agusi," *AfO* 8 [1932–33] 18:10–34).

Evidently, as it has been often observed,[46] this ceremony fits in well with the "western tradition" of covenant making and may be compared with the killing of a donkey, as in the Mari Age, or with the shedding of the blood of a sacrificial animal, as in the treaty of Yarim-Lim and Aban from Alalakh. But such a ceremony was not an obligatory part of the treaty making even in the west, and it does not appear in the Aramaic treaties from Sefire, contemporary with the treaty of Ashur-nirari with Arpad.[47] It would seem, then, that the normal procedure was to swear an oath in the presence of gods or of their symbols and pronounce an imprecation. Only in extreme circumstances, apparently, was the cutting of an animal employed. When concluding his treaty with Mati'ilu of Arpad, the Assyrian king must have resorted to the irregular western—not Assyrian—procedure, since a major western center was involved, Arpad being a vital economic foothold during the Assyrian expansion to the west in the ninth and early eighth centuries.[48]

Turning briefly to the biblical evidence, one cannot help noting that only extraordinary circumstances (the release of slaves during the siege of Jerusalem) led Zedekiah to impose the "covenant between the pieces," described in Jeremiah 34. The violators of that covenant were forewarned that they would become "like the calf which they cut in two so as to pass between the halves" (Jer 34:18–19). The similarity of this imprecation with the Abrahamic covenant in Genesis 15 is well known and has frequently been adduced.[49]

We have thus emphasized the continuity of a custom—the sacrificial killing of an animal in treaty making—from the early eighteenth to the sixth centuries B.C.E., a custom typical of the lands west of the Euphrates and of the western Semites in general and not to be found—as far as we know—in Babylonian, Assyrian, or Hittite treaty practices.

At this point a comment on the Hebrew term כרת ברית ("cut a covenant") is called for. This term, as it has often been pointed out,[50] corresponds to גזר עדן in Aramaic and כרת אלת in Phoenician (the incantation from Arslan-Tash);[51] all three have in common the notion that the treaty or an oath is "cut" as against "bound," *rakāsu*, "established," *šakānu*, etc., said of *riksu/rikiltu*. Similarly, in Ugaritic, perhaps under the influence of western

---

[46] See, conveniently, in McCarthy, *Treaty and Covenant*, 54–55 (2d ed., 91–92); Weinfeld, "Deuteronomy," 102–7.

[47] J. A. Fitzmyer, *The Aramaic Inscriptions of Sefire* (Rome: Pontifical Biblical Institute, 1967) 120–25.

[48] Cf. J. D. Hawkins, "Jaḫan," *RLA* 5, 238–39; H. Tadmor, "Assyria and the West," *Unity and Diversity* (ed. H. Goedicke and J. J. M. Roberts; Baltimore: Johns Hopkins University, 1975) 37–38.

[49] Bickerman, "Couper une alliance," in *Studies* 1:5, 24; Pedersen, "Eid," 49–50; S. E. Loewenstamm, "Zur Traditionsgeschichte des Bundes zwischen den Stücken," *VT* 18 (1968) 503; Kutsch, *Verheissung und Gesetz*, 42–46.

[50] Recently by Kutsch, ibid., 48–49, and Cross, *Canaanite Myth*, 266–67.

[51] *KAI* No. 222:7; No. 27:8–9 (see F. M. Cross and R. J. Saley, *BASOR* 197 [1970] 44).

Akkadian, the term for imposing an obligation under (vassal) treaty is *št mṣmt l* "establish a bond with PN,"[52] *mṣmt* being a *maqṭal* formation from *ṣamādu* ("to tie," "to bind") synonymous with *rakāsu*.

Thus, the idiom "to cut a covenant" would be an isogloss that separates the western from the eastern, or Mesopotamian, treaty terminology in which compacts were "bound" or "established" but never "cut." That this cultural and linguistic isogloss was typical not only of the West Semites but also of the ancient Greeks has been recognized long ago. The Homeric ὅρκια τέμνειν ("to cut oaths") and ὅρκια πιστὰ τέμνειν ("to cut faithful oaths," i.e., to swear a solemn oath [and sacrifice]) are indeed undisputed counterparts to the ancient biblical and West Semitic practices described above.[53]

This brief interlude on the semantic distribution of "cutting a covenant" as against "binding" it cannot be ended without an equally brief comment on the etymology of ברית. The etymologies that have been suggested are: (1) from the root ברה I ("to eat"), hence בריה ("food," "meal") in 2 Sam 13:5, 7, 10; *běrît* is then a communal meal, partaken of upon swearing the oath;[54] (2) from Akkadian *barû* ("to look," "to see"), hence *běrît* is a testimonial that is seen and is therefore binding, an obligation or pledge;[55] (3) from Akkadian *birītu* ("bond," "fetters"), hence *běrît* is a bond.[56] None of these etymologies, certainly not the last, explains why the Hebrew ברית is *cut*, not "set" or "tied," as the Akkadian *birītu* would demand. Perhaps that is the

---

[52] The evidence comes from the juxtaposition between the two versions, the Ugaritic and the Akkadian, of the vassal treaty between Ugarit and Hatti: ll. 16–17: *tpllm mlk r[b mlk ht] mṣmt lnqmd [mlk Ugrt] št* ‖ ll. 16–19: *Šuppilulimma šarru rubû šar māt Ḫatti rikilta ana Niqmanda šar māt Ugarit akanna irkus*, "Shuppiluliuma the Great King, King of Hatti, now set (the following) treaty-obligations upon Niqmadda King of Ugarit" (M. Dietrich and O. Loretz, *WO* 3 [1966] 208, 218). There must have been a distinction made between *ana PN rikilta rakāsu* ("to lay vassal treaty obligations upon PN," e.g., *PRU* 4, 52:6; 83:63; 103:10) and *rikilta birit PN₁ u PN₂ rakāsu* ("to establish a treaty between PN₁ and PN₂," e.g., *PRU* 4, 154:4; 158:2). The latter usage obviously refers to a parity treaty. Similar distributions exist, as we know, in biblical Hebrew: in vassal treaties (e.g., Josh 9:6, 15; 1 Sam 11) the phrase כרת ברית ל is usually employed, the subject of כרת being the sovereign, whereas in parity treaties *both* parties are said to have "cut the covenant": Gen 21:27; 31:44; 1 Sam 18:3; 20:16; 23:18; 1 Kgs 5:26; and see L. Köhler, "Problems on the Study of the Language of the Old Testament," *JSS* 1 (1956) 4–6; Jepsen, "Berith," 162–64; Kutsch, *Verheissung und Gesetz*, 22–26, 53–58.

[53] Already Gesenius in the first edition of his *Thesaurus* (1835) noted the correspondence between ברית and *horkia temnein*. For recent discussions see: Bickerman, "Couper une alliance," 133ff; J. F. Priest, "Ὅρκια in the *Iliad* and Consideration of a Recent Theory," *JNES* 23 (1964) 48–56; Weinfeld, "Covenant Terminology," 192; "Loyalty Oath," 400.

[54] E. Meyer, *Die Israeliten und ihre Nachbarstämme* (Halle a/S.: M. Niemyer, 1906) 558 n. 1; and more recently Köhler, "Problems," 4.

[55] First suggested by H. Zimmern in *Die Keilinschriften und das Alte Testament*, by E. Schrader, 3rd ed. (Berlin: Reuther and Reichard, 1903) 606, more recently by Kutsch, *Verheissung und Gesetz*, 32–39.

[56] W. F. Albright, "The Hebrew Expression for 'Making a Covenant' in Pre-Israelite Documents," *BASOR* 121 (1951) 22 n. 6; O. Loretz, "ברית—Bond—Bund," *VT* 16 (1966) 239–41; M. Weinfeld, "*Běrit*—Covenant vs. Obligation," *Bib* 56 (1975) 122–23.

reason why M. Noth[57] and G. R. Driver[58] independently suggested that *bĕrît* should be derived from the preposition *birit* ("between") in Akkadian, i.e., a treaty where the parties stand *between* the pieces of a sacrificial animal. A direct link would thus be established with *hayāram qaṭālum*, the killing of a donkey in Mari, and the covenant ceremonies of Genesis 15 and Jeremiah 34. One can accept the idea, though not the etymology. It would be rather strange if a preposition had become a key term or that an ellipsis had been misunderstood by its users. Therefore the most adequate etymology, I believe, would be to derive *bĕrît* from *bry* or *br'* in biblical Hebrew, said of cutting wood and corpses (Josh 17:15, 18; Ezek 23:47) and synonymous with כרת ("to cut"); the interchange in weak third radicals is well attested in Semitic. The credit for this suggestion goes to M. Held, who points out that this etymology is over seven hundred years old;[59] it was first suggested by Ibn Janah, the noted Jewish philologist of the eleventh century in Spain and was followed by Qimhi and Ibn Ezra.[60] In its *Namenbildung*, ברית is analogous to שבית (e.g., Num 21:29; Ezek 16:53), which likewise does not form a plural. It is then an old, frozen form whose original meaning had already been forgotten in the first millennium.[61]

To end our discussion of the material pertaining to the second millennium one further problem should be considered: Were the alliances mentioned so frequently in the political correspondence of the Mari Age verbal agreements, or were they actually put into writing? We have already noted several references to "the document of the 'touching of the throat,'" "the document (with an oath) by the life of the gods," "the document of the oath (and curse)."[62] However, not a single treaty document has so far come to

---

[57] M. Noth, "Das alttestamentliche Bundschliessen im Lichte einer Mari-Textes," *Gesammelte Studien zum Alten Testament* (München: Kaiser, 1957) 147–98.

[58] G. R. Driver in *JSS* 12 (1967) 107–8.

[59] Private communication and letter, 5 October 1980.

[60] Ibn Janah, *Kitāb al-uṣūl*, p. 114; Qimḥi, *Lexicon*, p. 50ª; Ibn-Ezra, Commentary on Gen 6:18 (second etymology). I am grateful to Prof. Moshe Held for this information.

[61] Lastly, in this connection, the extrabiblical attestations of *bĕrît* should be recalled: (a) The enigmatic TAR *be-ri-ti* in the heading of two tablets from Qatna, dating to ca. 1400 B.C.E., published by J. Bottero ("Autres Textes de Qatna," *RA* 44 [1950] 112, 114). W. F. Albright was the first to connect this with Hebrew ברית and to read the logogram TAR as *nakāsu/parāsu*, i.e., "cut, divide" (*BASOR* 121 [1951] 22), but the question is still open (see also J. A. Soggin, "Akkadisch TAR *beriti* und Hebräisch ברית כרת," *VT* 18 [1968] 210–15). (b) In several Egyptian documents from the reign of Rameses III, the defeated Libyans are portrayed as saying to each other: "Let us make a *brt* with [. . .]" and "they all make a *brt*, bringing their tribute." (See K. A. Kitchen, "Egypt, Ugarit, Qatna and Covenant," *UF* 11 [1979] 453.) Most authorities (ibid., 453 nn. 8–12) have consented that *brt* is a West Semitic loanword. Therefore, it could be connected with ברית and be understood as "compact among tribal groups and defeated people" (ibid., 457). This evidence would then be very close in time and social background to the arrival of the Israelites in Canaan, to the hill country of Shechem, where אל ברית, "El of the Covenant," had been the chief divinity (Judg 9:46).

[62] *ṭuppi lipit napištim* (e.g., ARM 2 No. 77:5); *ṭuppi niš ili* (e.g., ARM 1 No. 37:23); *ṭuppi ša*

light from any of the major Old Babylonian archives, including Mari.[63] Is this just an "accident of the spade"? Or could one perhaps surmise that among the rulers of the second millennium, in "a society of gentlemen," treaties were usually concluded orally—the symbolic ritual and the oath being considered sufficient guarantees—and that only specific and complex matters were put into writing and would thus be the exceptions rather than the rule? Supporting evidence for this suggestion comes from a recent study on the Babylonian marriage contract, the *riksātum*, which has convincingly demonstrated that the term does not necessarily indicate a written document; all it means is a "binding agreement, pact, covenant," or, in a broad sense, "contract, *verba solemnia*."[64]

And indeed, it was not in Babylonia but in the west that international treaties, especially those between major and minor powers, were commemorated in writing. The majority of the treaty documents from the ancient Near East that have survived originated in northern Syria and Anatolia, lands of the Hurrian and later of the Hittite supremacy. The oldest international treaty documents from that area are the parity treaties between Kizzuwatna—the Hurrian-Luwian state in southeastern Anatolia—and Hatti[65] and those between Kizzuwatna and Alalakh (about 1500 B.C.E. or slightly earlier).[66] Also from Alalakh comes another parity treaty between its king (Niqmepa) and that of the neighboring Tunip.[67] Irrespective of the question of what might have been the specific North Syrian (West Akkadian) contribution to the terminology of these and similar treaties, there can be hardly any doubt that it was in Hittite Anatolia that the treaty document was developed, becoming the sole basis for international relations in the lands encompassed by the Hittite empire.

Over thirty different treaty documents, Hittite and Akkadian—some still unedited—have come to light from the archives of Boghazkoy, Ras Shamra and Alalakh (level IV). Few of them are parity treaties; the majority belong to the vassal treaty type in which the bond—sometimes bilateral—between the overlord, "the Sun, the Great King, King of Hatti," and his dependents is reinforced by blessings and curses and sanctioned by divine witnesses.[68] However, not only treaties but also other very detailed provisions

---

mamīti or *ša rikilti u ša mamīti* (several references: *CAD* M I 190–91).

[63] The decree published by S. Greengus in *Old Babylonian Tablets from Ishchali and Vicinity* (Nederlands Historisch-Archaeologisch Institut, Te Istanbul, 1979) No. 3, 26, is not a political treaty and is therefore not discussed here.

[64] S. Greengus, "The Old Babylonian Marriage Contract," *JAOS* 89 (1969) 508–16.

[65] H. Otten, "Ein althethitischer Vertrag mit Kizzuvatna," *JCS* 5 (1951) 129–32; G. Meyer, "Zwei neue Kizzuwatna-Verträge," *MIO* 1 (1953) 108–29.

[66] Wiseman, *AT* No. 3 (= now also in E. Reiner's translation, *ANET³*, 532).

[67] Wiseman, *AT* No. 2 (= *ANET³*, 531–32).

[68] See Korošec, *Hethitische Staatsverträge*, 1–11; A. Goetze, *Kleinasien* (2nd ed.; Handbuch der Altertumswissenschaft III.1.2.2.1; München: Beck, 1957) 95–101; Kestemont, *Droit international*, 91–114.

were made in Hatti under oath and put into writing. These include instructions to temple and court officials and to commanders of fortresses throughout the empire. Those high functionaries of the state, as Goetze succinctly describes it, "are admonished to fulfil their duties and forewarned not to enter into treasonable activities against king and dynasty." Moreover, these functionaries "when taking office had to swear an oath like soldiers serving in the army and when doing so placed themselves under the vengeance of the gods invoked. The main theme of these oaths is the plea to remain loyal toward the person of the king and his direct issue."[69]

The prominence of the loyalty oath is especially evident in Phoenicia and Canaan, then under the Egyptian domination. Unlike the Hittite imperial system, in which the suzerain undertook an obligation—often under oath—to protect his vassal, the Egyptian system postulated—at least in theory—unilateral relationship.[70] The Amarna letters indicate that many, if not all, of the petty kings of Canaan swore loyalty oaths to the Pharaoh and were nominally his servants. They owed their throne to the Egyptian overlord, whose grace they repeatedly recall. Still, most significantly, the Amarna correspondence, though replete with references to vassaldom, never mentions a treaty document. We must therefore conclude that swearing a loyalty oath, which was reaffirmed from time to time, was considered a sufficient bond by the Egyptian suzerain and the Canaanite vassal alike. Evidently, the Pharaoh, the living god, did not have to sign treaties with his servants and vassals; to consolidate their fidelity he made them swear an oath, which might have been periodically repeated.[71] So did, for example, Thutmosis III to the Canaanites at Megiddo and Amenophis II to the Syrian princes at Qadesh: "They were made to take the oath and all their children as well."[72] Often the vassal's children were taken to Egypt as hostages, a rather effective tool to secure the loyalty of the Canaanite princes. For domination of this kind no treaty was needed and, in fact, none ever existed.

[69] A. Goetze, "State and Society of the Hittites," *Neuere Hethiterforschung* (see above, n. 9) 32; see also E. von Schuler, *Hethitische Dienstanweisungen für höhere Hof- und Staatsbeamte*, AfO Beiheft 10 (1951); and A. Goetze in *ANET*, 207–11, 353–54.

[70] Of special significance in this connection are the following studies: M. Liverani, "Contrasti e confluenze di concezioni politiche nell eta di El-Amarna," *RA* 61 (1967) 1–18, and W. L. Moran's as yet unpublished response on the political ideas in the Amarna Letters. I am grateful to Prof. Moran for putting the manuscript of his study at my disposal.

[71] See J. A. Wilson, "The Oath in Ancient Egypt," *JNES* 7 (1948) 129–36; K. Baer, "The Oath *sdf3-tryt* in Papyrus Lee I.1," *JEA* 50 (1969) 178–79; D. Lorton, *The Judicial Terminology of International Relations in Egyptian Texts Through Dyn. XVIII.* (Baltimore: Johns Hopkins University, 1974) 176–79; S. Ahituv, "The Alliance-Oath of the Canaanite Vassals to the Pharaoh," in *Studies in Bible and the Ancient Near East* (= S. E. Loewenstamm Jubilee Volume, ed. Y. Avishur and J. Blau; Jerusalem: Rubinstein, 1978) Hebrew section, 55–60, English section, 185.

[72] J. A. Wilson in *ANET*, 246ª (and see 238ª).

The First Millennium

Turning now to biblical Israel, we find that there can be little doubt that alliances between kings of equal ranks as well as the imposition of suzerainty—perhaps without any written treaty document—were known to the Israelites from the early stages of the formation of their state. One wonders to what degree the preceding Canaanite tradition of the loyalty oath to the Egyptian overlord affected the practice of the Israelites. Were they influenced by the local custom of contracting oral alliances and swearing loyalty oaths to Pharaoh, their suzerain, the sole owner of the land? Though we have no definite evidence, it may nevertheless be suggested that the customs of the semiautonomous Canaanite cities had an impact upon those current in early Israelite society.

Some of these Canaanite cities like Gibeon and her neighbors are reported to have concluded a "nonaggression pact" with the oncoming Israelites. Though aetiological in character and narrated under archaic guise, the story (Joshua 9) preserves some old, no doubt authentic, memories.[73] The pact between the Gibeonites and the Israelites resembles certain Hittite vassal treaties, especially those of the *kuiruana* type, in which also the suzerain undertakes upon himself mutual obligations under oath.[74] In another early monarchial tale (1 Sam 11:3) we hear that the king of the Ammonites agreed to conclude a vassal treaty with the people of Jabesh-Gilead, which he besieged, on condition that each one of them be maimed.[75] In the historical accounts of the monarchial period we read of several treaties between the king of Israel and Israel's neighbors. David and Solomon negotiated with the king of Tyre on a parity basis (2 Kgs 5:15–25), and at a certain stage parity treaty ברית אחים was concluded between them (cf. Amos 1:9). David imposed his sovereignty over several neighboring states, which became his tribute bearers (2 Sam 8:2, 6, 14). Similarly, Ahab imposed dominion on Mesha, King of Moab; the tribute of Mesha is even specifically recorded in 2 Kings 3. The rulers of Damascus and Samaria concluded treaties and violated them. The king of Judah bribed the king of Damascus to abrogate his treaty with Israel and come to Judah's rescue (1 Kgs

---

[73] A. Malamat, "The Doctrines of Causality in Hittite and Biblical Historiography," *VT* 5 (1955) 1–12; F. C. Fensham, "The Treaty between Israel and the Gibeonites," *BA* 27 (1964) 96–100 and in *BAR* 3, 121–26; J. M. Grintz, "The Treaty of Joshua with the Gibeonites," *JAOS* 86 (1966) 103–26; but see the critique of M. Haran, *Ages and Institutions in the Bible* (Tel-Aviv: Am-Oved, 1972) 201–17 (Hebrew).

[74] See Goetze, *Kleinasien*, 2d ed., 98 n. 7, p. 99; Kestemont, *Droit international*, 610 n. 39.

[75] A variant version of this story is preserved in a non-Masoretic Text of Samuel from Cave 4 at Qumran; see F. M. Cross, "The Ammonite Oppression of the Tribes of Gad and Reuben; Missing Verses from 1 Samuel 11 Found in 4QSamuel[a]," *The Hebrew and Greek Texts of Samuel* (ed. E. Tov; Jerusalem: Academon, 1980) 105–15 (reprinted from *History, Historiography, and Interpretation* [see below, n. 95]). See also P. K. McCarter, Jr., *1 Samuel* (AB; Garden City: Doubleday, 1980) 198–99.

15:18–20). In short, treaty making of every kind was a recognized custom in the area. Admittedly, however, we do not know whether any of these treaties was put into writing or, if so, what their written form was. Were they brief, as in Alalakh and Ugarit, or elaborate, as in Hatti?

In the quest for the origins of these treaties, and especially of the covenant between Yahweh and Israel, the OT scholar naturally turned to the Hittite vassal treaties, considering them the prototype of the later biblical phenomenon. More recently, however, the vassal treaties of Esarhaddon, King of Assyria, have become the point of departure for the comparison with the biblical covenant, especially as they are reflected in the book of Deuteronomy. Since a major part of the political history of Israel and Judah is tied up with the history of the Assyrian empire, it has been widely assumed that the practice, terminology, and formulation of the Assyrian vassal treaties, in addition to being known in Samaria and Jerusalem, were paramount in shaping the theology and language of the biblical covenant. It is for this reason that I propose to reexamine the history and transformation of the so-called Assyrian vassal treaty and comment upon questions of terminology and origins. Our comments will be limited to those issues that pertain to the west and relate in some way to biblical covenant research.

The term "Assyrian vassal treaty" should be used with great care. The main term for 'vassal treaty, adê, actually refers to a loyalty oath sworn by an Assyrian vassal.[76] It is true that riksu (u) mamītu—the term for vassal treaty in the second millennium—was replaced by adê (u) mamītu in the Assyrian empire. Yet adê is not an exact equivalent of riksu ("bond," hence "covenant"). In Assyrian usage adê is almost synonymous with the mamītu ("oath," "imprecation"; compare כרת אלת in Phoenician[77]). Likewise, it is "imposed" (šakānu), "taken" (ṣabātu), "sworn in" (tummû), etc. The concept is thus one-sided: the Assyrian sovereign does not "bind" himself—as the Hittite sovereign often did—but demands unconditional commitment on the part of his vassal and, later, of his subject in Assyria proper.[78]

---

[76] I. J. Gelb, BO 19 (1962) 161. The word is plurale tantum; the singular form adû of CAD A I 131 is merely a reconstruction, whereas the two alleged Middle Assyrian singular forms quoted in AHW 14ª (adû I) must be corrected. The first, a-di-a (KAJ 83:18), is to be emended, according to CAD A I 99ª, to a-di-a-<na>, i.e., adannu ("appointed time"); the second, a-di-an-ni (EAT No. 15:9), is to be read, in accordance with CAD A I 134ª, as adi anni ("until now").

[77] KAI No. 27:8–9 and n. 51, above.

[78] It should be noted also that adû B of CAD A I 134–35, translated there "majesty(?), power(?)," does not have to be classified as a separate entry. The lexicographical evidence adduced there shows that adê ša šarri, "King's oath," i.e., the oath taken by the life of the (reigning) monarch, corresponds to the formula niš šarri—oath sworn by the life of the king—common in Akkadian (CAD N I 291). What apparently happened is that toward the close of the Neo-Assyrian period, and mostly in the Neo-Babylonian period, the formula adê ša šarri became hypostatized and occasionally replaced niš šarri in legal usage. See also K. H. Deller, "Zur Terminologie neuassyrischer Urkunden," WZKM 57 (1961) 31–33, and J. Renger's review

No longer can there be any doubt that the term *adê* is not indigenous to Akkadian. Borrowed from Aramaic עדי (cst. pl. of עדן),[79] it quickly gained prominence in the Assyrian imperial usage, supplanting the traditional terms of the second millennium discussed above, such as *riksu, rikiltu, mamītu, ṭubtu, sullumû*.[80] These terms for treaty were also employed in the Assyrian chronistic tradition to describe the parity relations between Assyria and Babylonia from the fifteenth century to the beginning of the eighth century.[81]

No treaties, but one, have survived to illustrate these relations, oscillating periodically between border skirmishes, limited or full-scale wars, to "total peace": *ṭubta u sullumê gamru*.[82] The single treaty document surviving from that period (last quarter of ninth century) is a fragment, encased in stone, of a treaty between Shamshi-Adad V, son of Shalmaneser III, and Marduk-zakir-shum of Babylon.[83] Written in the Babylonian script it must

---

article of D. B. Weissberg, *Guild Structure and Political Allegiance in Early Achaemenid Mesopotamia* (New Haven: Yale University, 1967), *JAOS* 91 (1971) 496–97.

[79] I have elaborated on this and other Aramaic loanwords and institutions of the Neo-Assyrian period in "The Aramaization of Assyria: Aspects of Western Impact," in *Mesopotamien und seine Nachbarn* (Proceedings of the 25e Rencontre assyriologique internationale, Berlin, 1978, in press). The biblical cognates of עדן are עדות and once עדים (so in Isa 33:8 according to 1QIsᵃ; in MT: ערים), and see Fitzmyer, *Sefire*, 23–24.

[80] *sulummû* (once, *ṭūbu u sullummû*; see A. R. Millard, *Iraq* 30 [1968] 109:17) occurs, though not very frequently, in the royal inscriptions of the late eighth to seventh centuries; *mamītu* (often in the hendiadys *adê u mamītu*) is quite common in the royal inscriptions; *riksu* is no longer employed to designate treaty in a political sense, though it is used as a term for "bond" or "agreement" in documents of various types; *rikiltu*, however, had undergone a very distinctive transformation: it developed into a derogatory term, denoting "bond of conspiracy," hence "conspiracy" in general, just like קשר, its semantic equivalent in biblical Hebrew (Luckenbill, *Sennacherib*, 42:26; 64:24; Borger, *Asarhaddon* 13:5 and p. 41 n. to line 24). Finally, the *riksu* documents of the late Middle Assyrian palace-edicts (E. Weidner, "Hof- und Harems-Erlasse assyrischer Könige," *AfO* 17 [1956] 257–93) were not treaties or loyalty oaths but ordinances and regulations imposed by the king on his courtiers, mainly eunuchs, restricting their motions within the palace.

[81] Our main source describing these relations is an early eighth-century composition known as the "Synchronistic History," which was intended to be incised upon a monument marking the boundary between Assyria and Babylonia. Two such, as yet unpublished, boundary monuments—*tahūmu* in Assyrian (cf. תחום in Aramaic and late Hebrew)—came recently to light from eastern Anatolia. Though propagandistic and partisan in nature, the "Synchronistic History" is of great value, as the historical information there derives from contemporary authentic sources, most probably an Assyrian chronicle, focused on the Assyro-Babylonian relations (see Grayson, *Chronicles*, 51–56, and Tadmor, "Observations on Assyrian Historiography" in *Essays on the Ancient Near East* [J. J. Finkelstein Memorial Volume; Memoirs of the Connecticut Academy of Arts and Sciences 19; ed. M. de Jong Ellis; Hamden: Archon Books, 1977] 210–11). In another source concerned with the Assyro-Babylonian diplomatic relations, the king of Babylonia is admonished for not having kept the *rikiltu* and the *mamītu* and thus incurring upon himself and his country divine wrath and terrestrial punishment (see now P. B. Machinist, "The Epic of Tukulti-Ninurta I" [Ph.D. dissertation, Yale, 1978] 159–61).

[82] Grayson, *Chronicles*, 166:18; 167:21.

[83] In E. Weidner, "Der Staatsvertrag Aššurnirâris VI. von Assyrien mit Mati'ilu von Bît-Agusi," *AfO* 8 (1932–33) 27–29.

be the Babylonian version of the treaty, since it contains the stipulation that the Assyrian king obliges himself to surrender fugitives and report of any plots against Marduk-zakir-shum. Also the list of gods in the oath section, with Marduk and Nabu preceding Enlil and Ninlil, and the traditional Babylonian curses closely resembling those of the code of Hammurabi,[84] reflect the Babylonian attitude. Obviously, the document expresses the Babylonian supremacy, short-lived as it happened to be,[85] but since it is badly broken one cannot know whether the term employed there was *riksu/rikiltu* or *adê*.

It is important to remember that the entire corpus of the extant Assyrian *adê* documents is exceedingly small. It consists only of one complete text, two incomplete, and four or five fragments, some of them unpublished. The only complete text, the so-called Vassal Treaty of Esarhaddon, with its duplicates, which is the longest and, no doubt, the most eloquent among the vassal treaties of the ancient Near East, has been regarded— though without ample reasons—as paradigmatic for the whole genre. The earliest Assyrian *adê* document attested so far is the vassal treaty imposed about 755 B.C.E. by Ashur-nirari V upon Mati-ilu of Arpad.[86] Though only part of the text has survived, there is still enough there to give some insight into the structure and content of an Assyrian *adê* document concerned with the west. It begins with powerful imprecations and accompanying substitution rites, followed by apotropaic curses—all part of Mati-ilu's oath-taking ceremony. It ends (cols. V–VI) with a list of additional powerful curses that would befall Mati-ilu and his successors if they violated the *adê* (oaths) and with a list of gods, witnesses to the treaty. The only two stipulations that survived (cols. III–IV) are concerned with Mati-ilu's obligation to extradite Assyrian fugitives—probably political refugees—and to render military aid to Ashur-nirari when ordered to do so.

Another treaty fragment from the reign of Ashur-nirari, published recently by A. R. Millard, also contains the extradition clause aimed at any runaway instigator of rebellion.[87] A similar clause opens the text of Sefire III, one of the three Aramaic stelae containing the 'dy concluded between the same Mati-ilu of Arpad and בר גאיה, king of the still enigmatic כתך.[88] The other stipulations in the Aramaic stelae—the obligation to safeguard the royal succession of בר גאיה, to avenge any murder of his successors and to help reestablish his heir upon the ancestral throne, to report any rumor of a plot against בר גאיה[89]—are all in line with those of the Hittite vassal

[84] R. Borger, "Marduk-zakir-šumi und der Kodex Hammurapi," *Or* 34 (1965) 168–69.

[85] J. A. Brinkman, *Political History of Post-Kassite Babylonia* (AnOr 43; Rome: Pontifical Biblical Institute, 1968) 205–13.

[86] See above, n. 45.

[87] A. R. Millard, "Fragments of Historical Texts from Nineveh," *Iraq* 32 (1970) 174.

[88] J. A. Fitzmyer, *Sefîre*, 96–100; but see N. Na'aman, "Looking for *KTK*," *WO* 9 (1978) 227–28.

[89] Fitzmyer, *Sefîre*, 98:10–19; 100:21–23.

treaties. Thus, by way of the Aramaic intermediaries, the Neo-Assyrian *adê* documents continue the highly developed Syro-Anatolian and possibly also North Mesopotamian second millennium traditions.[90]

The loyalty oath form and terminology reached Assyria in a most appropriate time. The reign of Tiglath-pileser III inaugurated a series of new political relations, annexations, and subordinations—total or partial—on a very large scale. It was mostly in the lands west of the Euphrates, where the international relations were traditionally sealed by treaties and loyalty oaths, that Tiglath-pileser III[91] and particularly Sargon II imposed the *adê*-type vassal treaties. Very eloquent in that respect are the historical inscriptions of Sargon. They enumerate the rebels: the king of Carchemish "sinned" against the *adê* of the great gods, sent messages of hostilities and showed disregard for Assyria; the king of Shinuhtu in southern Anatolia forsook the *adê* and discontinued his tribute; Merodach-Baladan, the Chaldean, rebuked the *adê* of the great gods (*adê mamīt ilāni rabûti*), discontinued his tribute, made alliance with the king of Elam, and incited the desert tribes to rebel against Assyria. With the exception of Merodach-Baladan, all were punished accordingly; they themselves were captured and their countries were annexed to Assyria. The full formula of the treaty violation is applied in connection with Urzana, the king of Musasir. He is named "an evildoer and transgressor of divine oath, not submissive to my majesty, he sinned against the *adê* of Aššur, Šamaš, Nabu and Marduk and revolted against me."[92] Ursa (= Rusa), King of Urartu, is accused of having transgressed the borders set up by Shamash and Marduk and of violating the *mamītu* of Ashur. In contrast, Sargon himself is praised as a king "who abhors lie, who safeguards truth, does not transgress the borders set up by Ashur and Shamash." Thus,

---

[90] See the extensive summary of D. J. McCarthy in the second ed. of *Treaty and Covenant*, 122–53.

[91] E.g., Samsi, the queen of the Arabs, forsook "the oath sworn by Shamash" (*mamīt Šamaš*); her country was therefore invaded, her camp was set on fire, and she, "like a wild onager, escaped to the desert, the place of thirst" (see, provisionally, *ANET*, 383[b], 384[a]; more in my forthcoming edition of the Inscriptions of Tiglath-pileser III).

[92] A. G. Lie, *The Inscriptions of Sargon II King of Assyria, Part 1: The Annals* (Paris: Geuthner, 1929) 10:68, 72–73; 42:264–67. It should be noted that in these instances, and in many others, the king of Assyria appeals to his own gods—usually with a prayer—before arranging to punish the rebellious transgressor of the loyalty oath. Obviously, Ashur and Shamash, as well as the other Mesopotamian gods, were invoked as divine witnesses to safeguard the imprecation clauses. The problem of whether the local gods of the vassal king were also invoked in the written *adê* document is still unresolved for lack of conclusive evidence. However, it could be argued that except for the treaty with Baal of Tyre—which is a commercial treaty and hence an exception (below n. 103)—there is so far no definite proof that the local gods of the vassal not venerated by Assyria were invoked in the *adê* oaths. Yet, Adad of Aleppo, listed in the concluding oath formula of the vassal treaty with Arpad (above, n. 45), was considered, apparently from the second millennium onward, as a Mesopotamian deity and was revered by the Assyrian king (see the account of Shalmaneser III's campaign in his sixth year; *ANET*, 279b).

the king of Assyria claims that he is respectful of his obligations and does not encroach without just reasons upon the territory of his neighbors—in this case, the kingdom of Urartu.[93]

Coming to the historical inscriptions of Sennacherib, one notes that the enemies of Assyria, who admittedly rebelled and were subsequently punished, are never accused of breaking the loyalty oath. Only once is *adê* mentioned in his annals—in connection with Padi, King of Eqron.[94] However, it was obviously Sargon, not Sennacherib, who imposed upon Padi the Assyrian loyalty oath. Though one should always keep in mind that the absence of any references to the *adê* in Sennacherib's historical inscriptions may be owing to a change in scribal and historiographical conventions, still it is not unlikely that the text should be taken at its face value and that it actually reflects historical reality.

In marked contrast, in the reign of Esarhaddon every imposition of Assyrian suzerainty came to be expressed in terms of the *adê* oath, and every rebellion was considered an abrogation of these oaths. Moreover, at that very time there was a significant transformation in the use of the *adê* in Assyria proper: the loyalty oath was applied not only to foreign but also to internal relations: it came to express the loyal relationship between the emperor and his subjects in cases of irregular succession. To judge from the document, which we may call "Esarhaddon's *apologia*,"[95] this was first attested already in the latter years of Sennacherib. Assembling his sons, courtiers, and "the people of Assyria, rank and file," Sennacherib made them swear a loyalty oath to Esarhaddon, who was not in the line of succession:

> I was (indeed) the(ir) youngest (brother) among my elder brothers, (but) my own father . . . has chosen me—in due form and in the presence of all my brothers— saying: "This is the son to (be elevated to) the position of a successor of mine." . . . He called together the people of Assyria, young and old, my brothers (and all) the male descendants of (the family of) my father and made them take a solemn oath in the presence of (the images of) the gods of Assyria . . . in order to secure my succession.[96]

Indeed, it seems that extraordinary means were needed to legitimize this irregular succession. Sennacherib's decision must have created dissatisfaction among the royal princes, a feeling that was later to break out into open

---

[93] F. Thureau-Dangin, *Une relation de la huitième campagne de Sargon* (Paris: Geuthner, 1912) 25:156; 48:309–11.

[94] D. D. Luckenbill, *The Annals of Sennacherib* (OIP 2; Chicago: University of Chicago, 1924) 31:74 (= A. L. Oppenheim in *ANET*, 287^b).

[95] R. Borger, *Die Inschriften Asarhaddons Königs von Assyrien* (AfO, Beiheft 9; Graz, 1956) 39–45; and see now: Tadmor, "Autobiographical Apology in the Royal Assyrian Literature," forthcoming in *History, Historiography, and Interpretation: Studies in Biblical and Cuneiform Literatures* (Papers of the Institute of Advanced Studies, Hebrew University, Jerusalem; ed. H. Tadmor and M. Weinfeld).

[96] A. L. Oppenheim's translation, *ANET*, 289.

rebellion, culminating in the assassination of Sennacherib in 681 by Arda-mulišši (אדרמלך of 2 Kgs 19:37), probably his second oldest son.[97]

Surprisingly enough, a fragment of the actual *adê* document concluded by Sennacherib on behalf of his successor corroborates Esarhaddon's story, for which it was our only source until now.[98] We should be reminded that Sennacherib's father himself was not in the direct line of succession, having seized the throne from the line of Tiglath-pileser III, who in turn was not the rightful heir to the Assyrian throne. It would seem then that, well aware of the dangers, Sennacherib appointed an heir to the throne still in his life-time and resorted to a ceremonial imposition of the *adê* upon the royal house, court, and people. As the available evidence seems to suggest, it was the first time in the history of Assyria that the court and the citizenry were obliged to take a loyalty oath to the heir apparent. The originally western form of the loyalty oath with its provisions to safeguard dynastic succession must have answered the needs of the Assyrian monarchy, and thus in the eighth to seventh centuries the *adê* emerged as a powerful tool in the service of the monarchy.

Esarhaddon repeated, but much more effectively, what his father had done toward the close of his life. Fortunately we possess numerous letters written to the king by his astrologers, advisers, and state functionaries; and with the current advance in our understanding of the Neo-Assyrian dialect—owing mainly to the contributions of K. Deller and S. Parpola—we can make proper use of this important evidence. Esarhaddon's personality, as it emerges from the correspondence,[99] is that of a haunted king, obsessed by fears of sickness, treachery, and conspiracy. The memory of the assassina-tion of his own father would be enough to trouble a less superstitious, more stable person. To safeguard his throne, Esarhaddon constantly resorted to omens, checking and rechecking them. His main concern was his own safety and the safety of his dynasty. For that purpose an extreme step was taken. He appointed—"during his own lifetime"—two sons to succeed him: Ashur-banipal, the future king of Assyria and the empire, and Shamash-shum-ukin as the future king of Babylonia. Though Shamash-shum-ukin was older[100] than Ashurbanipal and had a priority in the claim to the throne of Assyria,

---

[97] See now S. Parpola, "The Murderer of Sennacherib," *Death in Mesopotamia* (Proceedings of the 26ᵉ Rencontre assyriologique internationale, Copenhagen, 1979 [Mesopotamia 8; ed. B. Alster; Copenhagen: Akademisk Førlag, 1980]) 171–82.

[98] E. Ebeling, *Stiftungen und Vorschriften für Assyrische Tempel* (Berlin: Akademie-Verlag, 1954) 9, No. 2.

[99] S. Parpola, *Letters from Assyrian Scholars to the Kings Esarhaddon and Aššurbanipal*, Part 1: Texts (AOAT 5/1; Neukirchen-Vluyn: Neukirchener Verlag, 1970).

[100] Parpola, *Letters from Assyrian Scholars*, No. 129:3–13: "Good health (to the King) my God! . . . You have girded a son of yours with a diadem and entrusted him the kingship of Assyria; your eldest son you have put to the kingship of Babylon, you have placed the first to your right, the second to your left side." (Compare Gen 47:13–14.)

Ashurbanipal was the beloved grandson of the queen mother, Naqia-Zakutu, Sennacherib's widow and the first lady of the empire.

In the spring of 672, in a state ceremony, loyalty oaths to the emperor and his immediate successors were imposed upon the courtiers and state functionaries, including the scribes who compiled the *adê* documents.[101] Somewhat later the oaths were imposed on the chieftains—now Assyrian functionaries—of the distant provinces of Media, areas that constituted a natural refuge for any possible contender to the throne; these chieftains came to express their allegiance on the occasion of the extraordinary installation of the heir apparent.[102] Outstanding as literary and legal masterpieces, these *adê* documents of Esarhaddon, with their lengthy, exorbitant maledictions, should not be considered typical examples of the Assyrian vassal treaty. On the contrary, they were born of necessity, resulting from an extraordinary situation—an exception rather than the rule. Neither can another document from the same time, the *adê* of Ba'al, King of Tyre, imposed by Esarhaddon,[103] be regarded as a typical vassal treaty. It is an unusual, and so far unparalleled, document concerned with questions of trading rights and maritime law specific to the "Tyrian problem" under Esarhaddon and Ashurbanipal. We may call it a commercial vassal treaty— vassal in the sense that it was one-sided and the king of Tyre was not free to reject it. Except for the term *adê*, it has very little to do with the other *adê* documents of the period. The closest parallel would be the maritime treaties between Rome and Carthage.[104]

The form and the style of the other surviving vassal treaties—all extremely fragmentary—show a few more common features. These treaties are: the fragment dealing with Yauta', the king of the Arabian tribe of Qedar, from the reign of Ashurbanipal;[105] and several unpublished fragments put at my disposal by S. Parpola.[106] Most of these fragments, including the one published by A. R. Millard,[107] share a few points in common with the vassal treaty of Ashur-nirari V and those of Esarhaddon: the dynastic clause, the obligation to extradite to Assyria any fugitive (designated as a "runaway slave"), and the provision to report to the suzerain whatever the

---

[101] Parpola, *Letters from Assyrian Scholars*, Nos. 1 and 2.

[102] Wiseman, *Vassal Treaties*, 4; 82; and see Cogan, *Imperialism and Religion*, 47.

[103] Borger, *Asarhaddon*, §69; E. Reiner in *ANET*³, 533–34; G. Pettinato, "I rapporto politici di Tiro con d'Assyria alla luce del 'Trattato tra Asarhaddon e Baal,'" *Revista degli studi fenici* 3 (1975) 145–60.

[104] *Polyb.* III 22, 8 (from 509/8 B.C.E.); 24, 12 (from 306 B.C.E.), and see F. W. Walbank, *A Historical Commentary on Polybius*, 1 (Oxford: Clarendon, 1957) 346.

[105] K. Deller and S. Parpola, "Ein Vertrag Assurbanipals mit dem arabischen Stamm Qedar," *Or* 37 (1968) 464–66. See now I. Eph'al, *The Ancient Arabs* (Jerusalem: Magnes Press, 1982) 146–56.

[106] I am grateful to Prof. Simo Parpola for having allowed me to study these fragments and to mention them here.

[107] Above, n. 87.

vassal had "heard or seen." This provision was effectively imposed throughout the empire in the age of Esarhaddon and Ashurbanipal—the "king's eyes
and ears" are frequently mentioned in the royal correspondence.[108] In fact,
at least one conspiracy against Esarhaddon was detected by these "eyes and
ears," and many other denunciations, whether true or false, were made.[109]

Having surveyed the development and usage of the adê oaths in the
Assyrian empire, it should be stated that the adê was not the sole and exclusive form of relationship between the Assyrian emperor and his vassals,
especially on the fringes of the empire where autonomous and semiautonomous kingdoms continued to exist. We have already stressed that the adê
form of relationship was not adopted before the middle of the eighth century; yet already from the fourteenth to the thirteenth century kings of
Assyria imposed vassalage on neighboring areas, mainly north and northwest
of Assyria. Usually the term for this type of dependence is ardūtu, a traditional term attested in cuneiform records at least from the beginning of the
second millennium. As in the cases of the Canaanite princes in the Amarna
period in their relations to the Egyptian overlord, so here the vassal had to
bring yearly tribute and—though not always—to perform labor service for
the king and his gods. Often this relationship was sanctioned by an oath
taken in the presence of Assyrian gods, as evidenced by the case of Šattuara,
the king of Hanigalbat, and Adad-nirari I or by that of the sixty captured
kings of Na'iri defeated by Tiglath-pileser I.[110]

Significant for our study is the fact that when the warring kings of the
ninth century, Ashurnasirpal and Shalmaneser III, ravaged the Aramean and
Neo-Hittite states of north Syria and southeast Anatolia, taking an oath is not
mentioned, and the Assyrian hegemony is said to have been imposed by
severe punitive measures.[111] Moreover, it is submitted that the gradual introduction of the adê loyalty oath in the eighth century neither replaced nor
abolished the traditional ardūtu relationship. It is also of significance that
the adê documents, insofar as they survived, do not include a clause of obligation to perform the corvée or to bring yearly tribute (biltu, maddattu).
Were these clauses self-evident, or were they drawn in a separate document,
as was done by the king of Ugarit and his Hittite overlord in the second

---

[108] A. L. Oppenheim, "The Eyes of the Lord," *JAOS* 53 (1968) [= E. A. Speiser Memorial
Volume, ed. W. W. Hallo] 174.

[109] S. Parpola, "A Letter from Šamaš-šumu-ukin to Esarhaddon," *Iraq* 34 (1972) 31, n. 52.

[110] E. Weidner, "Die Kämpfe Adadniraris I gegen Hanigalbat," *AfO* 5 (1928/9) 90:4–17; E. A.
Wallis Budge and L. W. King, *Annals of the Kings of Assyria*, 1 (London: British Museum,
1902) 69:12–70:16. (= A. K. Grayson, *Assyrian Royal Inscriptions*, 1 [Wiesbaden: Harrassowitz,
1972] §392; 2 [1976] §30).

[111] Note the statement in Ashurnasirpal's Annals: "They (= the conquered people) entered
servitude and I imposed upon them corvée" (Budge-King, *Annals*, 384:125 = Grayson, *Inscriptions* 2, §589, last sentence and n. 637).

millennium?[112] On the other hand, the swearer of *adê* was obliged to extradite Assyrian "runaway slaves" (very often political fugitives), and to render military help when it was needed. In the cases of Esarhaddon and Ashurbanipal, loyalty to the suzerain and safeguarding the throne against any usurper became the predominant motif.[113] Neither is there evidence that every vassal throughout the empire was obliged to take these oaths of loyalty upon his master's accession to the throne. The Median chieftains of Esarhaddon's vassal treaties might have been considered as belonging to Assyria proper.[114] In any event, the exact distribution of the two types of dependencies—the *adê* and the *ardūtu*—still remains to be investigated and defined.

This uncertainty also prevails when we come to the relationship between the Assyrian empire and the kings of Israel and Judah. Though the prophet Hosea speaks explicitly of a ברית,[115] it is not known whether the kings of Israel and Judah who paid tribute to Assyria—like Menahem of Israel[116] and Ahaz of Judah[117]—also took the loyalty oath. The relationship between Assyria and these vassal kings could be categorized as that of the *ardūtu* type rather than as based on a formalized vassal treaty, similar to that between Assyria and Arpad. In one case, however, the type of relationship between the vassal king of Israel and the Assyrian overlord is defined in the biblical record. According to 2 Kgs 17:3–5, Hosea ben Elah, Israel's last king, became "servant" to Shalmaneser V, and when his secret contacts with Egypt were disclosed he was punished and his capital besieged. Strangely enough, however, Sargon II in his account of the conquest of Samaria does not accuse the Samarians of breaking the loyalty oath but rather of siding with the enemy.[118] Nor is Hezekiah, the king of the

---

[112] *PRU* 4, 40–43.

[113] Hence the predominance of the extradition *topos* in Esarhaddon's treaty with Shubria (Borger, *Asarhaddon*, 103). That mountainous region, south of Urartu, harbored Assyrian political fugitives, if not Esarhaddon's personal enemies.

[114] See Cogan, *Imperialism*, 47.

[115] "Now they make covenant with Assyria, now oil is carried to Egypt," Hos 12:2. See Tadmor, "The Historical Background of Hosea's Prophecies," *Y. Kaufmann Jubilee Volume* (ed. M. Haran; Jerusalem: Magnes Press, 1960) Hebrew Section, 84–88; "Azriyau of Jaudi," *Scripta Hierosolymitana* 8 (1961) 249–50.

[116] Ibid., 251–52; M. Weippert, "Menahem von Israel und seine Zeitgenossen," *ZDPV* 79 (1973) 26–53.

[117] The embassy of Ahaz to Tiglath-Pileser III in 2 Kgs 16:7 is explicit: the term "servant and son" indicates vassaldom, as in the Amarna letters, but it cannot serve as evidence of an existing vassal treaty between Israel and Assyria. It could be argued that the sending of a "bribe," *šōhad*, to induce the Assyrian king to intervene and rescue the King of Judah is contrary to the assumption that a vassal treaty existed between them prior to the submission of Ahaz. And see Tadmor and Cogan, "Ahaz and Tiglath-Pileser in the Book of Kings," *Bib* 60 (1979) 491–508.

[118] "The Samarians, who agreed with (another hostile) king not to perform servitude (*epeš ardūti*) [and not to de]liver tribute and who started hostility. . . ." (Tadmor, "The Campaigns of Sargon II of Assyria," *JCS* 12 [1958] 34:25–28 [so, according to the version of the Nimrud

"strong land of Judah,"[119] accused by Sennacherib of breaking the *adê* but rather of not submitting to his yoke.[120] At a certain point in the campaign, Hezekiah yielded, paid a heavy tribute, and, according to Sennacherib's annals, sent personal messengers to Nineveh to pay homage. Here the term *epeš ardūti* ("to perform servitude") is employed.[121] An *adê* oath is not mentioned here, but it is specifically mentioned in relation to Sennacherib's campaign against Judah and Philistia—but there only in connection with Padi, the pro-Assyrian king of Ekron, who had been a faithful vassal (*bēl adê u mamīt*, "bearer of loyalty oath to Assyria") and whom Hezekiah had removed from the throne, thus committing "sacrilege" (*anzillu*) from the Assyrian point of view.[122] Again, if the differences in terminology are to be considered meaningful, then we must conclude that Hezekiah was not bound by a vassal treaty to Assyria.

In summary, though meager and far from conclusive, our evidence seems to favor the suggestion that the relations between Assyria and Judah prior to the reign of Manasseh were not based on a vassal treaty but rather were governed by the traditional *ardūtu*. Likewise, I believe that Manasseh and the rest of the twenty-two Syro-Palestinian and Cypriot kings mentioned as vassals in the inscriptions of Esarhaddon and Ashurbanipal[123] were mostly bound to Assyria by servitude, not by a vassal treaty, as far back as the time of Sargon. Sargon's successors would not have altered that status. Only in newly conquered areas, such as Lower and Central Egypt, was the *adê* imposed and perhaps records of *adê* written.[124] If our reconstruction is followed, this would mean that the royal chancellery in Jerusalem in the time of Manasseh did not possess a copy of Esarhaddon's *adê* document, which is believed to be a possible—if not direct—prototype of the covenant formulation in Deuteronomy.[125] Manasseh's idolatry, then, resulted neither from a vassal treaty nor from the alleged Assyrian religious coercion in vassal states, whose existence has been effectively disproved by evidence adduced independently by Cogan and McKay.[126]

Prism]). In contrast, the King of Carchemish—the conquest of which is described in the same prism-inscription just before that of Samaria—is said to have "sinned" by negotiating secretly with the King of the Mushki, thus violating the loyalty oath to Assyria. If indeed this alteration in terminology is not merely a stylistic variation but reflects historical reality, it would imply that from the Assyrian point of view the people of Samaria were not bound by any *adê*.

[119] Luckenbill, *Sennacherib*, 77:21 (*be-ru* read as *mit-ru*, with *CAD* M II 140).

[120] Ibid., 32:18–19.

[121] Ibid., 34:48–49.

[122] Ibid., 31:74–77.

[123] See conveniently in A. L. Oppenheim's translation, *ANET*, 291, 294.

[124] Ibid., 294–95.

[125] On the other hand, one should not exclude the likelihood that the vassal treaty formulas— indigenous to the west and especially the curse formulas—were common knowledge in the scribal and priestly circles in Jerusalem, as in any other major center of literacy in the ancient Near East. And see D. R. Hillers, *Treaty-Curses*, 84–85.

[126] Cogan, *Imperialism*, 72–88; nn. 3; 14; J. McKay, *Religion in Judah under the Assyrians*

The only king of Judah who definitely took the *adê* oath was Zedekiah, Judah's last and most tragic monarch. Ezekiel refers explicitly to Zedekiah's submission, rebellion, and impending punishment: "He (i.e., Nebuchadnezzar), King of Babylon, took one of the seed royal and made a covenant with him and imposed an oath on him," but the vassal prince "rebelled against him and sent his envoys to Egypt to get horses and a large army. Will he succeed? . . . Should he break a covenant and escape?" (Ezek 17:13–14, New JPS translation).

The calamities that befell Judah, the chastisement of Zedekiah, the destruction of his land and his capital with its temple, the exile of his people—all these were direct consequences of his infidelity as a vassal. The ultimate punishment of Judah is so far our only evidence that Chaldean Babylonia, Assyria's foe and successor, perpetuated the institution of the loyalty oath in the service of the empire.[127] To the best of our knowledge, Achaemenid Persia resorted to other means and neither employed vassal treaties nor administered loyalty oaths. When these powerful vehicles of rule reappeared—sometimes almost *verbatim*—in the Hellenistic world and the Roman empire, the *milieu* was entirely different; but it can hardly be denied that their roots lie in the procedures and formulas of the ancient Near East that we have attempted to describe here.[128]

Thus ends the history of the *adê*, the loyalty oath, in the ancient Near East. Borrowed from lands west of the Euphrates, it became a ruthless tool in the hands of the Neo-Assyrian and Neo-Babylonian emperors and was in fact instrumental in the final destruction of the west itself.[129]

732–609 B.C. (SBT II 26; London: SCM, 1973).

[127] On the transformation of the loyalty oath in Babylonia proper—the "*adê* of the King" becoming hypostatized, especially in legal procedure—see above n. 78.

[128] For the evidence, see especially Weinfeld, "Loyalty Oath," 396–405.

[129] My sincere gratitude to Frank Moore Cross for his most helpful critique of an earlier draft of this essay.

VIII

IS THE TEMPLE SCROLL A SECTARIAN DOCUMENT?*

Yigael Yadin

Several of the critical reviews of my study of the Temple Scroll, on which I worked for nearly a decade, were fundamentally positive, and by this I refer mainly to the fact that the reviews accepted my principal conclusions. At the same time there were scholars who took issue with several of the results. I shall deal here only with the reservations of Professor Baruch Levine, since they concern the main and basic conclusions of my study of this Scroll, which is the longest of the Qumran documents.[1]

His main contention is that the Scroll is not sectarian and contains no *hălākôt* deviating from those of rabbinic legislation. He makes this claim despite the striking similarity—which he too acknowledges—between the laws and language of the Temple Scroll and those of the Damascus Document. As a result, Levine arrived at the far-reaching conclusion about the Damascus Document that it too is *not* sectarian. (I shall return to this point later.) This means that Levine has reached the same general evaluation of the Damascus Document that was made by Professor Louis Ginzberg some sixty years ago. Were Levine successfully to prove his claim, he would certainly make thereby a revolutionary contribution not only to the understanding of the Temple Scroll but also to the entire field of Dead Sea Scrolls

---

* Translated by Victor Hurowitz.

[1] This paper will be devoted in its entirety to the reservations of Professor Baruch Levine concerning several of my most important conclusions, especially the one that the Scroll must be attributed to the sect of the Dead Sea Scrolls, which in my opinion is to be identified with the Essenes. This argument is important in principle both because of the important position of Professor Levine and because of the topic, which is fundamental to the study of the scrolls. I have preserved herein the lecture format and have refrained from citing superfluous references. In my argument with Levine I refer to his article: B. A. Levine, "The Temple Scroll—Aspects of its Historical Provenance and Literary Character," *BASOR* 232 (1978) 5–23. All references to Levine's reservations are to this article. The Temple Scroll has been cited consistently according to page and line number within the Scroll. On my own views see Y. Yadin, *Měgîllat Hammiqdāš* (3 vols.; Jerusalem: Israel Exploration Society, Institute of Archaeology of the Hebrew University, and the Shrine of the Book, 1977), to which I make frequent reference in this essay. In the commentary to the passage under discussion (vol. 2) the reader can find references to the detailed discussion in the introductory volume (vol. 1).

research. Nonetheless, it appears to me that one can refute the arguments presented in Levine's long and erudite article.

In my answers to his critique I do intend, among other things, to take advantage of the opportunity for bolstering several of my own conclusions and, incidentally, for rebutting his statements, which perhaps represent a wider school of thought. It seems to me that this school has difficulty digesting the revolutionary significance of the discoveries of scrolls from the area of the Dead Sea for Jewish history. Its most extreme representative is, of course, the late Professor Zeitlin.

About seventy years ago when the renowned scholar Solomon Schechter published the Damascus Document—or, as he called it, "Fragments of a Zadokite Work"[2]—the community of scholars in Jewish studies was 'excited and perplexed. These leaves from the Cairo Genizah, along with those of Ben Sira—which were likewise discovered in the Genizah and first identified by Schechter—were the first to break through a time barrier of two millennia. With healthy acumen and great courage Schechter managed to free himself from the scholarly consensus about the monolithic nature of Second-Commonwealth Judaism—except for the accepted division into three or four sects—and, as we now know, he was right on target: confronting him was a law code from a Jewish sect of the Second Temple period. This was a sect in the full sense of the word. Its laws were clearly at variance with those formulated by the rabbis—namely, "Pharisaic" law—found in the two Talmuds and in the Midrashim (see also n. 11 below). Schechter chose to present his views unequivocally: "I preferred to be blamed for my mistakes and be corrected, than be praised for my prudence of non-committal, which policy I do not always think worthy of a student."[3] Furthermore, as I have noted in a previous congress, he contended that several of the apocryphal books— such as Jubilees—were written by the same sectarian circles responsible for the Damascus Document (on this point as well, see below, n. 11). This opinion gains support in light of the discoveries at Qumran.

No sooner was the Damascus Document published by Schechter than the scientific community was swept over by a deluge of different suggestions and opinions. Several scholars proposed other identities, but they nonetheless accepted Schechter's view that at issue was a sect whose laws diverged from those of the "Pharisees." Among those who opposed Schechter's suggestion about a Jewish sect whose laws were different from those of the Pharisees was one of the greatest scholars of Talmud and Midrash, Professor Louis Ginzberg. Ginzberg published his commentary and conclusions in the *Monatsschrift für*

---

[2] S. Schechter, *Documents of Jewish Sectaries*, vol. 1: *Fragments of a Zadokite Work* (Cambridge: University Press, 1910; reprinted, with Prolegomenon by Joseph A. Fitzmyer, New York: Ktav, 1970).

[3] Ibid., v. Compare, on the other hand, the approach of my colleague Chaim Rabin, which is expressed in the introduction to his edition of the Damascus Document: C. Rabin, *The Zadokite Documents* (Oxford: Clarendon, 1954) vii–viii.

Geschichte und Wissenschaft des Judentums[4] prior to the First World War. In 1922 he collected his studies in a special book bearing the intriguing title *Eine unbekannte jüdische Sekte*, which he dedicated with great esteem to the memory of Schechter, despite their differences concerning principal conclusions and explanations. Even though he agreed that at issue was some sort of group or sect from the time of Alexander Jannaeus, he reached the conclusion that the *hǎlākāh* of the sect was *not* at variance with that of the Pharisees and that it was in no way related to those of the already known "heterodox" sects. This is how Ginzberg summed up his conclusions: "The *halakhah* of this sect conforms to Pharisaic views in all essential halakhic areas, and there is no point, relation, or influence of Sadducean, Dosithean, or any other heterodox sect known to us."[5]

Ginzberg's encyclopedic knowledge of rabbinic sources and his scholarly acuteness enabled him to iron out many difficulties in his attempt to harmonize with Rabbinic *hǎlākāh*. Despite the fact that he was mistaken in his fundamental approach to the sectarian nature of the Damascus Document— as is proven by the new finds as well (see below)—his book remains one of the most important studies of the Damascus Document.

I find it appropriate to open this essay with a reference to the Damascus Document since in several of the basic points of disagreement between Professor Levine and me there is a clear connection between the Temple Scroll and the Damascus Document. Curiously, there is much similarity between Levine's argumentation and that of Ginzberg, as I shall indicate at the conclusion of this paper. One should have been able to assume, I think, that views understandable in the 1920s, before the discovery of the Dead Sea Scrolls, would not be repeated in the same form. However, this is not the case.

One of the major points of similarity between the Damascus Document and the Temple Scroll, a point which serves as a focus for Levine, is the statement concerning *'îr hammiqdāš*, "the temple city" or "the city of the temple":

> A man shall not lie with a woman in the *temple city* thereby defiling the *temple city* with their menstrual-like impurity. (Damascus Document 12:1–2)

> And if a man lies with his wife and has an emission of semen, he shall not come into any part of the *temple city*, where I will settle my name, for three days. (Temple Scroll 45:11–12)

These two laws supplement each other and are even phrased identically. The Damascus Document prohibits sexual intercourse in the *temple city*, and the Temple Scroll prohibits *entering* the *temple city* by anyone who

---

[4] *MGWJ* 55–58 (1911–14).

[5] L. Ginzberg, *Eine unbekannte jüdische Sekte*, Pt. 1 (New York: Im Selbstverlage des Verfassers, 1922) VI–VII (my translation from the German); now in English edition: *An Unknown Jewish Sect* (New York: The Jewish Theological Seminary of America, 1976).

performed sexual intercourse outside the temple city before he is purified in
the way prescribed by the Scroll. This point is a focus, as has been stated, for
one of Levine's criticisms, since it is clear that acceptance of my proposed
interpretation forces one to conclude that both passages bespeak a sect with
extreme views wherever laws of purity are concerned. I shall return to this
point in what follows.

Does God Speak to Moses in the Temple Scroll?

Let us begin with Levine's first argument, which can in my opinion be
conclusively refuted. This argument touches upon the very *nature* of the
Scroll and its style as I defined them in the introduction to my book. First,
the Scroll presents us with Torah proclaimed by God in the first person, and
it includes numerous portions additional to what is in the received Pentateuch. Second, the words are addressed to someone who must be identified,
in my opinion, with Moses. For example, in the laws concerning the abattoir
in the inner court of the temple it is said: "And you shall make chains coming down from the ceiling of the twelve pillars" (34:15). Or again, in the
instructions concerning the area around the *hêkāl* it is said: "And you shall
make a place on the west of the *hêkāl* all around, a portico of standing
pillars for the sin offering of the priests" (35:10–11) and so on. In its description of the temple the whole style of the Scroll approximates—and at times
is even identical to—the style of Exodus where the building of the taber-
nacle is treated. There, too, God is speaking to Moses.

This fundamental nature of the Scroll as well as another matter about
which I have yet to speak led me, as I have stated, to the conclusion that the
Temple Scroll was for the sect a sort of second, additional Torah delivered
by God to Moses on Mount Sinai, just like the Masoretic one. This Torah was
revealed only to members of the sect. Obviously, if this conclusion is correct,
it is of consequence for the understanding of the Scroll. However, contrary
to my own contention that God speaks in the Scroll to Moses, Levine claims:
"[in] the entire Scroll . . . Moses' name is never mentioned, and for a specific
reason: The words of the Scroll are represented as God's own words, and the
role of Moses as the teacher of God's word to Israel has been meticulously
eliminated" (p. 6). Levine goes even further by stating absolutely and a
priori: "It is inconceivable that the Scroll contained any passages naming
Moses." It is regrettable that Levine hastily makes this statement on the basis
of his own preconception. "It is inconceivable"—who cannot conceive?

It is true that in the extant parts of the Scroll Moses' name is nowhere to
be found, and for this reason it does not appear in the concordance to the
Scroll prepared by my daughter Littal. However, I did not base my conclusion only on the stylistic identity between the Scroll and the book of Exodus,
or on common sense. Fortunately, several words have been preserved that
should convince even the most skeptical among us. Unfortunately, these

words escaped the eyes of Levine, perhaps because they appear in the technical parts describing the structure of the temple and dealing with the division of the chambers in the outer court. I am certain that Levine would not have written what he did had he noticed them.

This section discusses the allotment of chambers to the various tribes according to the gates of the court. So, for instance, it is stated:

> And from the Gate of Benjamin unto the Western Corner, to the children of Benjamin. From this corner unto the Gate of Issachar, to the children of Issachar. (44:15–16)

And when the Gate of Levi is treated previously, it is stated:

> And the whole area to the right and left of the Gate of Levi, to the sons of your brother Aaron. (44:5)

Who is the person who is Aaron's brother and to whom God speaks? Is it really necessary that there be preserved a sentence such as "And the Lord said to Moses: Speak to your brother Aaron" (Lev 16:2) for us to know that the reference is to Moses?

The Scroll contains some more allusions, but they too seem for some reason to have escaped the eyes of Levine. So, for example, it is said in the passages excerpted by the author of the Scroll from the book of Leviticus:

> And you shall warn the children of Israel of all the uncleanliness, and let them not be defiled by them, which I declare to you on this mountain. (51:5–7)

There can be no doubt, therefore, that the author of the Scroll places these words in the mouth of God as He addresses Moses.

The refutation of Levine's arguments about Moses automatically weakens his claims at the end of his article concerning the Temple Scroll and its relationship to the apocryphal books. At the same time, however, he is correct—and this I also stressed in my book—that the transposition into first person was intended to turn the whole Scroll into a Torah that God reveals to Moses, and not words uttered by Moses himself.

The Expression "The Temple City" ('îr hammiqdāš)

The second matter about which Levine and I disagree is that of the extreme laws of the Scroll concerning impurity and purity connected with the temple city, namely, the city in which the temple will be built. In the passages cited above from the Damascus Document and the Temple Scroll there appear, as already noted, severe prohibitions relating to the temple city. In the book of Numbers these prohibitions relate to the "camp." This series of prohibitions—with which I dealt at length in my book—includes restrictions concerned with entering the temple city:

> No blind man shall enter it all their days, so that they will not defile the city. . . . And any man who cleanses himself of his discharge . . . only then he shall come into the

> city of the temple. And any one unclean through contact with the dead shall not enter
> it (the city). . . . And any leper or diseased person shall not enter it. (45:12–18)

It is also appropriate to mention here the command to build latrines outside
the city:

> And you shall make them a place for a "hand," outside the city, to which they shall go
> out, to the northwest of the city—roofed houses with pits within them, into which the
> excrement will descend, so that it will not be visible at any distance from the city,
> three thousand cubits. (46:13–16)

Also of relevance in this matter is the command:

> And you shall make three places to the east of the city, separated one from another,
> into which shall come the lepers and the people who have a discharge and the men
> who have had a (nocturnal) emission. (46:16–18)

There is no stipulation providing for the assignment of a place for menstruating women or women after childbirth. However, in other cities—
which also, of course, are pure, although to a lesser degree—special places
must be set aside for this purpose:

> And in every city you shall allot places for those afflicted with leprosy or with plague
> or with scab, who may not enter your cities and defile them, and also for those who
> have a discharge, and for women during their menstrual uncleanness. (48:14–16)

The prohibition against menstruating women's entering the other cities
disproves Levine's contention that the Scroll's laws concerning defilement
apply solely to the temple compound and not to the entire city. The other
cities contain no temple, and nevertheless they are to be kept pure and are
subject to laws of purity to which there exist no parallels in normative rabbinic *hǎlākāh*. To this one can add a long row of prohibitions concerning
sacred and profane slaughtering in the temple city and its environs. Levine
deals with these restrictions at length, and since they are germane to the
issue I will cite them here:

> And the city which I will hallow by settling my name and my temple within (it) shall
> be holy and clean of any unclean thing with which it may be defiled; everything that
> is in it shall be clean, and all that will be brought to it shall be clean: wine and oil and
> all foodstuffs and all *mûšqeh* shall be clean. All skin of clean animals that will be
> slaughtered within their cities, they shall not bring into it; but in their cities they may
> do with them their work for all their needs; and into the city of my temple they shall
> not bring (them), for their (degree of) cleanness is according to (the degree of clean-
> ness of) their flesh. And you shall not defile the city in which I settle my name and my
> temple. . . . And you shall not defile my temple and my city in which I dwell with the
> skins of your abominations. (47:3–18)

In the introduction to the Scroll I explained in great detail the difference between this strict approach and the lenient one that crystallized
within rabbinic circles. The latter diverged from—as the late Professor
Gedalyah Alon put it—the plain meaning of the prohibitions that were

appropriate to desert conditions, tending to make them suitable for urban conditions. From Levine's reaction to the words of Alon quoted in my book, it appears that he does not accept Alon's position.

The prohibitions in the book of Numbers are perfectly clear, and all of them are connected with the *camp*. Rabbinic *hǎlākāh* sought to confine the prohibitions to the temple alone and solved the problem by imposing upon Jerusalem a division into three "camps": Divine Presence, Levites (including the temple and the temple mount), and the camp of Israel (including the city within the walls). In so doing, the *hǎlākāh* did not give a consistent interpretation to the word "camp," and the prohibitions regarding the "camp" were applied sometimes to the camp of Levites and other times to the camp of Israel. Thus Alon states: "And even the Tannaitic interpretations of the Pentateuchal pericopes which speak about expelling the impure from the camp, which are taking them to refer only to the camps of Divine Presence and of Levites, are not very close to the plain meaning of Scripture."[6]

However, the Scroll's prohibitions regarding "the temple city," "my city," "my temple city," or "the city which I have chosen to cause my name to abide there" clearly indicate that the laws were determined in accordance with the literal meaning of the biblical text and that all prohibitions concerning the camp were applied to the temple city in its entirety. Several of the prohibitions were extended to the other cities as well. The Scroll presents, therefore, a different, extreme approach. This is accordingly a central concern in Levine's discussion where he attempts to refute my conclusion that the Scroll reflects sectarian Torah.

How does Levine attempt to counter this assertion? One of his principal arguments is that the term "the temple city" (*'îr hammiqdāš*) in the Scroll and in the Damascus Document does not indicate the city in which the temple is found but only the *temenos*, that is to say, the temple and its courtyards and that all of the prohibitions about "the temple city" do not therefore apply to the city itself. It is interesting to note that for the same reason Ginzberg was forced to explain away this difficulty in his commentary to the Damascus Document, only in his opinion—which was not accepted by the scholarly community and which was expressed very cautiously—the term refers to the original "city of David," which is to be identified with the "temple mount" of rabbinic parlance.

Levine noticed, of course, that several of the prohibitions that I mentioned apply not only to "the temple city" but to "my city" as well and especially to "my temple city" (*'îr miqdāšî*). He even acknowledges that in these instances one cannot claim that reference is only to the temple courtyards. But from this he arrives at the strange conclusion that *'îr hammiqdāš* is not synonymous with *'îr miqdāšî* or *'îrî*: "The designation *'îr miqdāšî*, 'the city of My temple,' is synonymous with *'îrî*, 'My city,' whereas . . . the designation *'îr*

[6] G. Alon, *Mehqarîm BěTôlědôt Yiśrāēl*, vol. 1.

hammiqdāš refers only to the temple complex itself. The two terms ought not to be confused" (p. 15). I must admit that it is difficult to argue with this statement, for it seems to me that it has no basis on any grounds, including linguistic grounds! Is there really a difference between "'*îr hammiqdāš*" and "'*îr miqdāšî*"? Does the former term mean, as Levine says it does, "Temple City" in some technical or specialized sense, while the latter means "the city of my temple" in the sense of the whole city of Jerusalem? I believe that the answer is negative from numerous standpoints, and firstly from the linguistic one. As for '*îr hammiqdāš*, clearly this must be taken to mean "the temple city," and the linguistic structure is well known.[7] On what basis does Levine translate '*îr miqdāšî* as "the city of *my temple*" and not "*my city* of the temple"? Does *bêt tĕpillātî* (Isa 56:7) mean "the house of my prayer"? Rather, it should be rendered "my house of prayer." Does *har-qŏdšî* (Ps 2:6) mean "the hill of my holiness" or "my holy hill"? Does '*îr qŏdšĕkā* mean "the city of your holiness" or "your holy city?"[8]

Before we proceed with our discussion of this term it would be worthwhile to ask why Levine is alarmed by the Scroll's position that the entire city where the temple is located is holy and consequently must be kept pure. Is this such an innovative conception of the sect? Has it no basis at all in Scripture? I discussed this subject in my book and cited several passages that bear on this issue, such as: "Put on your robes of majesty, Jerusalem, *holy city*! For the uncircumcised and the *unclean* shall never enter you again" (Isa 52:1). It has already been pointed out by Professor M. Haran that Second Isaiah is the only prophet to call Jerusalem '*îr haqqōdeš*—the holy city—and only in his words does the Lord call Jerusalem "my city," just as in the Scroll.[9] To all this we may add the words of the prophet Joel: "And Jerusalem shall be holy; nevermore shall strangers pass through it" (4:17).

The term "the holy city"—or "Jerusalem the holy," as it was known during the First Revolt—was not an abstract expression in the minds of its coiners but one of practical significance: the holy city is holy because of the temple within it, and therefore it must be kept pure. At that time there was no argument about the actual sanctity of the city but about the degree of purity that was to be maintained in it and in its various parts. Apparently the sect of Qumran—the Essenes—was among the most extreme where this matter was concerned.

---

[7] See E. Kautzsch and A. E. Cowley, *Gesenius' Hebrew Grammer* (2d ed.; Oxford: Clarendon, 1910) § 127a.

[8] For additional examples see Gesenius, § 135n. We are told there: "When the genitive, following a construct state, is used periphrastically to express the idea of a material or attribute . . . , the pronominal suffix, which properly belongs to the compound idea (represented by the *nomen regens* and genitive), is, like the article (§ 127), attached to the second substantive (the genitive) e.g. *har-qŏdšî* prop. *the hill of my holiness*, i.e. my holy hill. . . ."

[9] M. Haran, *Between Ri'shonot (Former Prophecies) and Hadashot (New Prophecies)* (Jerusalem, 5723) 96ff.

From the linguistic as well as the halakhic standpoint there is no basis, as we have stated, to distinguish between *'îr hammiqdāš* and *'îr miqdāšî*. Yet Levine's claims can be refuted in another way: on the basis of the Scroll's terminology itself. The area bordered by the temple courtyards—and which is called, according to Levine, "*'îr hammiqdāš*"—is called in the Scroll *hammiqdāš* (the temple). It is clear that the reference is not to the sacred structure itself, which the Scroll calls *habbayit* (the house/temple) or *bêt YHWH* (the house/temple of the Lord). The author of the Scroll uses the vocable *miqdāš* in order to designate the entire *temenos*. Let me cite several examples.

The instructions to build the temple are presented from the inside outward: the structures in the inner court, including the *bayit* (the house/temple), the *hêkāl*, the inner court, the middle court, and the outer court. Only afterwards is the city itself mentioned. Then, after the commands concerning the outer court—namely, the courtyard enclosing the *temenos*—it is said:

> And you shall make a terrace around, outside the outer court, fourteen cubits wide, according to the entrances of all the gates. And you shall make twelve steps to it, *for the children of Israel to ascend to it to enter into my temple.* (46:5ff.; emphasis mine, of course)

It is clear that the term "my temple" indicates here the complex that is enclosed by the outer court—"the Temple City," if you will, according to Levine. In the continuation the matter is stated even more clearly:

> And you shall make a fosse around the temple, one hundred cubits wide, which will separate *the holy temple from the city,* so that they may not come suddenly *into my temple* and desecrate it. They shall consecrate *my temple* and fear *my temple,* for I dwell among them. (46:9–12)

There is no basis to Levine's contention that, since according to the other sources the moat (*ḥêl*) was inside the *temenos*, the author of the Scroll deviated, apparently, from his order of description out of his desire to emphasize that this moat was outside the temple but not outside the temple city. On the contrary, the author of the Scroll points out that the moat—like the terrace (*rōbed*)—was connected with the entrance to the temple, and he stresses that its function was to separate between "the holy temple and the city." The terminology of the Scroll—and of additional sources—is therefore: the temple and the courtyards are the "temple" or "the holy temple"; "the city which I chose to cause my name to abide therein" is "the city of the temple" or "my city" or "my city of the temple."

One can find in the Scroll other examples, but it seems to me that those already cited may suffice. If I have refuted Levine's claims on these points, the edifice that he constructed upon them falls automatically. Nonetheless, it is appropriate to deal with one more point that Levine raises on the present topic. Even Levine is forced to acknowledge that the passage which prohibits bringing skins of pure animals that were not slaughtered in the temple and that were used as containers for wine, oil, etc., into the "city where I have caused my name and my temple to abide therein" (47:3–18) applies to the entire city. However, Levine offers a curious explanation: the intention here is not to keep the city pure of any defilement, items by which a person might be defiled, but rather the regulation is

> an attempt to muster support for the Jerusalem temple cult by encouraging Jews who do business in Jerusalem to donate sacrifices. By prohibiting delivery of liquids and foodstuffs to Jerusalem in any except sacrificial animal skins, the Scroll was saying to the temple's purveyors that if they wished to market their goods in Jerusalem and to do business with the temple, they would have to patronize the temple! (pp. 15–16)

It is possible, to be sure, that this was really the intention behind the prohibition, but Levine also noticed that within the explanation provided by the Scroll appear sentences such as:

> And the city which I will hallow by settling my name and my temple within (it) shall be holy and clean of any unclean thing with which *it may be defiled*; everything that is in it shall be clean. (47:3–6)

> And you shall not defile the city in which I settle my name and my temple. (47:10–11)

These sentences are unambiguous and intend to explain the matter of the skins—no matter what the "practical rationale" behind the prohibition may have been—out of the obligation to guard the city from every "defilement by which they may become defiled." Yet on this Levine remarks that the Scroll's frequent use of terminology relating to purity and impurity is only aimed at achieving a dramatic effect!

To be sure, there are many other considerations against Levine's attempt to distinguish between prohibitions on impurity that apply to the "Temple City" and those that apply to "my city of the temple" and "my city." I will not discuss them here, for this was already done successfully by Professor Jacob Milgrom in his answer to Levine's reservations on the matter.[10]

Is the Scroll's Calendar That of the Qumran Sect?

To this topic Levine devotes a very lengthy discussion, and he answers the question posed in the title to this section in the negative. He rejects my assertion—and not only my conjecture—that the calendar presupposed by the Scroll's holidays is that of the Qumran sect, the Essenes. This calendar, whose principles and details are set out in the book of Enoch, is the basis for all the events and holidays in the book of Jubilees. Levine's claims could have been summarized in half a page, but his discussion spreads over several pages, in which he examines fundamentally several issues—such as the meaning of the vocables *šābûaʿ*, *šabbāt*, and *mimmoḥŏrat haššabbāt*—some of which are not

[10] J. Milgrom, "'Shabbath' and 'Temple City' in the Temple Scroll," *BASOR* 232 (1978) 25–27.

relevant to the matter at hand. (The reason for this lengthy discussion is Levine's correct assumption that the readers of his article are incapable of reading my book, which is in Hebrew.) In the course of this discussion he cites long passages from the Scroll and from the Bible in English translation, along with whole paragraphs of transliteration into Latin characters.

I must admit that I was hesitant about responding to Levine on this subject because at the end of his long treatment and after he has reached his negative conclusion (about which he seems not to be entirely convinced), he writes:

> Even if one had explicit evidence that the Scroll's author was operating on the Qumran-Jubilees calendar, the precise provenance [sectarian or not—Y. Y.] of the Scroll would have to be established independently. After all, the book of Jubilees and the Qumran sect shared the same calendric tradition, and yet it is not being suggested that the book of Jubilees is one of the writings of the Qumran sect, strictly speaking. (p. 11)[11]

This implies that, even if I were successfully to refute Levine's claims and prove the correctness of the conclusion in my book, Levine will claim that this is not conclusive concerning whether the Scroll is a Qumran sect composition. Despite my own hesitations, I decided to deal with the subject because, if the Scroll's calendar *is not* that of the Qumran sect, the Scroll *ipso facto* is not of this origin.

The calendar under discussion is based on the following principles: There are twelve months of thirty days each with an additional day following every period of three months, all adding up to a 364-day year. The first day of the first month falls on Wednesday—the day on which the heavenly luminaries were created—and as a result of following this calendar the holidays will always fall on the same day of the week.

In a special chapter of my book I dealt with the holidays and reached the conclusion that the author of the Scroll used this calendar. How? One of the Scroll's many novel features relating to the calendar holidays is the institution of two additional feasts of first fruits—the first fruit of wine and that

---

[11] This statement as well is incorrect, for today there are many scholars who lean toward the conclusion that both the book of Jubilees and other works were written in the Qumran sect or by others akin to it. Already Schechter, with his typical daring and brilliant analysis, wrote about this subject in his introduction to the Damascus Document (p. xxvi): "One result . . . seems to me to be beyond any doubt. And this that it is among the sects severed from the general body of Judaism in which we have to look for the origin of such Pseudepigraphic works as the Book of Jubilees, the Book of Enoch, the Testaments of the Twelve Patriarchs, and similar productions,—and *not* in Pharisaic Judaism. This fact was recognized more than half a century ago by Beer, who thus expressed himself with regard to the Book of Jubilees:—'Its whole type is a peculiar one, and is apparently based on a sectarian foundation.'" Even so I cannot help quoting one more sentence from Schechter which is directly relevant to the argument at hand: "And surely this is the only possible view which could be formed of this class of writings by any scholar who has ever made a proper study of Rabbinic literature, such as the Mishnah, the Talmud, and the 'great Midrashim'" (ibid.).

of olive oil—and of an important feast entitled "the feast of the wood offering." It is furthermore clear that the author of the Scroll considered the day of raising the *ômer* as the holiday of the first fruits of barley. Levine concentrates his main arguments on the calculation of days between the first fruits feasts, and deals in particular, as already stated, with the meanings of the terms *šābûa'*, *šabbāt*, and *mimmoḥŏrat haššabbāt*.

The Pentateuchal method of counting the days and determining the time for the first wheat holiday appears in the book of Leviticus:

> And from the day on which you bring the sheaf of wave offering—the day after the sabbath—you shall count off seven weeks. They must be complete: you must count until the day after the seventh week—fifty days. (23:15–16)

This is to say, a counting of the holiday of first fruit will depend upon the day on which the *ômer* ("sheaf") will be waved. This day is defined once again prior to the verses we just cited, just after the commands about the Paschal offering and the festival of unleavened bread:

> When you enter the land which I am giving to you and you reap its harvest, you shall bring the first sheaf of your harvest to the priest. He shall wave the sheaf before the Lord for acceptance in your behalf; the priest shall wave it on the day after the sabbath. (23:10–11)

The various Jewish sects were divided, as is well known, over the meaning of "the day after the sabbath." The Pharisees, as is expressed in the rabbinic legislation, held that the intention is the day following the first day of the Passover, while the Sadducees, the Boethusians, the Samaritans, and the Karaites held that the day in question was the morrow of the first Saturday following the Paschal offering.

From the calendar of the book of Jubilees and the literature of the sect it turns out that the counting of the *ômer* was not to commence according to any of the aforementioned methods but on the morrow of the first Saturday following the entire seven days of the Passover holiday, namely, on the twenty-sixth of the first month. According to this calendar, the day of the wheat first fruits would always fall on a Sunday on the fifteenth day of the third month. In the following way the author of the Scroll explains the method for calculating the feasts of first fruits:

The first wheat

> And you shall count seven full sabbaths from the day that you brought the sheaf [of the wave offering; you shall c]ount to the morrow after the seventh sabbath, counting fifty days. (18:10–13)

The first wine

> [And] you shall [count] from the day that you brought the new cereal offering to the Lo[rd,] [th]e bread of new fruits, seven weeks; seven full sabbaths [there shall be un]til you count fifty days to the morrow of the seventh sabbath. (19:11–13)

The first oil

> And [you sha]ll count from that day on seven weeks seven (*l.* 15) times, nine and forty days; seven full sabbaths until the morrow of the seventh sabbath, (*l.* 16) counting fifty days. (21:12–14)

In other words, according to the method followed by the author of the Scroll, the holiday of first fruits was counted twice, both as the last day of the counting that preceded it and as the first day of the counting that followed it. From all of the passages it becomes clear that this way of reckoning is "seven weeks seven times" which are "seven complete weeks" (7 X 7), namely, "forty-nine days," and "you shall count off until the day after the seventh sabbath" (49 + 1), that is, fifty days.

According to the approach of the Scroll's calendar, the day of waving the sheaf falls on Sunday, and all feasts of first fruits likewise fall thereon. Sunday is also the day when one begins counting the days from one holiday to the next. Clearly, according to the Scroll's terminology, "*šabbāt*" here is a week that begins on Sunday and ends on Saturday, in contrast to "*šābûa'*", which designates any period of seven days, not necessarily commencing on a Sunday.

Levine's long discussion of these terms—which is interesting in itself—is not always relevant to the subject under study. The main question he poses is: On what basis does Yadin decide that the counting for these holidays actually did in fact begin on Sunday, and in particular on Sunday, the twenty-sixth day of the first month? For according to rabbinic interpretation, the words *mimmoḥŏrat haššabbāt* do not refer of necessity to Sunday, and it therefore must not be determined absolutely that the Scroll held differently. In his opinion, I cannot make this claim on the basis of those sections that were preserved, and a strong case can certainly not be built thereupon.

It is true that the passage defining the day of sheaf waving has not been preserved in its entirety, and for this reason I wrote in my introduction that there is room to *assume* that in the paragraph not preserved "there was a more precise definition of the words *mimmoḥŏrat haššabbāt*" (p. 82). Very unfortunately, also unpreserved was the sentence containing the actual words "*mimmoḥŏrat haššabbāt*," but I have no doubt that the text did in fact contain them. Although I cannot prove this with certainty, this fact does not disprove my conclusion that we are dealing with the Qumran calendar. At the same time, I find surprising Levine's claim that the author refrained from using these specific terms in specifying the beginning of the counting for the holidays of first fruits:

> These words, *mimmoḥŏrat haššabbat*, which are the ones that actually make the point about initiating the counting on a Sunday, are nowhere to be found in any of the Scroll's preserved formulations. In later periods, those Jewish sects who disputed the Rabbinic calendar, such as the Karaites, justified their divergence by insisting on the

literal interpretation of the word *šabbāt* in Lev 23:11 and 15a, and yet the Scroll's author, who is alleged to be an advocate of the Qumran-Jubilees calendar, failed to avail himself of three perfect opportunities to make the same point! (p. 10)

Furthermore, Levine reaches the conclusion that this "deletion" was intentional and aimed at verifying the rabbinic approach according to which Saturday is not intended.

I must admit that this argument of Levine is most surprising. If we assume that counting the *'ômer* began on "the day after the sabbath," even though we do not know how the author understood the word sabbath in the missing passage, it would be illogical, both materially and stylistically, once again to define the method of reckoning. Thus the Scroll states:

> . . . from the day that you brought the sheaf [of the wave offering; you shall c]ount to the morrow after the seventh sabbath. . . . (18:11–12)

> [And] you shall [count] from the day that you brought the new cereal offering to the Lo[rd,] [th]e bread of new fruits, . . . to the morrow of the seventh sabbath. (19:11–13)

> And [you sha]ll count from that day . . . until the morrow of the seventh sabbath, (*l.* 16) counting fifty days. (21:12–14)

These statements are certainly sufficient for calculating the holidays. It would have been rather strange had the author of the Scroll added in every instance, for example, words such as "from the day on which you bring the sheaf for the wave offering, from the day after the sabbath" or "from the day on which you bring the new *minḥâh*, from the day after the sabbath." Milgrom has already refuted Levine's claims on this matter.[12]

Even so, I did not claim in my book that on the basis of what was preserved in the Scroll I am able to determine—and not merely surmise—that the calendar of the Scroll is that of Qumran. This conclusion was reached in another way, but for some reason Levine does not accept it clearly. This is what I wrote in the introduction (vol. I, p. 95):

[12] Levine does not, as already said, accept this proof and satisfies himself with one or two general comments, without reaching any conclusion on the topic of discussion. So, for instance, he writes: "Yadin further notes that a fragment from Qumran Cave 4, cited by Milik, gives the 22nd of Elul as the date for 'the set-time of the oil' (*mô'ēd haššemen*), another name for what the Scroll calls *mô'ēd hayyiṣhār*. Now it is significant that the 22nd of Elul comes at the end of three cycles of 49 days each, commencing on the 26th of Nisan!" (p. 8). If this were actually the case Levine would have had to admit the validity of my position, but despite his statement just quoted Levine claims: "It is, therefore, [after discussing the meaning of '*šabbāt*' and '*šābûa*''] difficult to understand just how Yadin is able to conclude on the basis of the three cited formulations in the Scroll that its author is speaking of seven weeks, each beginning on a Sunday and ending on a Saturday, and that consequently the Scroll's calendar began its cycles from the 26th of Nisan, a Sunday" (p. 9). I am at a loss to comprehend Levine, for the fact that the fragment published by Milik and the Scroll are identical he dismisses with the general conclusion: "All that we know, therefore, is that the liturgical calendar of the Scroll shared certain nonbiblical 'set-times' with the Qumran sect. We have no way of knowing, however, how limited or how widespread such celebrations were at the time" (p. 10).

It is possible that we would not have been in a position to describe the method of the author of the Temple Scroll [in counting and fixing the various first fruits feasts] were it not for a tiny fragment from Qumran, which enumerates the feasts according to months and days [mentioned by J. T. Milik, "Le travail d'édition des manuscrits du Désert de Juda," VTSup 4 (Leiden: Brill, 1957) 25]. In this fragment it is stated: "On the twenty-second of this month (the sixth month) the Feast of Oil." Obviously, Milik was not in a position to identify this festival and therefore he merely commented: "de caractère agricole." However, it was immediately clear that this date—the twenty-second of the sixth month—results from a double count of forty-nine days from the feast of the first wheat, according to the Qumran calendar. Thus we now possess the missing links, with the help of which we can ascertain for sure that the author of the Scroll followed the Qumran calendar. . . . Only on the basis of this calendar with all its details will the Feast of Oil—discussed in the Scroll, with its detailed manner of counting—fall on the twenty-second of the sixth month!

And indeed, from the table mentioned the following facts clearly emerge (counting backward from the twenty-second day of the sixth month): all holidays of first fruits fall on Sunday; from one holiday to another there are fifty days if we count the holiday of first fruits as the last day of the count that precedes it and as the first of the count that follows it; the day for starting to count the 'ômer falls on the twenty-sixth day of the first month, Sunday, or in other words, the day after the sabbath—*mimmoḥŏrat haššabbāt*—according to the plain meaning of Scripture.

Herein, as has been said, lies the decisive proof that the calendar of the Scroll is that of Qumran, the book of Jubilees, and the book of Enoch. I have therefore proven, so it seems to me, that Levine's claim is not warranted. Milgrom, too, has already proven this in his aforementioned article.[13]

The Temple Scroll and the Damascus Document

I opened this essay with the Damascus Document, and with it I shall also conclude. Levine was unable, as we have seen, to ignore the fact—which I already discussed in my book—that there is great similarity, even identity, between several passages and laws in the Scroll and what is said in the Damascus Document. I cited in full the passages that prohibit entry into the temple city (or city of the temple) to anyone who has lain with a woman and has not purified himself for three days.

To this matter, like the matter of the calendar, Levine devotes much space in his argument with me, but in the end he comes to the conclusion that on the basis of the similarity the Damascus Document itself *is not* a product of the Qumran sect! On first thought I should be able to ignore Levine's claims, because his conclusion is so extreme that it contradicts the opinion of most students of the Dead Sea Scrolls, and dealing with it therefore would seem to have no place in a limited discussion of the Temple Scroll.

---

[13] See above, n. 10.

Even so, it is proper to conclude with this issue in order to show that his desire to demonstrate conclusively that the Temple Scroll is not sectarian is likely to distort unintentionally even the most obvious facts. First I will quote a central paragraph in Levine's argumentation on this subject:

> There is yet another *caveat* affecting Yadin's legal comparisons: They center predominantly around the Zadokite Document. (The same is true, by the way, with respect to the linguistic and terminological parallels which he adduces elsewhere in his discussion.) There seems to be a particular affinity between the Scroll and the Zadokite Document which is not generally shared by the other acknowledged writings of the Qumran sect. Instead of assuming that such comparisons with the Zadokite Document reinforce the Qumranic provenance of the Scroll, perhaps we ought to assume that *neither the Scroll nor the Zadokite Document* was authored by the same group which produced the *sĕrākim*, the Thanksgiving Scroll, and others. This possibility needs to be explored in a separate investigation. (p. 12, emphasis mine)

Despite this conclusion Levine goes on to "examine three important legal comparisons discussed by Yadin" (ibid.). He begins with a clear comparison that I suggested concerning laws of incest.

> And they marry each man the daughter of his brother and the daughter of his sister, though Moses said: "Thou shalt not approach to thy mother's sister; she is thy mother's kin." The rules against incest are written with reference to males but apply equally to women. Hence, if the brother's daughter uncovers the nakedness of her father's brother, she is considered his adopted kin. (Damascus Document 5:7–11)

It is true that this prohibition is adopted by Samaritans, Falashas, the Church, and Moslems. However, I already pointed out in the introduction to my book (vol. I, pp. 284f.):

> It is interesting that the Temple Scroll deals with this subject in a way similar to the Damascus Document, which anchors this law to the prohibition against taking the mother's sister immediately after the adamant prohibition against marrying one's father's sister or mother's sister. It is worthy of note that that in the Damascus Document is identical with that of the Temple Scroll, and probably is copied therefrom.

The second comparison I suggested is the passage in the Damascus Document:

> They are caught in two: in whoredom they take two wives in their lifetimes. . . . And about the prince it is written: "Let him not multiply wives unto himself," but David had not read in the Sealed Book of the Law. (4:20–5:2)

Similarly, the Scroll states concerning the king:

> And he shall not take upon her another wife, for she alone shall be with him all the days of her life. (57:17–18)

In my book (vol. 1, pp. 272ff.) I dealt with these two passages at length, for their content is identical and their formulation is similar; I also explained there that the meaning of "*bĕḥayyêhem*" in the Damascus Document is "*bĕḥayyêhen*." In this matter, too, Levine claims that despite the similarity there is still no proof that the author of the Scroll and the author of the Damascus Document belonged to the same sect, for it is possible that this prohibition was very common.

The third topic with which Levine deals is related to the severity of the laws of purity, especially in connection with the expression "the temple city," or "the city of the temple," which occurs only in the two scrolls. I have already discussed his arguments on this point.

Despite Levine's attempts to minimize the importance of the parallels, in the end he reaches the conclusion that even the Damascus Document does not derive from the sect! Within the limits of this lecture, I shall not respond to this conclusion, for it may well be taken for granted that the argument with Levine on this issue will be taken up by most scholars of the scrolls. At the same time, I cannot help observing that in the Damascus Document as well as in the *sĕrākîm* and in the *pĕšārîm*—which Levine considers typical products of the Qumran sect—there is mention made of esoteric matters relating to the sect that are linguistically identical, such as "*serek*," "*môreh haṣṣedeq*," and "*mĕšîḥê (māšîaḥ) 'ahărōn wĕyiśrāēl*." Thus it is impossible to separate the Damascus Document from the sectarian writings, and this is attested as well by the numerous fragments of the Damascus Document discovered in the Qumran caves. Consequently, the identity between the Temple Scroll and the Damascus Document (as well as other arguments put forward in my book) shows that the former, too, was composed by a member of the sect, and perhaps even—as I suggested in my book—by the Teacher of Righteousness himself.

In my lecture before the Thirty-Fifth Congress of the Israel Exploration Society I stressed that one of the difficult problems confronting scholars of Judaism and Christianity who undertake a study of the writings of the Qumran sect is the psychological barrier. Suddenly new revolutionary material is discovered which demands an absolute departure from time-honored conceptions. It appears to be very difficult to overcome this barrier, which still presents itself to scholars of the scrolls, including such a distinguished one as Professor Levine. Therefore, the challenge now facing scholars is to illuminate with the help of the scrolls one of the most important periods in our history: the twilight of the Second Commonwealth. This is possible only if we can place ourselves in the context prior to the destruction of the Second Temple and prior to the spiritual, historical, and religious shocks which it created.

CONTRIBUTORS

Gillian Feeley-Harnik, Assistant Professor of Anthropology, Williams College.

Langdon Gilkey, Professor of Theology, The Divinity School, The University of Chicago.

Hans Küng, Professor of Ecumenical Theology and Director of the Institut für Oekumenische Forschung, University of Tübingen, West Germany.

Edmund Leach, Professor of Anthropology, emeritus, King's College, Cambridge University, England.

Martin Marty, F. M. Cane Distinguished Service Professor of American Church History, The University of Chicago.

J. Hillis Miller, Professor of English, Yale University.

Hayim Tadmor, Professor of Assyriology, The Hebrew University of Jerusalem, Israel.

Yigael Yadin, E. L. Sukenik Professor of Archaeology, The Hebrew University of Jerusalem, Israel.